Dedication

We dedicate this book to the memory
of Ivor Kamlish (1931-2019).
He designed every volume in this
series over a period of 25 years.

King's Cross Central, Somers Town, Euston

ISBN 978 1 913213 02 2

Printed and bound in Great Britain
by The Ludo Press Ltd, London

Front cover:
The St Pancras Renaissance Hotel,
2020 (photo by Eve Barker)

This book is one of a series of fourteen that survey the history of all parts of the London Borough of Camden. The present volume is a complete revision of one that appeared in 2002. Since then, so much has happened in the area and so much new historical information has become available that the book has been extensively reworked and enlarged. The earlier volume is in part an historic document in its own right, now that two of the three railway termini that dominate the area have been reborn, and that major new buildings have transformed the former railway lands, while encouraging regeneration elsewhere.

The present volume looks at that small part of the original parish of St Pancras, Middlesex, which was its historic heartland. It covers the area from Euston Road in the south to Agar Grove in the north and from Hampstead Road in the west to York Way, the border with Islington, in the east. This takes in the huge new development that is King's Cross Central; the district around Euston Station, currently much affected by HS2 works; and the residential streets of Somers Town and Bedford New Town.

We explore our survey area in nine walks, starting with St Pancras and King's Cross Stations and the land in between, once industrial but now home to offices and restaurants. It forms part of King's Cross Central, earlier site of the largely off-limits King's Cross Goods Yard. This had lain semi-derelict until restoration and redevelopment began, once the Channel Tunnel Rail line into St Pancras Station was opened in 2007.

Flooding from the Fleet had discouraged significant development in our area before the late 18th century, and much of the first housing north of what is now the Euston Road was aimed at the lower classes. Bisected by the Regent's Canal, which from the start encouraged industry along its banks, and then cut about by railways, the streets were never likely to be fashionable, although the Bedford Estate once had hopes for the new town it built on Fig's Mead, north of Somers Town. The standard of housing in Somers Town itself degenerated over time although early on it attracted waves of immigrants fleeing political convulsion in Europe – first French émigrés, later Spanish political exiles. To the west, Euston Square was initially a desirable address before Euston Station was built and slowly expanded.

Despite its often lowly status the area has had its fair share of notable residents. Writers have included Dickens; Shelley and his wife Mary, author of *Frankenstein*; the latter's parents William Godwin and proto-feminist Mary Wollstonecraft; the satirist John Wolcot (*alias* Peter Pindar); Leigh Hunt; and Wordsworth. Among artists were painters Walter Sickert and Spencer Gore; the engraver Charles Heath (of Penny Black fame); and the sculptor E H Baily. Political figures a-plenty have lived in the area – the Venezuelan statesman Andrés Bello; the Italian patriot Mazzini; even Lenin, to name but a few. The actress Alison Steadman and her husband Mike Leigh were residents, and comedians Dan Leno and Kenneth Horne were born here. The first Pearly King, Henry Croft, lived and died in the area, which was home to such varied characters as the inventor Henry Bessemer; the film pioneer Cecil Hepworth; and the England cricketer Fred Titmus.

We gratefully acknowledge the assistance of all the staff of Camden Local Studies & Archives Centre (CLSAC), especially its Archivist Tudor Allen. We also thank Margaret Stobo both for her contribution to the 1st edition of the book and her extensive local knowledge of Somers Town. Particular thanks go to Steve Job for his expert customisation of the street maps.

The St Pancras research team
Sheila Ayres (Routes 4 and 5)
David Hayes (Routes 6 and 7)
Ruth Hayes (Routes 8 and 9)
Steve Denford (Team leader; Routes 1, 2 and 3)

A survey of streets, buildings and former residents in a part of Camden

Streets of St Pancras

King's Cross Central, Somers Town, Euston

compiled by
Camden History Society

edited by
Steven Denford and David Hayes

designed by
Eve Barker

CAMDEN HISTORY SOCIETY

Diagram of the walks

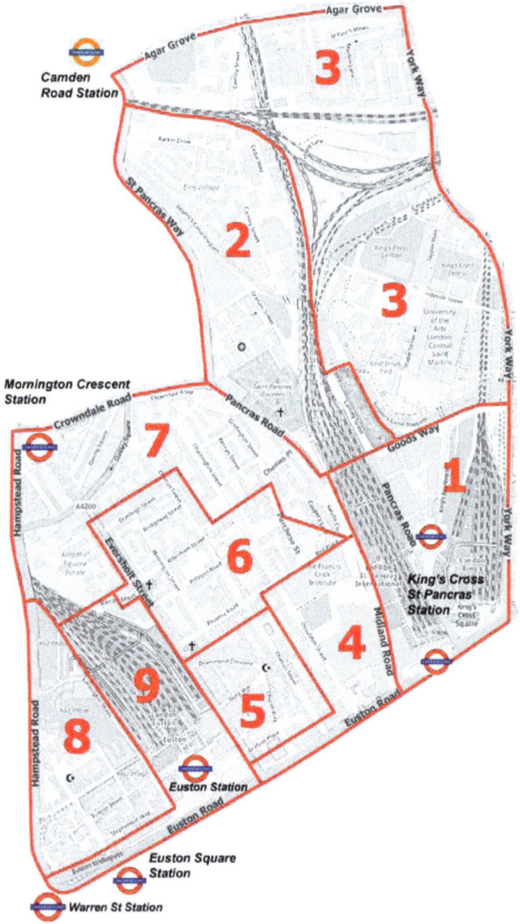

Contents

List of illustrations

Illustrations numbered

3, 15, 20, 21, 27, 31, 34, 35, 36, 40, 41, 43, 44, 50 are reproduced by courtesy of Camden Local Studies & Archives Centre
1, 2, 4, 6, 14, 16, 18, 19, 23, 24, 25, 26, 33, 37, 46, 48, 49, 54, 55 Wikimedia Commons
5, 7, 8, 9, 12, 17, 30 Wellcome Images
13 Islington Local History Centre
10, 11 London Metropolitan Archives

Historical overview

The parish of St Pancras once stretched some four miles north to south from Highgate Village to the borders of Holborn and St Giles. Its historic heartland, upon which we focus in this book, was centred on the parish church.

Occupying a knoll by the River Fleet St Pancras Old Church was probably built as early as the 4th century. It is thought to have been rebuilt and rededicated to St Pancras at the time of St Augustine's mission to England in 597. Pancras or Pancratius was a 14-year-old Roman martyred in 304, who became the patron saint of the young, and avenger of false oaths and perjury; William the Conqueror made Harold swear by St Pancratius.

A small settlement grew up around the church. The parish was recorded in Domesday as Pancras, by which name the locality was long known. By the 14th century, and may be forced by the constant flooding of the Fleet to seek drier ground, the villagers had migrated north to the area now known as Kentish Town. A chapel-of-ease was erected there and the old mother church became neglected, long used only for weddings and funerals.

Our survey area remained sparsely populated until the later 18th century, as open country with a few scattered houses and wayside inns. Dairy farms supplied milk for the metropolis and hay was grown for its horses. Londoners used the area as a rural retreat, frequenting its tea gardens or taking the waters at Pancras Wells beside the Fleet. There were few roads, mostly running south to north: the ancient road to Hampstead (now Hampstead Road); Gray's Inn Lane (now Pancras Road and St Pancras Way); and Maiden Lane (now York Way). Fig Lane (Crowndale Road) provided the only east-west link. Haunted by highwaymen the roads were regarded as dangerous, especially after dark.

Presaging change was the advent of the New Road from Paddington to Islington. Authorised by Act of Parliament it was constructed in 1756 and maintained by two Turnpike Trusts. Intended as a by-pass it quickly became the boundary of the capital.

As London expanded northwards many local fields were given over to the making of bricks, supplied both to local builders and to a wider market. Dust heaps arose for the disposal of the capital's waste, a smallpox hospital was opened in Battlebridge in 1767 and two West End parishes (St Giles-in-the-Fields and St James', Piccadilly) established overspill burial grounds in the district, each later converted by St Pancras Vestry into public gardens.

Beginning with ribbon development along the New Road around 1780, our area was gradually built up, as landowners leased the land to speculative house builders in the hope of maximising their incomes. (See Land Ownership on p 9). Development was slow and fitful, held back by successive slumps in the building trade.

In 1783 Lord Somers leased his Brill Farm estate for house building, the first phase of which was completed in the next decade. Somers Town when first built was indeed a self-contained new 'town', separated from London by acres of open fields. It was intended as a respectable suburb, but the leases granted by the noble lord gave him little influence over what was erected. Although early houses had generous gardens, many of these were soon built over with poor-quality housing.

In later housing developments, from the Regency onwards, landlords sought to learn from this mistake, attempting to exercise more control over what was built. West of Somers Town, in one corner of the Lord

Southampton's estate, Euston Square and its environs were laid out as a northward extension of Bloomsbury, and with First-Rate houses lining the square itself. To the north, the Duke of Bedford developed his Fig's Mead estate primarily as a middle-class suburb, whose street pattern was deliberately designed to minimise contact with neighbouring Somers Town. The building of 'Bedford New Town' and the development of the Brewers' estate immediately to the east of it were finally completed only around 1860.

By that time much of the district had been transformed yet again in the transport revolution of the 19th century. The Regent's Canal opened to traffic in 1820 passed through our area en route from Paddington to the Thames at Limehouse. Wharves and warehouses were set up along its banks. The canal's importance was soon eclipsed by the advent of the railways, three of which built their termini in close proximity along the New Road, renamed Euston Road in 1857. London's first intercity line, the London & Birmingham (later London & North Western), opened its Euston Square (Euston) Station in 1837. Fifteen years later the Great Northern Railway established its terminus at King's Cross. For a few years this was shared by the Midland Railway (MR) until it gained a station of its own alongside: St Pancras opened in 1868. Determined to outshine its rivals it fronted the station with its magnificent neo-Gothic Midland Grand Hotel. The approach lines of the MR's 'London Extension' not only cut controversially through the old parish churchyard but also destroyed much of Somers Town and wiped out the short-lived (and much defamed) Agar Town. A vast tract of land on the eastern side of our area was progressively given over to railway use, with numerous goods and coal depots, engine sheds and many acre of sidings.

Other landmarks in the area's transport history were the construction beneath the Euston Road of the Metropolitan Railway, the world's first underground line, opened in 1863; and the arrival of the local tramway network in 1872. Run by the London Street Tramways Company, this was originally horse-powered, electrified in 1909 and replaced by trolleybuses shortly before WWII.

The district's excellent transport links attracted industry. A major gasworks bordered the Regent's Canal while lighter industries thrived in the area's many yards and mews. The presence of industry and the smoke and noise from the railways ensured that the area would never be fashionable. No provision had been made to house those displaced by the building of the railways. They could only pour into the already overcrowded area nearby. Somers Town evolved into one of London's most notorious slums.

In 1889 St Pancras, previously governed by the parish Vestry, became a Metropolitan Borough, later renowned for its left-wing politics. It was eventually absorbed into the new Borough of Camden in 1965.

The 20th century saw major change in Somers Town, first through slum clearance. Bug-infested houses were replaced by innovative blocks of flats, some municipal, others erected by the St Pancras House Improvement Society, founded in 1924 and later renamed the Saint Pancras Housing Association (SPH); it is now part of Origin. We cannot here do justice to its remarkable work, for the full story of which the reader is referred to *Housing is Not Enough* by Malcolm Holmes.

During WWII the local railway infrastructure was a prime target for enemy bombers and neighbouring residential streets were also hit. After the war damaged and blighted housing was replaced by further blocks of council and SPH flats. Some original houses nevertheless survived to benefit from rehabilitation and gentrification later in the century. Others have been put to corporate use: national charities and trades unions which have long had their headquarters in the district have more recently been joined by many firms from the creative industry sector. The area has become known as the Knowledge Quarter from its cluster of knowledge sources, from the British Library with the world's earliest manuscripts to the Francis Crick Institute with the very latest medical research.

The local residential population has always been mixed. Early Somers Town attracted many people of a radical persuasion, including atheists, republicans and Chartists. Ever cosmopolitan the area has found favour with many immigrants from overseas. Somers Town was colonised first by aristocratic and other French émigrés and later by Spanish refugees. There has been a significant Irish presence ever since the arrival of the navvies to dig the canal. Since the 1970s our area has seen an influx of Bangladeshis and others from the Indian subcontinent and more recently many from Africa, who made up more than 10% of Somers Town's population in 2001. The diversity of cultures is showcased in the annual START festival.

In the railway lands to the north the demise of wagon-load freight, the collapse of the household coal trade, and the end of steam traction left an expanse of post-industrial wasteland whose future was endlessly debated over several decades. Work on a masterplan approved by Camden Council finally began in 2008. This was after the Eurostar tracks were constructed into Saint Pancras Station, which was given a magnificent refurbishment fitting its status as the gateway to Europe, the terminus of High Speed One lines. Over the last few years King's Cross Central – a mixed development of shiny offices, living spaces, shops, restaurants and bars amongst new public squares and gardens – has transformed the former railway lands and made them what would have seemed an unlikely tourist attraction. At the time of writing it is not clear whether the redevelopment of Euston Station and the surrounding area because of High Speed Two will have a similar effect.

Land ownership

Of the medieval manors underlying our area (see diagram), two were 'prebends' of St Paul's Cathedral. Property was granted by the Dean and Chapter to a 'prebendary', who in turn could lease land to a third party under an arrangement known as copyhold, so called because each party to the agreement held a written copy.

Attached to the old parish church was St Pancras Prebendal Manor. A survey in 1649 described the prebend farm of Pancras as 75 acres of pastureland lying between Battlebridge (King's Cross) and what is now Agar Grove. Three further fields abutting Maiden Lane (York Way) were held by St Bartholomew's Hospital. That area known as Allensbury evolved into the Railway Lands which we explore in Route 3. The manor house is believed to have been sited in the northwest corner of the manor, east of Gray's Inn Lane (now St Pancras Way). The lawyer William Agar bought the site in 1810 and erected a fine mansion called Elm Lodge for himself and his family and in 1816 leased the the manor from the prebendary William Beloe. By this time it did not include the land south of what is now Goods Way, which in the 18th century was called the Drakefield estate (Route 1). From 1840 Agar's widow and his son sublet plots of land on 21-year leases to working men and others for the building of the once notorious Agar Town, whose former territory we visit in Route 2.

Further west and mostly outside our survey area lay the prebendal manor of Tottenhall, a large manor extending from Fitzrovia to Highgate. Its manor house was at Tottenham Court, near modern Tolmers Square. Leased by the Crown, then appropriated by Parliament and reclaimed at the Restoration, it had to be sold because of Charles II's extravagance. Acquired by the Earl of Arlington, the copyhold was inherited together with property at Euston in Suffolk by his daughter Isabella. She married Henry FitzRoy, the 9-year-old illegitimate son of Charles II, who became Earl of Euston and 1st Duke of Grafton. In 1780 the soldier Charles FitzRoy, younger brother of the influential 3rd Duke, became Baron Southampton. In 1767 he had succeeded in purchasing the freehold of 255 acres of manorial demesne at a bargain price of £300 per acre, paving the way for the later development of the area around Euston Square (Routes 8 & 9).

Extending south of Fig Lane and eventually bisected by the New Road was a third area, known conventionally as the Lay Manor of St Pancras. There is some doubt if it really existed as such; no lay manor has ever been identified. The so-called manor was once owned by the London Charterhouse.

After the Dissolution land ownership here became very fragmented. Mostly south of our area was the Battlebridge estate, but the construction of the New Road left just over an acre north of it.

Also clipping the southeast corner of our area was part of one of two estates bequeathed by benevolent Tudors for the benefit of public schools and vested in City livery companies. This was the Skinners' Sandhills estate, given by Sir Andrew Judd in 1572 to benefit Tonbridge School in Kent. Three years later a brewer Richard Platt gave land west of what is now Pancras Road to the Brewers' Company to endow a school at Aldenham, Herts. Two further estates were owned by peers of the realm. Brill Farm was bought in 1628 by Charles Cocks of the Middle Temple, whose namesake was in 1784 created Baron Somers of Evesham and on whose land was built Somers Town (Routes 4, 5 & 6). Immediately to the north was Fig's Mead owned by the Russell family (Dukes of Bedford), better known as landlords of nearby Bloomsbury, and who here developed Bedford New Town (Route 7). Most of the landowners mentioned above – or people and places connected with them – are commemorated in the names of streets and buildings we shall encounter on our walks.

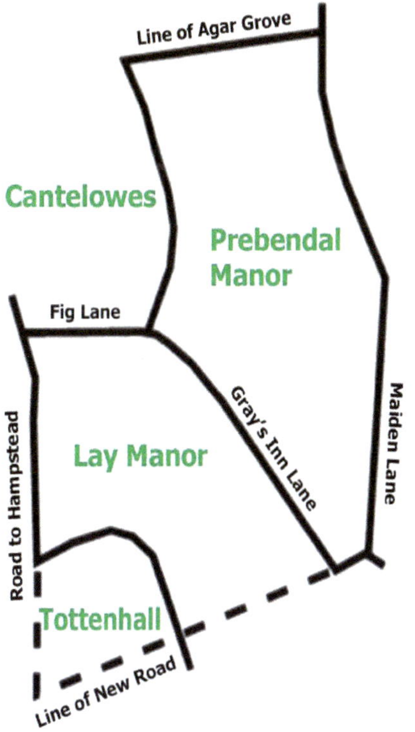

Medieval manors in St Pancras

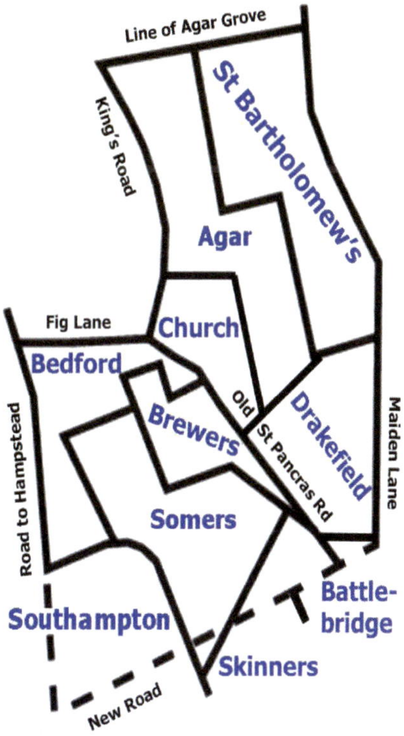

Georgian estates in the same area

Present street names and their origins

*= (location of) property of the Dukes of Bedford

Agar William, C18-C19 local landowner
Aldenham Herts. birthplace of Richard Platt, and public school he endowed
Allensbury Eastern part of St Pancras Prebendal Manor, owned by St Bart's
Ampthill Small Bedfordshire town *
Bagley Bottle and glass merchant
Barker Tom, Mayor of St Pancras 1958-59
Barnby Sir Joseph, C19 composer and conductor
Beaconsfield Benjamin Disraeli, Earl of, patron of the body that built nearby Beaconsfield Buildings
Bergholt Place name used by two villages in Constable Country
Blakeney Norfolk salt marshes (coincidentally?) drained by Agar Creek
Bridgeway Variant on earlier (?Duke of) Bridgewater
Brill The Brill, farm and farmhouse
Broadfield Northernmost field in Allensbury
Camley Variant on earlier Cambridge
Canal Street approaches the Regent's Canal
Cardington Village near Bedford *
Cedar Arbitrary arboreal reference
Chalton Place name, earlier often spelt Charlton; significance unknown
Charles Charles FitzRoy, 1st Baron Southampton, landowner
Charrington Brewing company; street built on Brewers' estate
Chenies Buckinghamshire manor house *
Chill Cooling Pod
Christopher ? Christopher Kite, local sanitary and heating engineer
Churchway Ancient footpath to old parish church
Clarendon Clarendon Square once adjoined
Cobourg Prince Leopold of Saxe-Coburg (sic) married Princess Charlotte in 1816
Coopers Nearby former Coopers Arms pub; or the craft of making casks for beer
Crace John Gregory, interior decorator of St Pancras New Church
Cranleigh Cranleigh Houses, 1930s flats
Crofters Recalls rural occupation
Crowndale Farm near Tavistock, Devon *
Doric Euston Station's lost propylaeum ('Doric arch')
Drummond Lady Caroline, relation of Lord Southampton, or John & Charles, his bankers
Euston Euston Hall, Suffolk seat of Dukes of Grafton
Eversholt Village near Woburn Abbey *
Exmouth Admiral Lord, hero of Napoleonic Wars
Foundry Former Wailes' iron foundry nearby
Freight Former British Rail Freight Depot
George George FitzRoy, 2nd Baron Southampton, landowner
Goldington Village near Bedford *
Goods Road led to GNR Goods Yard
Gower Earl of, father-in-law of 4th Duke of Bedford
Grafton Duke of, head of FitzRoy family and local landowner
Granary (Square) Great Northern Railway warehouse (Street) Midland Railway ale/ grain store
Hampden Former Hampden Street (after John Hampden, C17 Parliamentarian)
Handyside Andrew, ironmaster & civil engineer, whose firm built the Goods Yard canopies
Harrington Earl of, father-in-law of 7th Duke of Bedford
Hurdwick Another farm near Tavistock *
King's Leads from King's Cross Station
Lancing Sussex seaside town
Lidlington Village near Ampthill *
Maiden Midden (refuse heap); or an image of the Virgin Mary
Medburn Farm at Aldenham
Melton 3rd Lord Southampton a Master of the Quorn (Melton Mowbray) hunt
Midland Pre-1923 railway company that built adjoining St Pancras Station
Millbrook Another village near Ampthill *
Neville Edith, Secretary of St Pancras Council of Social Service
Oakley Oakley House near Bedford *
Ossulston A 'hundred' of the County of Middlesex
Penryn Town in Cornwall
Phoenix ? Street 'rose out of the ashes' of local dust heaps
Platt Richard, C16 brewer and landowner; benefactor of Aldenham School
Ploughmans Recalls rural occupation
Polygon Late-C18 'experimental' 16-sided building
Purchese Frederick, St Pancras churchwarden and LCC member
Reapers Recalls rural occupation
Regnart Family members were presidents of Maple & Co.
Rossendale Anthony Greenwood, Baron Greenwood of Rossendale, Labour politician, d.1982

(St) Pancras	Patron saint of children (inter alia), martyred 304 AD
St Paul's	Local parish named for canons of St Paul's Cathedral who once owned the land
Stable	Former GNR Goods Yard stables lie beneath the street
Starcross	Devon village across Exe estuary from Exmouth
Stephenson	Robert, engineer of the London & North Western Railway
Tapper	? Wheeltappers, testers of railway wagon wheels for flaws
Tolmers	One (defunct) source of the New River
Weavers	Recalls rural occupation
Weir	Alexander, local paving commissioner
Wellesley	Arthur, Duke of Wellington
Werrington	Manor on Devon-Cornwall border *
Wilberforce	Mrs, character in the locally-set film, *The Ladykillers*
Wollstonecraft	Mary, proto-feminist writer & Somers Town resident
Wrotham	Kentish village
York	Destination of Great Northern Railway

Route 1

A tale of two termini

Circular walk from King's Cross
St Pancras Underground Station

This is an area dominated by two well-known London railway stations, King's Cross and St Pancras. The latter's role as the terminus for Eurostar trains to and from the Continent has put St Pancras firmly back on the map. At the start of the Millennium the area was frankly squalid and known for drug and alcohol abuse and prostitution. The restoration of both stations and the redevelopment of the area in between is an exemplar of 21st-century urban renewal.

Emerge from King's Cross St Pancras Underground Station and find a seat in the extensive new piazza in front of King's Cross Station. **King's Cross Square**, paved with York stone, was completed in 2013 and on weekdays is often alive with stalls selling all sorts of street food.

It abuts London's very first by-pass, laid out in the 1750s as the New Road, from Paddington to the City, intended for drovers from Wales and the North bringing their animals to the livestock market at Smithfield. It was also an impetus to development.

Until that time the area north of the road had largely been fields given over to hay. In the 19th century a Royal Commission recommended that the New Road should be the nearest to central London that railways should penetrate, and three railway companies built their London termini along it. The London and Birmingham Railway was first at Euston in 1837 and here side by side are King's Cross, opened by the Great Northern Railway (GNR) in 1852 and St Pancras, opened by the Midland Railway (MR) in 1868. Eleven years earlier the New Road had become **EUSTON ROAD**.

The name King's Cross derives from a memorial of sorts designed by Stephen Geary (p 16) and erected at the junction of what are now Euston Road, Gray's Inn Road and York Way. It was close to the turnpike at the end of Pancras Road that was demolished in July 1864 (leading to a huge increase in traffic). A statue to the late George IV, raised above a Greek Doric base, the 60-ft high structure **[1]** was projected in 1830 but not completed until

1836. It proved as unpopular as the monarch. The shoddy statue was taken down only six years later and its base, used at first by police but then as a beer shop, was removed as a public nuisance in 1845. At the time the GNR was planning its station and chose to call it King's Cross, rather than the centuries-old name for the area, Battlebridge. According to local legend, but on no evidence whatsoever, the name recalled the battle between Queen Boudicca and the Romans. 'Battle' was most likely a corruption of Bradford, or Broad Ford, a crossing of the River Fleet. Battlebridge had by the 19th century acquired a rather sordid reputation so the change of name was welcomed by many, particularly builders and developers. It was many decades later claimed that one local developer, William Forrester Bray, had suggested the name King's Cross soon after George IV ascended the throne in 1820.

The GNR was incorporated by Act of Parliament in June 1846, during the period of railway mania. Its main purpose was to connect York to London, with authorised capital of £8.1 million. After some delay the land for the station, by then largely covered with streets and buildings, was acquired. As a temporary measure a terminus opened on 7 August 1850 alongside a new goods yard further north on the west side of Maiden Lane (now York Way), which we visit in Route 3.

The plain brick exterior of the permanent station was built in 1851-52 by Lewis Cubitt, brother of the famous builder Thomas. Its two semi-circular lunettes reflect the arches of the roofs behind, separated by a 120-ft clock tower that is surmounted by an Italianate roof. The clock by Dent & Co. was originally built for the Great Exhibition of 1851. In that year *The Builder* recorded Cubitt's remark that 'the building will depend for its effect on the largeness of some of the features, its fitness for its purpose and its characteristic expression of that purpose'. Its functional architecture was widely admired in the 1960s when the popularity of St Pancras station, its neo-Gothic neighbour, was at a low ebb. Early photographs show the arcade which formed the lower part of the facade, but this became masked by a clutter of small buildings, huts and shelters, nicknamed the 'Indian Village', removed for the construction in the 1970s of a large covered concourse. The recent complete overhaul of the station, which we will visit later, has created the present square.

1 King's Cross statue of George IV, by George Shepherd 1835

To the left of the station is the Great Northern Hotel (p 31). Both cover the site of the former Smallpox Hospital **[2** p19**]**. This had been founded in July 1746 in Windmill Street, off Tottenham Court Road, for the reception of infected patients with 'casual small pox' and for free inoculation of the poor. Patients were housed in a variety of buildings for several decades thereafter, including a leased building in Cold Bath Fields. In 1763 the freehold of four acres on the Drakefield estate at Battlebridge was bought from Thomas Saltonstall (d.1782), but as soon as the foundations of a hospital were laid the inhabitants of St Pancras, Kentish Town, Hampstead and Highgate took legal action. The Court ruled that if they could suggest another equally remote site the hospital should move, but none was suggested. A new building opened just for inoculation on 9 December 1767.

A smallpox hospital had been set up in Coldbath Fields, Clerkenwell but the building leased there was unfit and patients were transferred to the inoculation building. A separate Small Pox Hospital designed by James Johnson was built in 1793-94, at a right angle fronting Pancras Road. The patients moved in in June 1794. Vaccination was introduced in 1799, by Dr William Woodville, a physician with the hospital for 14 years until his death there in 1805. He had assisted Edward Jenner, the pioneer of vaccination, in his researches but it was Woodville who undertook the first large-scale trial of the method and proved its efficacy. He was also a noted botanist, the author of an influential book, *Medical Botany* (1790) and maintained at his own expense a botanic garden within the grounds. Perhaps surprisingly, the 2-acre open space in front of the hospital was marked on the 1801 parish map as a 'Pleasure Ground'. At that time the land immediately north and east of the hospital was still farmed, and included a narrow field beside Maiden Lane called Cat's Head Acre (p 28).

In 1802 the London Fever Hospital opened in Gray's Inn Road. In 1816 it moved into the Smallpox Hospital with 60 (later 120) beds, while the Smallpox and Vaccination Hospital took over the old inoculation building to the east (expanded in 1840-41). Fever Hospital patients mainly had typhus and scarlet fever. Only servants and the 'decent poor' were admitted; wealthier patients were treated at home. Dr Southwood Smith served as a physician to the Fever Hospital from 1824 until his death in 1861 and his observations strengthened his advocacy of sanitary reform.

The resources of the two hospitals were severely stretched as they were the only two isolation hospitals in the capital. The arrival of cholera in London in 1832 made the situation even worse and applicants were often turned away. When the GNR bought both sites, offering £20,000 in compensation, the hospitals were forced to move again: the Smallpox Hospital to Highgate Hill (on the site of Whittington Hospital) and the London Fever Hospital to Liverpool Road, Islington. The 'superior building materials' of the latter (e.g. Portland stone cornice and York stone paving) were auctioned off in 1850.

A description in 1851 of the area between the New Road and the land as far north as the Regent's Canal talked of immense destruction in preparation for the new GNR terminus. Behind the hospitals little houses laid out from 1806 on the Drakefield estate (p 26) had been razed. The street layout to the north of the Smallpox Hospital's site was however largely retained in the rebuilding that occurred after King's Cross Station opened in 1852.

The curving plan of the hotel follows the former line of **PANCRAS ROAD**, originally a medieval track to Kentish Town. It was known by Victorian times as Old St Pancras Road, progressively assuming its present, uncanonised, name during the 1870s. The road ran alongside the ancient River Fleet, one of the 'lost rivers of London', which still flows from the northern heights to join the River Thames at Blackfriars. This is now no more than an underground drain contained in iron pipes but a thousand years ago the invading Danes sailed beyond here. Samuel Bagster, a local resident, remembered it as having been (c.1760) 'a clear ever-flowing rivulet of five or six feet wide and about a foot deep, unless when swollen by long continued rain'. This stretch of the road on the low-lying plain beneath St Pancras Old Church was prone to serious flooding, earning the area the name Pancras Wash. In medieval times people moved away from St Pancras to Kentish Town because of the flooding and in the 1679 flood 'cattle floated on the stream to Clerkenwell'. In 1809 and again in 1818 the whole area between the church was covered with sewage-laden water 3 ft deep.

Pancras Road once ran across the new square. In Its lower reaches here, facing the hospital grounds, was Weston Place. This was a long row of small houses developed in the 1790s by William Weston, who lived at No.18 and was receiving a tidy £27 per annum in rent for each by 1814. In that year Joanna Southcott, the religious fanatic, died of a brain tumour having resided for several years at No.17, in lodgings paid for by clergymen who promoted her prophecies. She published some 65 pamphlets which were widely circulated, and was one of the most popular writers of her time. She claimed shortly before her death that she was pregnant with a second Prince of Peace, miraculously conceived, she being a virgin and in her sixties. Another contemporary resident was the miniature painter John Barrow, to whom the young Theodore Lane (c.1800–1828), painter and etcher, was apprenticed. The architect Stephen Geary, who designed Highgate Cemetery and the King's Cross, was based at No.22 in the late 1820s. The broker William Colton lived at No.4; he was a police informer who gave, and possibly manufactured, evidence in a large number of larceny trials in the 1820s and 1830s. After King's Cross Station opened, the easternmost houses in the terrace were pulled down in 1852 to create a shortcut from Pancras Road into the New Road. Total demolition followed in 1871 so that Pancras Road could be straightened to run alongside the new St Pancras Station. In its last days Weston Place had coffee houses and pubs – including the Royal York, the York Arms and the Iron Duke - to cater for railway travellers.

The small area south of Weston Place (just over an acre) formed the northern tip of the Battlebridge estate. Fronting the highway in the late 18th century were two small terraces - Dyer's Place and Pershore Place - and behind them was a rope walk. By the mid 1820s, when the estate had been sold for development, they had been rebuilt in grander fashion as Egremont Place. The Venezuelan statesman and writer Andrés Bello was living at No.9 from 1826 until 1829, when he left London for Chile. The photographic entrepreneur Richard Beard lived at No.6 in 1835-40. He opened Europe's first public photographic studio in Regent Street in 1841 and soon after purchased the sole patent rights of the daguerreotype process in England and Wales. The Nonconformist preacher Robert Forman Horton, was born in Egremont Place in 1855. The terrace was renumbered as Nos.2-34 Euston Road in 1857. The sculptor brothers William and Thomas Wills were at No.12 until 1865, before they moved to No.168. They exhibited jointly at the Royal Academy and created the statue of Richard Cobden at Camden Town. No.18 was the home of Baron Anselmo José da Costa Ricci, the Portuguese attaché in London. Former Egremont Place was pulled down at the same time as Weston Place, having already lost a few of its houses when the 1852 cut through was formed.

Now walk towards St Pancras Station, whose clock tower soars ahead, 270 ft high. On the gable alongside it is a black statue of Britannia, standing helmeted and armed with a trident. Cross Pancras Road by the traffic lights, and in the wall to the right of the stairway is a disused drinking fountain, opened on 27 Aug 1877 by the widow of Robert Hansler, JP for Middlesex.

Walk up the stone steps that are surmounted by an ironwork sign and pause at the top to take in the full splendour of the 565-ft-frontage of the building, which houses the **St Pancras Renaissance Hotel**. This is surely one of the most romantic scenes London has to offer, one of the largest and finest buildings in the Gothic style in the world.

Built as the Midland Grand Hotel, it was designed by Sir George Gilbert Scott, who had won an architectural competition launched in May 1865. Work started in 1868 after the train shed had been erected (which dictated the siting of the entrances and gives the lie to the oft-repeated story that Scott simply recycled his rejected design for the Foreign Office). The hotel took eight years to complete, opening partially in 1873 but not fully until 1876. This was largely because Scott was forced to change his plans. He wanted high standards of finish while the MR urged economy; they were answerable to their shareholders. He omitted one storey, used slightly cheaper materials and removed intended statuary.

Scott was a rich man who did not need to and never had done any railway work but here was a chance to build a secular building in a style that he thought was next to godliness. He borrowed ideas from many medieval Gothic buildings across Europe - the western tower is based on the Cloth Hall at Ypres in Belgium - and ensured there was plenty of naturalistic ornament adorning the structure. It is a delight to run the eye over the highly decorated Gothic surface. Dragons abound: in the spandrels of the support for the large oriel window in the centre, underneath brackets, in some of the capitals. On the bases of the columns dividing the windows are figures supporting coats of arms, which include the City of London and Midland towns associated with the railway. As a cost-saving measure, niches above are empty.

The materials used were as far as possible from places accessible to the MR - hence Nottinghamshire brick, Leicestershire slates and Derbyshire iron and 14 different types of stone from quarries in the Midlands.

The Midland Grand Hotel had over 300 bedrooms, a 100-ft dining room, a vast reading room and a dramatic Grand Staircase. The latest technology was used in the design of hydraulic lifts, central heating, bathroom and kitchen planning and fire-resistant construction. An innovation in the 1890s was the ladies' smoking room, equipped with an electrophone, which linked up to eight guests at a time by telephone line to live concerts and church services. A men's room had a column printer that relayed Stock Exchange news and racing results. The guests were not necessarily railway travellers, but anyone who appreciated and could pay for the richly decorated rooms furnished by Gillow. One such was Scott's hedonistic son George Gilbert Scott Jr, who died at the hotel of cirrhosis of the liver in 1897. Other guests during the hotel's heyday included Marie Lloyd, the music hall artiste, who had a suite of rooms on the second floor; Dame Nelly Melba, the opera singer and Jesse Boot, founder of Boots the chemists, as well as half the peerage. It is said that when the Shah of Persia stayed staff ensured that no chambermaid under the age of 45 entered his rooms. The hotel accommodated less well-off customers too, in rather spartan rooms on the upper floors.

The hotel's golden years lasted until WWI. During the war, the hotel was damaged on the night of 17 February 1918 when five bombs were dropped from an immense Zeppelin-Staaken biplane, killing 21 people and injuring 22 more sheltering by the entrance arch.

In December 1922 the London, Midland and Scottish Railway, the largest of the several large companies created by the Railways Act of 1921, assumed control but rival hotels like the Ritz stole its business and profits fell. It was becoming obsolete because it had been built at a time before en-suite facilities and when an army of staff (some 150) was needed to tend its coal fires and clean everything by hand. The hotel closed in 1935, when it became railway offices and was renamed St Pancras Chambers. Crude and insensitive adaptations to the interior were made, which nevertheless helped preserve some of the original decoration (behind partitions).

British Rail vacated the building in 1985 when it failed its fire certificate and for the next two decades it lay empty. At this time it was popular as a film location. From *Hell* (2001) and *Batman Begins* (2005) were both filmed here.

The exterior was meticulously cleaned and restored by British Rail in a project costing some £10 million and completed in March 1995. The following year British Rail was privatised and London and Continental Railways took over.

The top two roof storeys, which after 1935

had been used for rail staff, were converted into private apartments collectively known as St Pancras Chambers by the Manhattan Loft Company, owned by entrepreneur Harry Handelsmann. This helped to fund the cost of transforming the rest of the building into the five-star St Pancras Renaissance Hotel. Work started in 2006. Handelsmann collaborated with Marriott Hotels and heritage specialists Richard Griffiths Architects and interior designers GA Design.

The hotel mainly occupies the western arm of the building, where the Midland Grand's stunning public rooms have been lovingly restored. At the far side the imposing public entrance to the old Hotel facing Euston Road is now a gilded bar. Under the departures arch, where taxis once deposited passengers, is the extensive glazed hotel lobby, called the Hansom Lounge. A new wing designed by RHWL in a faux Gothic style was built alongside Midland Road (p 77) to house most of the hotel's bedrooms.

The plot of land on which St Pancras Station and the hotel were built was originally part of Sandhills (a property mostly south of the line of Euston Road), which in 1572 was vested by Sir Andrew Judd in the Skinners' Company as trustees for the benefit of Tonbridge School. It was still grassland on a map of 1785 but during the 1790s the livery company began the development of the area. Along what was then the New Road good-sized, 4-storey terraced houses - Judd Place East - were built, set back since no buildings were permitted within 50 ft of the roadway. Behind, on what was called Skinners' Field, smaller streets – Skinners' Place, Hertford Street and Smith's Place grew up, as far as the southern portion of the Brewers' estate. In Smith's Place in June 1830 Joseph Grantham aged 31 became the first Metropolitan police officer to be killed on duty. He attempted to break up a fight between two Irish labourers and was savagely kicked, dying of his injures; his assailant was sentenced to just 7 months in prison. Smith's Place contained a Ragged School from the late 1850s.

On the boundary between the Skinners' and Brewers' estates lay Weston Street, full of shopkeepers and tradesmen, with a Perseverance public house at No.9, and leading to the Brill (p 75). Here was Weston House, a building of some pretension, advertised as an establishment for insane ladies in the late 1830s. It was run by the surgeon Hugh Welch Diamond, who had lived here since at least 1827. Diamond became a passionate photographer; he is best remembered for the many photographs he took in the 1850s of his insane patients. By this time he had left Weston House, which had become home to the Westminster and North West London Penitent Female Asylum (established in 1837). This aimed to convert 'fallen women' and get them work as servants. Its Superintendent was Lieutenant Blackmore who from 1858 helped set up the London Female Preventive and Reformatory Institution at No.200 Euston Road (p 154), which continued the Asylum's work.

Judd Place East, facing the New Road, was home to the painter Charles Catton the Elder (1728–98) who died there. He was coach-painter to George III and a founder member of the Royal Academy. Sophia Collet, writer and campaigner for women's rights, was born here in 1822, the daughter of the merchant John Dobson. The publisher and topographical engraver William Bernard Cooke, who worked with Turner and Constable, was at No.13 in Regency times. Edward Irving, the controversial and charismatic Presbyterian minister of the nearby Regent Square Church, was living at the same house in 1830, when the Presbytery of London found him guilty of heresy. The sculptor Thomas Milnes lived at No.3 (later No. 40 Euston Road) from 1845-1861. While there he was asked to model the lions for Nelson's Column, but the commission was given to Landseer. Next door, at No.4, the organ builder George Maydwell Holditch had his works from 1850. He built the organ for Lichfield Cathedral.

2 The Small Pox Hospital (drawing, 1807). From the site of St Pancras Station, with a view of the houses along the east side of present-day Pancras Road. The original Smallpox Hospital (1767) is on the left, what became the Fever Hospital to the right.

Judd Place East was also home to the church of St Luke's. The district of St Luke's King's Cross was created in 1849 and at first was served by a temporary church in the grounds of the former Smallpox Hospital **[2]**. This was dismantled in 1851 as the site was needed for King's Cross Station. In 1856 a new church, designed by John Johnson in a 14th-century Gothic style with seating for 1,200 people, was begun here but funds ran out. It was finally consecrated on 30 May 1861. Four years later it was taken down, the stones sold and re-used for a congregational chapel also designed by Johnson in Wanstead, opened in 1867. The MR paid for a replacement church of St Luke's in Oseney Crescent, Kentish Town.

Judd Place East became Nos.36-62 Euston Rd in 1857 and soon afterwards shops appeared in the front gardens. All the buildings were cleared by the MR, including Nos.44&46 which had housed a pioneering industrial school, called the Boy's Home for the Training and Maintenance by their own labour of Destitute Boys not convicted of crime. The school opened in a rented house here in February 1858 but moved in 1865 to Chalk Farm.

Now walk though the arch into **St Pancras International Station**, to admire the daring sweep of the train shed. Designed by William Barlow, Engineer in Chief to the MR, and built 1866-68, it was and remains an engineering marvel. Wrought-iron lattice arch ribs spring from platform level and rise over 100 ft to meet in a slightly pointed apex, a four-centred arch of the late Gothic type and very stable. Indeed the ribs were erected before the walls went up. They cover what was then the largest enclosed space in the world; it was also the tallest. The shed is 690 ft long and 245 ft wide. Each girder is embedded in the ground below the station floor which acted as a tie to the arch, a daring concept that had not been attempted on such a scale before. It was probably suggested by Rowland Ordish who assisted Barlow. John Julius Norwich wrote that 'in all England there is no more triumphant affirmation of the power, vitality, self-confidence and sheer panache of the Victorian age'.

The tracks are raised 20 ft above Euston Road so that trains could run on the level from Camden Town, without the need to tunnel under the Regent's Canal as the GNR had done at King's Cross. The pillared vaults beneath were designed to store Burton beer barrels, a highly lucrative traffic for the MR. There was a hydraulic lift at the northern end of the station, between present Platforms 7 and 8, to take the barrels up and down. The Undercroft was tailored so precisely to the needs of the brewing industry that the 720 cast iron columns supporting the platforms in a grid pattern were spaced precisely to allow three hogsheads of beer to sit between them. The station could be said to be literally built on beer; the Undercroft had a capacity of 28 million pints. The delivery and storage of beer here ended in 1964 with the last steam train from Burton on Trent, superseded by road haulage. The huge space was latterly taken over by taxi cleaning and servicing businesses and cab drivers could enjoy refreshments at Doug Sherry's Big Red Bus café.

The Undercroft is the heart of the new St Pancras. The lead architect for the reconstruction, Alistair Lansley, persuaded English Heritage, which supervised the project, to allow four sections of the Undercroft roof to be removed so natural light could stream into the new shopping mall and the ticket and check-in desks, and escalators inserted. This was achieved by laying a concrete raft on top of Barlow's wrought iron beams to take the load.

The renovation of the train shed cost £800 million and took five years to complete with 5,000 workers involved. It was part of a £5.8 billion project to build a high-speed route to the continent and transform the station into a new transport hub, a gateway to Europe. Now known as High Speed One, the Channel Tunnel Rail Link (CTRL) works changed the face of the immediate area and made the station a destination in its own right. The station was opened officially by the Queen on 6 November 2007 and Eurostar began rail services eight days later.

The iron work is once again painted sky blue (as it was from 1877) and proudly bears the legend 'manufactured by the Butterley Company, Derbyshire'. Also restored is the glazing of the roof. Built using a huge mobile scaffold, this originally had an estimated 2.5 acres of glass. The glass was damaged in wartime bombing on St Pancras Day, 12 May 1941 and subsequently reduced to two narrow strips. There are again 18,000 panes of glass laid out in a ridge and furrow fashion, as in the former Crystal Palace.

The clock was always a place for people to meet so under it has been placed Paul Day's 9m-high bronze sculpture, *The Meeting Place.* The couple embrace but don't kiss; that was considered too daring. The models for the couple were the sculptor himself and his (French) wife. Walk round the piece to take in the frieze of wartime and underground scenes.

The original station clock was made by Dent and Co. It was decommissioned in the 1970s and reputedly sold to an American collector but as it was being taken down it fell to the ground and shattered. Roland Hoggard, a railway employee, took away the pieces (by train) and in his Nottinghamshire garden painstakingly restored the clock. When Dent was asked to make a replica the company used it for the blueprint, and the 91-year-old was invited to the Royal opening of the station. The replica is made of aluminium, with visible parts in slate and the hands painted with 22-carat gold.

Walk over to the former Booking Office, the name incised into the stone lintels. Now part of the hotel, it was designed separately by George Gilbert Scott and opened in 1869. Elaborately decorated in medieval baronial style, it originally had an open-trussed timber roof on carved hammer beams, but this was damaged in WWI and later replaced. The ticket desks with their linen-fold wooden panelling were then moved to the opposite side of the hall. These have been retained to form a drinks bar.

By the entrance a memorial to the 150 MR employees who worked in and around the station and who died in WWI was unveiled in November 2018 to mark the centenary of the end of the conflict. The 4-metre-tall memorial is comprised of a series of job titles that represent those who left their work to fight and die for their country. The artist Fabian Peake used vitreous enamel which has historically been used for signage by railway companies.

Looking back towards the clock, note the artwork suspended from the roof, part of a commission known as Terrace Wires which changes annually. In 2019 this was a 20m-long light installation by Tracey Emin depicting the words, 'I Want My Time With You', which the artist said had an anti-Brexit message.

If St Pancras was the patron saint of the district, then the statue of Sir John Betjeman over to the left presents him as the patron saint of St Pancras Station. This is not entirely fair. The poet and architectural writer campaigned to save the building when British Rail planned to tear it down, but Pevsner and the Victorian Society were much more instrumental in securing the station's Grade I Listing in November 1967. The large disc around the statue contains some of Betjeman's poetry. The sculptor Martin Jennings called him 'a scruffy icon of English neglect' and this is reflected in his attire, with his baggy trousers and broken shoelace.

Continue along what is called The Grand Terrace. All evidence of the railway track that was once here has gone. During the Cold War it was dedicated to the use of the Joint Services Air Trooping Centre, which organised special trains for troops to get to Luton Airport for flights to West Germany.

To your right walk past the 300-ft Champagne Bar, said to be the longest in Europe, and on the left the Pancras Grand restaurant, both managed by Searcys. Beyond, the walkway ends at the platforms for domestic services run by East Midlands Trains. These stand to the side of those for Eurostar trains, which alone use Barlow's train shed. Eurostar trains have eighteen carriages, which necessitated the doubling in length of the original platforms. A flat-roofed, wider extension has been added, carried on four lines of columns. There is a clear separation of old and new, echoing the way the Barlow shed stops short of the hotel, where a glazed screen was placed to reduce noise and smoke.

Go down the escalators into the Undercroft, now known as The Arcade, which houses a long arcade of shops and cafés, and turn 180 degrees towards the entrance to Thameslink. This railway runs through a curved tunnel built by Barlow under Midland Road (p 77) and the train shed, linking with the Metropolitan Railway and so enabling coal from the Midlands to be delivered to the south of London; this proved a valuable trade for the MR. The new station below, which opened at the end of 2007, replacing King's Cross Thameslink, is served by trains from Brighton to Bedford. It also has links to Cambridge and Peterborough via a pair of bored tunnels running under the Regent's Canal that were constructed during the CTRL works and which meet the East Coast main line at Belle Isle junction, just north of King's Cross.

Turn right to walk past the food outlets of the Sourced Market (surmounted by departure boards) to the far end of the new extension where high-speed domestic trains (javelins) to Kent make use of the CTRL tracks. St Pancras International was the first station in the world to be simultaneously served by British, French and Japanese designs of high-speed train.

As we leave the station by the **PANCRAS ROAD** exit, spare a thought for the many people who lost their homes in its original construction. The northern end of the station lay on the southern part of the estate of the Brewers' Company, who had obtained an Act of Parliament in 1811 to pave and improve it. This led to the removal of a tile kiln (shown on the 1801 parish map when it was part of a large brickfield) and the growth of streets, all subsequently demolished to make way for St. Pancras Station: Denton Street; Smith Street; and Perry Street. Denton Street was home between 1823 and 1830 to one of the many Spanish Liberals who had fled here after the absolutist Ferdinand VII was restored: Don Manuel Gurrea, a General who was later to die in the First Carlist War in 1837. Perry Street may have been named after Benjamin Perry (1780-1850), who lived and died in the largest building, Broxted House; he was born in Broxted, Essex. He was the owner of three pubs nearby, the famous Brill House (p 76), the Independent at No.25 Brewer Street, and the Friend at Hand in Platt Terrace that fronted Pancras Road until it too was pulled down to build the station.

In the early 1820s the surgeon John Davies lived in Platt Terrace. At St Pancras Infirmary in 1823 he performed a pioneering plastic surgery operation (without anaesthetic) on a 40-year-old shoemaker from Suffolk called Capon, whose nose had disintegrated through taking mercury for syphilis. Davies cut skin from Capon's forehead to reconstruct the nose. Another resident of Platt Terrace in 1829 was Esther Hibner, hanged for starving to death a young child farmed out to her by the local workhouse.

The richly decorated side wall of St Pancras Station has undercut capitals and lions' heads terminating drip moulds above the arcading. New brickwork is evident. Sixty million bricks were used to build the original station and hotel, but for the renovation a further one million bricks were kilned in the Midlands to the dimensions and colours of the originals. The roof not only bears new panes of glass but also new slates; a quarry was opened in Ffestiniog in Wales (the original in the Midlands had long since closed) to mill 300,000 new ones of the same colour.

Cross by the lights to the **German Gymnasium** opposite. This was built in 1864

3 The German Gymnasium in action (drawing, 1866). Note the climbing ropes hanging from the roof trusses.

by Edward A Grüning for the German Gymnastic Society, founded in 1861 by Ernst Ravenstein, a geographer and cartographer. Ravenstein (p 143) helped set up what was probably the first purpose-built gym in the UK **[3]**. It opened in January 1865, initially for Germans, but within a decade at least a half of its 1,100 members were English. The National Olympian Association held the indoor events of their first Olympic Games in the Gymnasium in 1866. These games continued annually here until the White City games in 1908. The gymnasium was then wound up and the premises sold to the GNR as office space. The building was damaged during a daylight aeroplane raid by Germans in July 1917. The Gymnasium was originally larger; its entrance was removed during CTRL works and the frontage reconstructed. The interior was renovated in 2015. The original laminated timber arches supporting iron spandrels span the breadth of the hall, a construction used also for the original roofs of King's Cross Station, and still sport the hooks to which climbing ropes were attached. The building now houses, appropriately perhaps, a German restaurant.

Walk left to reach **The Stanley Building**, the only surviving block of a group of five model dwellings. It dates from 1864-65. Not only is it one of the oldest examples of working-class flats in London (although no longer used as such), it is also an early example of the use of concrete, because it was cheap and reduced the risk of fire. Erected by the Improved Industrial Dwellings Company (of which Lord Stanley was Chairman) and to a design adapted from Prince Albert's model cottages for the Great Exhibition, the blocks housed 104 families in completely self-contained accommodation. One of the blocks was destroyed by WWII bombs, one was pulled down for road widening, another fell victim to the CTRL works, while the fourth was pulled down when Pancras Road was realigned to its present course once St Pancras International had been completed. Stanley Buildings was condemned in 1968 as unfit for human habitation but survived to be leased for short life community housing in the 1980s and 1990s. Mike Leigh (p 114) set his 1988 film *High Hopes* here. In the film the lead character takes his old mum to the roof (used for clothes drying and children's play areas) to see trains pulling out of St Pancras. 'It's the top of the world', she exclaims. The block has been restored and given a modern addition to house serviced offices.

This passageway is the only reminder of several parallel and once narrow turnings off Pancras Road, which were laid out in the late 18th century to the north of the Smallpox Hospital. Before the coming of the railway this part of Pancras Road was known as Pancras Place. Nearest the hospital stood a turning called Paradise Row (which several historians have erroneously stated to be part of Agar Town, which lay further north). In 1827 an inhabitant, a local hog-dealer named Charles Martin, was gored to death by a large boar he was driving along Maiden Lane. At No.31 Pancras Place the Somers Town Self-Supporting Dispensary was operating in 1843, charging one shilling for a consultation 'to meet the requirements of the middle and working classes', though how many of the latter could afford this is doubtful. A dispensary of the same name was based in Chalton Street (p 95) towards the end of the century.

Houses built in the vicinity quickly deteriorated, and had by the Victorian period become an 'awful rookery'. A report of 1850 talks of sixteen houses in Pancras Place in a filthy state, never painted or repaired, each let to five or more families, with partially uncovered cesspools, and if one was taken down all would fall. Fall they did within a few months, as much of the area was cleared by the GNR and then rebuilt. The street layout off Pancras Road was retained, although Paradise Row was replaced by GNR stables and Pancras Place was renamed Stainton Terrace from

1865 to 1872, after the landowners, the Stainton family.

South of the gymnasium was a passage called Weller's Court (before 1852 Weller's Place), while where we stand was Clarence Passage, now much enlarged; it contained a corner pub called the Duke of Clarence, which was later used as a homeless hostel by the Simon Community. North of Stanley Buildings was Stanley Passage (known as Red Lion Passage until 1937). Houses between Clarence and Red Lion Passages, including a diminutive Scalesbury Place (described by the Medical Officer of Health in 1856 as 'quite unfit for human habitation'), were swept away to form Stanley Buildings.

All these turnings initially led into Pancras Walk, parallel to Pancras Road and which once looked across open fields towards Islington. By the mid-19th century this had become cobbled Cheney Street, renamed Cheney Road **[4]** in 1937, so called after William Cheney, its builder. With its industrial Victorian feel, overlooked by gasholders, it was beloved of filmmakers, providing a setting for the van robbery in the Ealing comedy *The Ladykillers* (1955). It also attracted the artist Käthe Strenitz who spent many years in the late 20th century sketching images of this area and the railway lands to the north, capturing the desolation of the post-industrial landscape. The London Metropolitan Archives holds a collection of her artwork donated by her family after her death in 2017.

4 Cheney Road looking towards King's Cross Station 1977. The rear of the German Gymnasium is on the right. Photo by Geoffrey Skelsey

Now walk ahead and into **PANCRAS SQUARE**, opened in 2015. A giant pin oak tree marks the entrance. Water tumbles down green lawns between the tall office buildings, which are part of the huge King's Cross Central development (for more, see Route 3).

Here was once Pancras Gasworks, formally opened by Sir William Congreve in June 1823 for the Imperial Gas Light and Coke Company, which had purchased the southernmost part of the estate of William Agar (p 43). The Regent's Canal had opened a little to the north in 1820 and quickly attracted industry along its banks. A short branch canal was dug leading into the gasworks and a large wharf developed. In 1828 the company was found guilty of illegally extracting, over several years, large quantities of water (950 tons daily) from the canal through pipes laid below the surface.

The gas was manufactured by burning vast quantities of coal and the stench must have been overpowering. In 1860 the Gasworks was expanded when several acres alongside what is now Camley Street (p 49) were purchased and the gasometers were increased in height to cope with the huge demand for gas before there was competition from electricity. At this time the Gasworks was held to be the largest and finest in the world. By 1904, when the company ceased to manufacture gas here, the site was 11 acres in extent. The surrounding retort houses and other buildings were demolished in 1921, but the gasholders remained in use until 1999. Most were dismantled in 2001 and stored on site before reuse (see p 54).

The Gasworks' contaminated land was cleaned of tar and coal before construction of the present blocks began. Pancras Square's central landscaping sits on top of a steel podium deck that accommodates an underground, shared delivery space for the buildings. They are all served by the district heating network (p 54).

The first block along the left side of the square is 5-storey **No.7**, wrapped around The Stanley Building. Designed by Studio Downie Architects, it was completed in 2016. The University of Warwick's London hub is here, fittingly based in an area being touted as London's 'Knowledge Quarter'.

No.6 is an 11-storey block with black metal beams, designed by AHMM (Allford Hall Monaghan Morris), with an impressive atrium. It provides offices for some 2,500 Google staff working on products such as Android and YouTube. It opened in 2016. All food and drink in the cafes and canteens is provided free, but there is a gym surrounded by a 90-m running track, with massages available afterwards. There are also sleep pods for those needing a nap!

Beyond it is **No.5**, a major community building for the London Borough of Camden, opened to the public in 2014. It was designed by Bennetts Associates, with each façade treated differently. It includes a leisure centre, swimming pools, library, café and customer services centre. It also houses most Camden Council office-based staff and was funded by a major reorganisation and sale of old office buildings across the borough.

Terminating the square on its northern side is **No.4**, designed by Eric Parry, with a façade of glass, glazed ceramic and patinated steel. The last is said to recall 'the heroic engineering of the Industrial Revolution'. Its private roof garden is a moorland landscape. The building opened in 2018 and provides the HQ of Universal Music UK.

On the right side are three blocks rising up the slope, each one a little taller and wider. As in other blocks there are shops and restaurants at street level. **No.1** was completed in 2013 and has twisted iron columns to reflect the site's heritage. Designed by David Chipperfield Architects, and called The Gridiron, the building provides serviced office space over eight floors. The fashion house Louis Vuitton has its UK HQ here. The ground floor gives direct access to King's Cross St Pancras Underground Station. 11-storey **No.2** was completed in 2014 to a design by the master planners of King's Cross Central, Allies & Morrison. It has a white precast stone outer masonry layer and a metal and glass inner layer arranged on a grid. Among those based here is PRS for Music, the organisation that represents over 100,000 songwriters, composers and music publishers.

Walk up to No.2 and turn right between it and **No.3**, designed by Porphyrios Associates, completed in 2016 and now let to global communications group, Havas. They've called it the HKX Building. It has a 1930s feel.

Turn left into **KING'S BOULEVARD**, which is the central spine of the King's Cross Central development south of the canal, with an expansive pavement for pedestrians. Major retailers have moved in to the ground floor shops.

The laying out of King's Boulevard entailed the destruction of an east–west street called Battlebridge Road, abutting the southern edge of the Gasworks. This in turn had destroyed Suffolk Street, one of the residential streets developed after a 99-year lease had been granted on the Drakefield estate in 1806. The streets to the south were Northampton, Norfolk and Ashby Streets (with small China Walk off the latter), all bounded on the west by Pancras Walk (later Cheney Street) and on the east by Upper Edmund Street. In 1850 the GNR purchased the freehold from James Pope, but was slow to acquire individual leases. The area was densely populated, with more than 300 people living in Suffolk Street alone; on the 1851 census most of the men worked on the railway or at the Gasworks. The construction of the tunnel for the Hotel Curve (p 31) in 1861-62 inflicted structural damage upon a number of properties in the district, which obliged the Company to buy up those houses worst affected. The GNR drew up plans for the partial redevelopment of the estate during the mid-1860s and had bought up all the remaining leases by 1870. It had agreed to establish a road connection between Suffolk Street and York Road (now York Way), and decided to lay out Battlebridge Road a little to the north. The roadway and viaduct across the GNR tracks was completed in 1873.

It was some years before all the properties in former Suffolk Street were torn down; the Freemasons' Arms pub lasted until 1885 and a handful of inhabited dwellings remained on the 1891 census. They were razed later in the year and Culross Buildings was built in Battlebridge Road to house those displaced by the enlargement of King's Cross Station. Named in honour of Lord Colville of Culross, the GNR Chairman, the block was a rare example of a tenement style of flats applied to railway housing. It had a basement for railway workshops and mess rooms, accessible only from the rear (by the railway tracks). It featured in the film *Nuns on the Run* (1990). The street also contained other buildings put up by the GNR: Culross Hall, which in 1898 became one of three mission halls run by the GNR as centres for religious guidance and recreation, and No.41, built as a canteen. All these buildings were demolished in summer 2008.

The northern part of King's Boulevard lies over the retort houses of Pancras Gasworks, later replaced by a stone yard, garages, and also railway stables, as the land had been bought by the GNR. Its successor the LNER never found the money to build a projected motor maintenance depot. This was finally constructed by British Rail in 1955. It was abandoned in the 1980s and its disused buildings and equipment was taken over by a collective of artists calling themselves the Mutoid Waste Company. Inspired by the *Mad Max* films they made giant post-apocalyptic sculptures welded from scrap machinery and cars. They were evicted by the police in 1989 although the depot buildings survived until the new Millennium.

The street ends at **GOODS WAY**, where it opens up into a small plaza that gives a fine view of development north of the canal. During WWII there was a piggery at this point, whose ruins stood here until the depot was built.

The western section of Goods Way to our left has been realigned; it used to bend away southwards. It was initially part of Wharf Road, which crossed the canal into the King's Cross Goods Yard by the former Somers Bridge, close to the Coal Office (p 56), the curving brick buildings over to the left. The road was renamed Goods Way in 1921, after the eastern section had been laid out over the Gasworks and extended to York Way (to which we walk, right). The canalside wall has now been removed.

Before the recent redevelopment Goods Way was notorious for prostitution. Many of the working girls were local drug addicts although some travelled here by train. Their clients were mostly kerb crawlers, including in 1991 the Director of Public Prosecutions, Sir Allan Green.

On the north side in the 1960s a petrol

station was built, redesigned in 2012 as a restaurant and cultural venue, The Filling Station. It closed in 2016 and was replaced by an apartment and sales gallery for Gasholders London (p 59), which has since become the Chapel Down gin works. Walk past it.

On reaching **YORK WAY** take a few steps to the left for the view from **Maiden Lane Bridge**. The first bridge over the canal was built in 1819. It was widened and rebuilt in 1852, 1923 and most recently in 1998, but parts of the original fabric, including some fine cast iron work, were retained. Underneath stop gates were installed during WWII to prevent flooding of the railway tunnel into King's Cross in the event of bombing; each night these gates were pulled shut. Note how the canal widens near the bridge – on its southern bank barges moored at two flour mills (the Albion Mills), built here in 1869 and in operation until the milling trade went into decline in the late 1880s. They were probably named after the nearby Albion pub (on the corner of former Stephenson Street to the south). Numerous inquests were held there into the deaths of people who drowned in the canal, which was popular with swimmers and suicides.

Across the road (in Islington) towers King's Place with a serpentine glass frontage, designed by Dixon Jones in 2008. Office space – for *The Guardian* and *The Observer* newspapers - finances the public facilities which include two galleries and two concert halls. It stands on the site of Belmont Wharf, where dust contractors were prosecuted in the 1850s for keeping huge heaps of 'hard and soft core' that damaged the health of St Pancras residents.

In existence since at least 1300, York Way has had many names. The Elizabethan antiquary John Norden said that, 'deep and dirtie' in winter, it was at first called Longwich Lane. It was occasionally known as Black Dog Lane, as it led to the Black Dog inn at Highgate. By the 18th century it was always Maiden Lane, so-called either from a corruption of 'midden', or dunghill, or from an image of the Virgin Mary which might have stood beside the lane before the Reformation. That the name 'Mayde Lane' was recorded as early as 1467 lends some credence to the latter, less inelegant theory. A public house called the Maidenhead once stood at Battlebridge, on the lane's southeast corner.

Maiden Lane was renamed York Road in 1853 after the opening of King's Cross Station and Goods Yard, for which the lane had been doubled in width; the GNR railway went from London to York. The road was renumbered in 1881, with odds on the St Pancras (west) side, and in 1938 was given its current name, York Way.

By the 19th century the land along Maiden Lane had become a semi-industrial twilight zone. Dickens wrote in *Our Mutual Friend* that the area was 'a tract of suburban Sahara, where tiles and bricks were burned, bones were boiled, rubbish was shot, dogs fought and dust was heaped by contractors'. A drawing of 1843 by George Scharf shows carpet grounds here, with carpets slung across large wooden posts and beaten by women wielding 6-ft poles.

Cross Goods Way at the traffic lights and walk south as far as the next set of lights, alongside a brick wall. In the early 19th century two cul-de-sacs led off west from Maiden Lane ending at Pancras Gasworks: Stephenson Street and Congreve Street. They had been built by the Imperial Gas Light and Coke Company after 1823 on land it had leased from the Governors of St Bart's at the southern tip of Allensbury (see p 50). Noted as an unhealthy district during the cholera epidemic of 1849, the small houses in both were demolished over the next two years by the GNR. The company was however tasked under its Act of Parliament to retain Congreve Street at its own expense as a bridge, over the new tracks, to the Gasworks; it was removed in 1911 after the latter ceased operating.

In 1850 the GNR had also pulled down several little streets further south for its permanent station: Union Place, separated by open ground from Maiden Lane; Essex Street; part of Norfolk Street; the east side of Adden Place with Vernon's Buildings; Spencer Place; Victory Place; and the main thoroughfare, (Lower) Edmund Street. In 1828 Thomas Creswick, the landscape painter, had settled in Edmund Street. At No.12 the printer and freemason George Claret set up a printing press in 1835. He published a book *The Whole of Craft Masonry*, which explained lodge rituals. At the time the Grand Chapter considered this a heinous crime. William Treen was a spoon maker who lived at No.3 Essex Street; he was tried at the Old Bailey on 17 October 1833 for forging the mark of the Goldsmith's Company on two spoons, but as he had only pawned rather than sold them he was acquitted. The open ground by Union Place – once known as Cat's Head Acre - was the site of a gigantic dustheap **[5]**, which provided ash for nearby brickmakers and gainful employment for 'sifters' who lived locally. Its towering grey mass is depicted in an 1837 watercolour by E H Dixon, with the trees of the Smallpox Hospital's grounds behind it. The dust heap was removed in 1848. It has been said it was sold for a princely sum to Russia to help make bricks to rebuild Moscow but that confuses this dust heap with another that had stood south of the New Road at the top of Gray's Inn Road on the Battlebridge estate and removed in 1826.

5 The Great Dust Heap, King's Cross 1837 (watercolour by E H Dixon). The Smallpox Hospital grounds behind and houses in Union Place to the right

Pause at the first gap in the wall. Set into the brickwork on the far side is a St Pancras parish boundary stone, dated 1853. At this point Battlebridge Road (p 25) once provided the only east-west route north of King's Cross until Goods Way was laid out in 1921, when the long viaduct over the tracks here was dismantled. The cobbled ramp (left, behind the locked gate) was the former cab road into the station.

From this spot one can admire the train sheds of **King's Cross Station**, the work of the architect Lewis Cubitt. As planned, there was a departures and an arrivals shed, separated by a spine wall and each with just one platform. Both were roofed in laminated wood, inspired by the work of the French engineer, Colonel Emy. The timber rotted and had to be replaced in wrought iron in 1866-67 on the east side, and twenty years later on the west. The ribs rise from dignified brick arcades, the thrust on the east taken by the 3-storey block, formerly offices, along York Way. Each round-arched roof has a span of 105 ft, covering an area 800 ft long, 210 ft wide and 72 ft high. The roofs were supposedly modelled on the imperial riding school in Moscow. They were restored as part of a major regeneration project (p 30) from 2008-12, letting light flood back into the station. Solar panels were added and placed at the apex of the lanterns to minimise visual impact.

When the station first opened on 14 October 1852 it was the largest in Britain, but soon could not cope with the amount of traffic. This increased after 1858, when the GNR allowed its rival the MR to run trains into the station. This arrangement was stipulated in an Act of Parliament which the GNR had supported in the hope that the MR would not build a London terminus of its own. It was frequently said that Midland trains were deliberately held back by GNR signalmen, giving their own company's trains priority. The MR withdrew as soon as its own station at St Pancras opened in 1868.

By then further platforms had been built at King's Cross, including one just outside the station, although this did little to alleviate the congestion. The other ramp, on your right, leads down to its site. York Road Station, opened on 1 June 1866, had a single platform used by southbound trains linking up with the Metropolitan line. The platform had to be resited after tunnelling works in 1878, but the station continued in use for nearly a century. It had its own booking office, removed after the station closed on 15 March 1977, upon electrification.

Look through the railings to get an idea of the railway's approach to King's Cross Station. The passage under the canal (which was placed in a cast-iron aqueduct) cost the GNR a small fortune and presented great problems of limiting gradients and clearances; early steam trains had a fearsome climb out of London. The original two-track **Gas Works Tunnel**, with its semi-circular portal, also became a serious bottleneck as traffic increased. It was supplemented in 1878 by the now disused tunnel on the east and in 1892 by another on the west. Further tracks to the west were added in 1922-23 to form the GNR's Passenger Locomotive Depot on the excavated site of the canal basin of the former Gasworks.

Now retrace your steps along York Way and Goods Way to regain **KING'S BOULEVARD**. Between the railway tracks and the street the Internet giant Google is building its UK HQ in a 'groundscraper', as long as the Shard is tall, for 4,500 staff. Google scrapped the initial plans for being 'too boring' and then employed Olympic cauldron designer Thomas Heatherwick, working with Danish architects Bjarke Ingels Group (aka BIG). This is the first building Google has had designed for itself outside America and the immense pile will house several major sports facilities, with a landscaped roof terrace, including a 200m running trail. Before construction work began in 2017 the site here – which had been used as a car park for the station - was used from 2015 for a temporary theatre (e.g. for productions of *The Railway Children* and David Bowie's *Lazarus*), supported by Google.

King's Boulevard ends in **Battlebridge Place**, a paved area opened in 2012. What looks like a huge birdcage is the artwork *Identified Flying Object* by Jacques Rival, moved from its earlier site on Goods Way. Colourfully illuminated at night, its bars are wide enough to walk through and the public is encouraged to have a go on the swing.

Battlebridge Place lies on the site of a large 3-storey warehouse that stood along the passageway called Weller's Court. Initially the King's Cross Patent Wheelworks, erected in

1858 and sold in 1866, it later became a printing works. Next to it King's Cross Market, a 'people's market', had been formed in 1868 with 86 outlets. It was not a success and in April 1870 Eley Brothers **[6]** opened a huge cartridge case manufactory on the site. They became the first ammunition manufacturers to become a public company, in 1874. They subsumed the printing works but closed their factory here in the early 1890s, when the property was bought by the GNR. In the 20th century the area was for many years a car park, but some of the small buildings fronting Pancras Road long survived, including the Earl Russell pub at No.2.

We are at the north entrance to **King's Cross Station.** As noted earlier, the expansion of passenger facilities on this west side of the main terminus entailed the demolition of a number of residential streets. The suburban platforms were built in 1875 and extended westwards in 1895 by the reconstruction of the west wall (along the line of King's Boulevard) and the construction of a new roof.

Entering the station, we walk past both the Suburban Platforms (9-11) and the stairs up to the Parcel Yard, a converted parcel sorting office spread over two floors; it is said to be the largest station pub in Britain. On 11 May 1941 two 1,000-lb bombs chained together demolished much of the western range of offices. Luckily it was early Sunday morning otherwise casualties could have been horrendous. As it was 12 people died.

In 2005 a £450 million restoration plan was announced to transform King's Cross Station. It was restored in 2008-13 by Network Rail, with the support of the Railway Heritage Trust and in the end cost £547 million. The station's main new feature is the extraordinary vaulted semi-circular roof over the new Western Concourse, designed by John McAslan & Partners, who drew up a master plan in 2005. It rises some 20m and spans the full 150m length of the surviving Grade-I-Listed Western Range, whose brickwork and masonry has been restored. 16 steel, tree-form columns radiate from a tapered central funnel that masks the booking hall. The original entrance to the station was on this side, where a porte-cochère once stood to protect passengers arriving by carriage, but a concourse was built in the 1970s facing Euston Road, now removed.

6 Cartridges made by Eley Bros.

There is always a long queue for photos at Platform 9¾, where one may imagine catching the Hogwarts Express, with the inevitable shop alongside with Harry Potter-themed merchandise. There are other 'legends' associated with King's Cross, all equally spurious. Some say that at Battlebridge in AD 61, Boudicca fought her last battle with the Romans, and that she is buried under Platform 10. Others hold that the ruins of Troynovant, Britain's mythological and ancient capital, lie under the station. Here, too, King Arthur would have drawn the sword Excalibur from the stone.

Beneath the Departure board is an oval plaque with the closing lines of the poem The *Whitsun Weddings* by Philip Larkin, inspired by a journey from Hull to King's Cross.

At one end of the Booking Office is a stone plaque recording the renovated station's formal opening by Transport Minister Justine Greening on 14 March 2012 (the exterior was completed in 2013). The plaque itself is an old worn step from a stairway in the Western

Range. At the far end is a 2016 statue by Hazel Reeves of Sir Nigel Gresley, replacing a blue plaque and erected on the 75th anniversary of his death. Gresley was a chief engineer of the GNR and its successor (from 1923), the London and North Eastern Railway. He had offices at the station and designed many stylish and modern steam locomotives, including *Flying Scotsman* and *Mallard*, holder of the world steam speed record. His lasting invention in rolling stock was articulation, still much used today (e.g. on Eurostar trains).

On the opposite side of the concourse is a passage that gives access to the GNH Bar and to the **Great Northern Hotel**, whose exterior we saw earlier. In his plans for King's Cross Lewis Cubitt set aside an area for a hotel, but it was not built until 1852-53 and finally opened in May 1854 on a 21-year lease to the hotelier Joseph Dethier; the GNR took over in 1875. Dethier had been closely involved in the hotel's design. It was one of the first to include rooms on the 'continental system': bedrooms en suite with sitting rooms. The *Official Illustrated Guide* to the GNR in the 1860s stated 'good wines, excellent viands, lofty well ventilated bed-rooms and extremely moderate charges are among the advantages of this first-class hotel'. The cost of full board, at 14s (70p) a night, was however in the upper range of London hotels of the time. Modernised between the wars and sold by British Rail in 1983, the hotel was in service until 2001, then the oldest purpose-built hotel in central London. It owed its longevity to its simple, hence easily maintained, layout and fireproof construction. In 2013, after a £40 million facelift, it reopened as a luxury boutique hotel, with many of the original features retained.

Cubitt designed the hotel to look inwards towards the station across a large flower garden, away from the tenements of Somers Town. Over the years the garden was annexed by station buildings and became used by taxis. It latterly served as a car park and was known as Station Place. It was removed to build the present concourse. Before WWI there was also a garden in front of the hotel, leading down to Euston Road.

In 1863 the world's first underground railway, the Metropolitan line, was opened from Paddington to Farringdon and a few months later the tunnel connections from the Great Northern (already built) were opened. Northbound trains had to negotiate the Hotel Curve, a notoriously dark, smoke-filled greasy climb upwards, where on at least one occasion a train slid backwards into the one behind. They then had to reverse into the main station until in 1878 an extra suburban platform was provided at York Road Station for their use. Large scale OS maps show the line went neatly between the station and the hotel, and not under the hotel itself, as is sometimes supposed.

At the southern end of the station concourse, the access to platforms 0 to 8 has replaced the ground-floor office where the infamous fraudster Leopold Redpath once worked. For eight years, as the GNR's registrar of stocks and shares, he cooked the books undetected, defrauding his employers of nigh on £½ million. Finally rumbled in 1856, he was put on trial and found guilty was transported to Australia for life.

Go through and from the gate-line look along the platforms towards the tunnels under the canal outside the station. Admire the two main shed roofs, before exiting the station into **King's Cross Square** once more.

Over to the left is Henry Moore's *Large Spindle Piece* from 1974. Turning right, you can enter the Underground for your journey home, but just before the steps down, note the blue plaque on the wall of the mainline station recognizing both the architect who first built it and the organisations that have given it a new lease of life.

Route 2

The St Pancras Heartland

Circular walk from King's Cross
St Pancras Underground Station

This walk leads us through the heartland of St Pancras and over the site of Agar Town, renowned in early-Victorian times as a slum and which was obliterated by the Midland Railway (MR) in the 1860s.

From King's Cross St Pancras Underground Station take the Regent's Canal exit and emerge into Battlebridge Place (p 29). Walk towards St Pancras International but stay on the east side of **PANCRAS ROAD**, past the German Gymnasium and further along the offices of Google and Camden's community hub (all described in Route 1). Cross by the traffic lights, turning left under St Pancras International, before following the road to the right at the next lights as it resumes its original course.

Its west side here is described in Route 7. Lining the road on the east side was a row of MR coal drops erected in the 1860s and rebuilt in the 1950s. They were later used as garages and workshops, including a toy shop featuring a very prominent ship's figurehead, until pulled down when St Pancras International was developed in the first years of the 21st century.

This was once the site of Pancras Wells, a fashionable 18th-century spa, one of several along the banks of the Fleet or 'River of Wells'. It was first mentioned in 1697, when Edward Martin, keeper of the adjoining tavern The Horns, promoted its waters and the extensive gardens with long straight walks shaded by avenues of trees. In 1700 its two pump-rooms offered a choice of purgative or chalybeate (iron-rich) water for 3d a day or half a guinea (52½p) for the whole season. The virtues of its waters in curing such diseases as the King's Evil (scrofula) were well publicised: 'it cleanses the body and sweetens the blood, and is a general and sovereign help to Nature'; it was also intimated it helped with venereal disease. The proprietors bottled the waters for sale in London, and a print of 1729 shows various stones voided by Mr Harrod of Islington after drinking the waters for a few days.

The spa's fortunes fluctuated during the 18th century. There were complaints in 1722 of scandalous company and it was probably closed in 1751 when there was a boarding school for young gentlemen run by John Bolt on the site. Old Bailey records which detail many highway robberies nearby show it was open again in 1754, and by 1769 its two Long Rooms were advertised as able to 'dine 200 completely'. Facing competition from the Adam & Eve tavern nearby, the spa felt it necessary to warn people that 'to avoid mistakes St Pancras Wells is on that side of the church yard towards London'.

The spa had closed by 1797, when a map shows houses built over its gardens. Church Hill climbed gently eastward, overlooking the churchyard. After 1800 the street was continued southward as Essex Place (otherwise Back Walk), linked to the main road by diminutive Dorset Place and King's Place, and leading into Spann's Buildings. Put up by Charles Spann (d.1829), owner of some very poor property (Spann's Place) in Somers Town, this row of 23 cottages was a local centre of clay pipe manufacture. At No.12 lived Francis Kerby, who published widely in the 1810s and 1820s on theoretical chemistry and was curator of instruments to two of the most eminent professors at London University from 1828 until his death in 1835. His son Frederick made telegraph instruments before emigrating to the US in the 1840s. At the foot of Spann's Buildings, on Pancras Road, the Agar Town Ragged School was set up in 1846 in an old skittle alley next to the Olive Branch pub. It had free spaces for up to 100 infants and 80 boys and girls. It was run for several years by Robert Clemenger, later Vicar of St Thomas, Agar Town (p 65), who by all accounts was very popular throughout the local area. At an inquest held in 1854 it was reported that he had dived into the canal to save a child from drowning.

Along Pancras Road itself was Church Terrace, and further south, Church Row; the spring that had given rise to Pancras Wells was enclosed in one of the latter's private gardens, close to the Wheatsheaf public house. The meteorologist William Marriott was born at No.8 Church Terrace in 1848. He was a prolific author, with more than 100 publications to his name. In 1814 Percy Bysshe Shelley, his future wife Mary, and her stepsister-in-law Claire Clairmont (later mother of Byron's illegitimate daughter Allegra) stayed briefly at No.5 Church Terrace after their return from Europe. Shelley was in debt, and hiding from the bailiffs. To pass the time, the party dabbled in chemical experiments and let off fireworks in the garden.

More scientific experiments took place two doors away at Baxter House. From 1841-66 it was occupied by the inventor Henry Bessemer. In a small 'factory' erected in the back garden he manufactured his famed bronze powder, an inexpensive substitute for the gold powder used by japanners, which made him a fortune and enabled him to buy a Highgate home. He then used Baxter House as a workshop, constructing a centrifugal machine for separating molasses from crystals of sugar. Here he later conducted experiments that led to the patenting of his celebrated 'converter', whereby steel could at last be cheaply manufactured, by blowing air through molten pig-iron. He also had a 'secret' factory in the area. It was by the canal in Cambridge Street (p 47), shown as 'Besemeer's Glass Factory' on the 1851 census.

Church Terrace and Church Row and the little streets behind were all swept away for the building of the MR's coal drops, mentioned above.

Walk alongside St Pancras churchyard beneath tall plane trees and alongside its brick wall built c.1820 and topped with railings. We soon reach the steps to the splendid entrance gates, added in 1891, and walk up to **St Pancras Old Church**, the historic heart of St Pancras **[7]**. There may possibly have been a Christian place of worship here, beside the River Fleet, since Roman times. The discovery, in 1848, of an altar stone said to be 6th-century, suggested that the church was rebuilt and rededicated at the time of St Augustine's mission to Britain in 597 (Pancras being Augustine's favourite saint). There is a 9th-century reference to a church and the

7 St Pancras Church and Wells. Engraving c.1750 by J Roberts after J B C Chatelain

boundaries of the parish may have been fixed then; it almost certainly predated the Norman Conquest. The building itself was first mentioned in 1183, with records of visitations during the 13th century. It was thoroughly repaired between 1331 and 1350 but then lay neglected and unaltered, as the centre of village life shifted to Kentish Town.

When the new St Pancras parish church opened on what is now Euston Road in 1822 the old parish church became a chapel of ease and an interpretation board on the right shows what it looked like in 1827. The relentless increase in population as London expanded led to it being enlarged and insensitively 'Normanised' in 1847-48 by Alexander Gough of Gough & Roumieu. The old square tower was demolished and its material used in extending the nave 30 ft westward and adding a spire on the south side. Further, more sympathetic restorations, took place in 1925, 1948 (after WWII bomb damage) and 1978 (by Quinlan Terry, when the parish room was created at the west end). The present church has a timber-framed and pebble-dashed belfry, and a slate roof at the front but pantiles over the chancel. If rather ugly outside, the interior is delightful. In the church are some impressive wall monuments, including one from 1637 with busts of William Platt and his wife and another from 1672, topped by easel and brushes, to Samuel Cooper, the miniaturist who painted Cromwell 'warts and all'.

The old church had long been used primarily for marriages. It witnessed the marriage of William Godwin to his first wife, Mary Wollstonecraft in 1797; that of the pantomime clown Joseph Grimaldi, to his second wife, in 1801; and, in 1718, that of the 'thief taker' Jonathan Wild to his third. In 1760, Laurence Shirley, the 4th Earl Ferrers, famously executed for the murder of his steward, was buried under the tower, although his remains were later removed to his family's seat in Leicestershire.

After visiting the church turn left (or if the church is shut, right) by the gate beside a tomb and along a path through what was the churchyard but is now maintained as part of **St Pancras Gardens**. Burials in St Pancras churchyard whose graves are no longer visible include Jonathan Wild, following his execution at Tyburn in 1725 (his body was subsequently stolen and the coffin abandoned in nearby Fig Lane); Giacomo Leoni, architect, in 1745, well known for his editions of Palladio and Alberti; Francis Townley, executed for his part in the Jacobite rebellion of 1745; William Woollett, engraver to George III, in 1785 (who has a memorial in Westminster Abbey); Chevalier D'Éon **[8]**, political writer and transvestite, sometime double agent of Louis XVI, who died in poverty in the guise of a woman in 1810; Captain John Mills ('the last survivor of the Black Hole of Calcutta') in 1811; William Franklin, son of Benjamin, but unlike his father, whom he had assisted in his experiments with lightning, a leading Loyalist, in 1813; and in 1821 John Polidori, Byron's physician and author of *The Vampyre*, the first published modern vampire story in English.

8 Chevalier D'Éon (a 1792 painting by Thomas Stewart after Jean-Laurent Mosnier)

The churchyard, used for burials for centuries, became densely packed with bodies. Records indicate that between 1689 and 1854 88,000 burials took place, over 32,000 in the final 23 years. During this latter period trench burial was commonplace: 15 or so coffins would be stacked in a trench which was left open for a week before more coffins were added and then a thin layer of soil placed over them. The ground was raised several feet by the accumulation of bodies and fungus grew inside the church. Intensified by the cholera outbreak of 1849, an order-in-council in 1855 discontinued burials. By then St Pancras Cemetery had opened in East Finchley.

Walk ahead with a row of four upright tomb stones in the distance. One is inscribed in French to the Marquise de Tourville and the Vicomtesse de Buffevent, both émigrés. The burial ground was popular with French refugees who died in this country after the Revolution. It was believed that masses were said for their souls in a church dedicated to St Pancras in the south of France. Bigot de St Croix, Louis XVI's last minister, was also buried here.

Take the first left turn up steps along a tree-lined path, with the church to our left. Among the surviving table-tombs, now mostly illegible, is a charming gravestone featuring a bar of musical notation. It is to Samuel Webbe, a prolific composer of 'glees', and the first librarian of the Glee Club in 1787; for 37 years he was also organist of the Sardinian Chapel in Lincoln's Inn Fields. There is a large pink-granite memorial to numerous members of the Rhodes family, which once farmed land locally (p 50) and was prominent in parish affairs for several generations. The monument was erected in 1890 by the family's most famous son, Cecil Rhodes, founder of Rhodesia (now Zimbabwe and Zambia). At its base is a record that he was buried in the Matoppo Mountains, now the Matobo Hills, Zimbabwe.

St Pancras churchyard was originally quite small, arcing round the church. It was enlarged in 1727 when waste ground to the south and east known as the Pindle was bought and a curving ditch filled in. This made the southern boundary straight, as it is today. Further land to the east was purchased in 1792, authorized by Act of Parliament. 'The New Burying Ground' comprised two acres divided into what were called the First, Second and Third Grounds.

It was through the New Burying Ground that the MR cut a swathe in 1866-67, en route to its new St Pancras terminus. This left what was known as the Third Ground, which was bought by the company in 1889 to widen its lines into St Pancras. During the Channel Tunnel Rail Link (CTRL) works in 2002-03 a detailed archaeological survey was made of the Third Ground. Many of the graves were identified as those of French refugees, including the bodies of some senior clergy. One was the Archbishop of Narbonne, Arthur Dillon (1721-1806), son of an Irish Jacobite, complete with a gold-sprung set of false teeth made of the finest porcelain. His body was reinterred with great ceremony at Narbonne in 2007.

The displacement of graves during the CTRL works was undertaken with care. The same could not be said of the MR's works in 1866. The workmen were not told what to do with bodies they dug up. Macabre scenes of disinterred, dismembered corpses caused a national outcry and questions in Parliament. Work was suspended, but later allowed to proceed under supervision. The excavation for a link tunnel to the Metropolitan line (later used by Thameslink) was undertaken at night and behind screens. However, an attempt by the MR in 1874 to sweep away the rest of the churchyard and the old church was firmly resisted.

Overseeing the relocation of bodies, as assistant to Arthur Blomfield, was a young Thomas Hardy, then living in London as a trainee architect. He later described the experience in his poem *The Levelled Churchyard*:

We late-lamented resting here,
are mixed to human jam
And each to each exclaims in fear,
'I know not which I am!'

The remains were reinterred in a 40-ft-deep burial pit, specially consecrated in 1866 by the Bishop of London. The Coroner's Court (see below) was later built over it.

Take the first path on the left to walk behind the church. Over to the right is a large railed ash tree, which has grown up through gravestones left in a dome-shaped pile. This is known as the Hardy Tree, although most of the stones are not in fact from St Pancras churchyard but from neighbouring St Giles Burial Ground. A corner of the latter was also partially affected by the MR works, but no memorials were removed at the time.

Between the workhouse (whose former blocks overlook the gardens to the north) and St Pancras churchyard the land – once called Parsonage Close - was acquired by St Giles parish as a suburban cemetery and consecrated in June 1803. A 7-ft-wall was built around it, indicated on the large-scale OS map of 1871. Among the huge numbers buried here was John Flaxman the sculptor in 1826. The burial rate shot up in the 1840s: 10,000 between 1843 and 1845 and 3,000 in six months during the 1849 cholera epidemic. The stench was said to be appalling, and there were frequent complaints of body snatching and body burning to make more space. This led to a special parliamentary enquiry in 1850 to investigate 'alleged revolting practices'. A pall of smoke and smell was found to be hanging over the burial ground. It was closed down in 1855.

The most famous tomb here stands in the circular railed enclosure ahead. It was designed by Sir John Soane (1753-1837), 'architect of the Bank of England'. He lies buried with his eldest son and his wife Elizabeth. She died in 1815 and Soane then built this distinctive monument, in marble with a heavy Portland-stone canopy. Steps lead down to a vault beneath. If its shape looks familiar it is because it seems to have been the inspiration for Sir Giles Gilbert Scott's design for the iconic red 'K2' telephone box. It is one of only two Grade-I-Listed grave monuments in London (the other is the tomb of Karl Marx at Highgate).

On the lawn beyond is a selection of gravestones. By the path is the grave of William Jones (1776-1836), 'for many years master of a respectable school in this parish' - the Wellington House Academy, attended by Dickens; it inspired Creakle's school in *David Copperfield.* Beyond it is the standing tomb of the early feminist Mary Wollstonecraft (1759-1797), author of *A Vindication of the Rights of Woman*, and her husband William Godwin (1756-1836). Their remains were reinterred in Bournemouth, where their daughter Mary, author of *Frankenstein*, was buried in 1851. Over her mother's grave here in 1814 Mary and the poet Shelley had declared their love for each other. The prominent 8ft-high slab is a memorial to John Walker (d.1807), compiler of the still in-print *Rhyming Dictionary of the English Language.*

Walk towards the small red brick Gothic building over to the right. It was built in 1886 by architect Frederick Eggar as the **Coroner's Court**, a function it still retains. Inquests held here have included those for the victims of the fire at King's Cross Underground Station in 1989 and those of the London terrorist bombings in 2005. Next to it is the **St Pancras Public Mortuary**, modernised in 2015 by Paul Murphy Architects. It adjoins the Geffen Public Health Annexe. Dennis Geffen was Medical Officer of Health for St Pancras from 1944 to 1959, as a bronze circular plaque records.

Continue around the northern edge of the gardens and by the side of St Pancras Hospital (p 39). The dormitory blocks date from the 1890s and if they look forbidding this was because this was St Pancras Workhouse. Then walk over to the centrepiece of the gardens, the Grade-II*-Listed **Burdett-Coutts Memorial**. Angela Burdett-Coutts was famous for the amount of money she gave to charity. She was the richest woman in England after Queen Victoria, who in 1871 created her a Baroness in her own right. She was also the Lay Rector of St Pancras, and bore the costs of this memorial which lists several dozen (once) notable people whose graves had been removed. Surrounded by railings, and guarded by four beasts, it boasts an easily missed vertically mounted sundial, a stepped pedestal and floral mosaics.

Adjoining the monument railings on the west side is an upright tombstone recalling the members of the local Purchese family (cf. Purchese Street, p 119). On the north side, set in the ground, is a small memorial to the composer Johann Christian Bach, the eighteenth child of his better known father. Dubbed the 'English Bach', he settled in London, became musician to Queen Charlotte and helped popularize the piano. He died in debt in 1782 and was buried in a mass grave at St Pancras.

Over to the left is an iron water fountain, painted blue, surmounted by a round temple in imitation of the Temple of Vesta. It was presented by William Thornton, senior church-warden in August 1877. Two months earlier the two cemeteries had been opened as gardens, laid out by St Pancras Vestry after it had secured an Act of Parliament in 1875 to take control of the land and had received a gift of £100 from Baroness Burdett-Coutts. It had moved quickly to prevent the MR acquiring the land using powers of compulsory purchase.

Now walk down to the entrance which is flanked by a tile-hung Arts & Crafts lodge called **Gardener's Cottage**. This bears a plaque recording that St Pancras Gardens were completed by arrangement with the MR in 1890-91 and inaugurated on 15 July 1891 - although they had been a public space since 1877. The MR was given the green light by the Vestry to widen its tracks over the remaining parts of the New Burying Ground and to remove the residual memorials there.

The building was restored as part of a Heritage Lottery Fund grant awarded in 1997. After a lengthy consultation process final plans were approved and work began in early 2000 to renovate the gardens, including replanting, floodlighting and restoration of gates and monuments.

On the site of the lodge was once the Adam & Eve inn, here from at least 1700. An advert in 1786 says it was 'fit for the reception of the genteelest company', although Palmer wrote that it was the 'common resort of holiday folk' because of its trap-ball ground. Its tea-gardens witnessed several notable ballooning events: in 1802, a Frenchman named André-Jacques Garnerin made Britain's first planned parachute fall from a balloon – bailing out at over 8,000 ft above Bloomsbury, he crash-landed at the Adam & Eve; in 1850 and again in 1854 the noted aeronaut Charles Green made a spectacular balloon ascent; and in 1855, a well publicised ascent by a Monsieur Gardonia ended abruptly when his balloon hit a bandstand and, falling out, he hit his head on a monument in St Giles Burial Ground.

The last three ascents were made from a relocated Adam & Eve. After the St Giles Burial Ground opened on the site of its gardens (the former Parsonage Close), the old inn was demolished in 1805 and replaced by a brick chapel, bounded by iron gates; when the Burial Ground closed in 1855 the chapel became St Pancras National School. At the southern end of a row of houses named Eve Terrace, fronting the road south of the chapel, a new Adam & Eve was soon built (at No.1), retaining just a small part of the old gardens. The remnant was initially laid out for bowls but after King's Cross Station was built became known rather grandly as the Great Northern Pleasure Grounds, complete with a bandstand. It was flanked to the south by a terrace of tiny dwellings, running at right angles to the road, called Eve Place, very close to the church. At No.6 Eve Place the comedian Dan Leno was born, as George Wild Galvin, in 1861. He was regularly top of the bill in music halls. Charlie Chaplin called him the greatest comedian since Grimaldi. Eve Terrace was home until 1864 to Mrs Frances Southgate, with whom the wealthy engraver Richard Golding (p 110) had lived for over 20 years until shortly before his death in 1865. She was the prime mover in getting his body exhumed to determine whether his medical attendant, Dr Part, who was executor and main beneficiary of his will, had poisoned him.

The Adam & Eve pub (run in the 1850s by an Irish comic called Thomas Lee), Eve Place and Eve Terrace were demolished and their sites incorporated into St Pancras Gardens in 1889-90. The National School was also pulled down and its entrance gates reused here.

Leaving the gardens, turn right past the South Wing of St Pancras Hospital. The wing was built as an extension to St Pancras Workhouse and opened in March 1885 with beds for 500 old and infirm women. It was designed by H H Bridgman, who claimed the interior was 'cheery and comfortable'. The block replaced a row of terraced houses called Cook's Terrace (until 1849 Cook's Row). They are shown in James King's *Kentish Town Panorama*, which depicts properties lining the road at the start of the 19th century. King asserts that the houses were built by a Captain Cook of Hampstead, although the Dean and Chapter of St Paul's gave a 7-year renewable lease of the ground to a Somers Town butcher called William Cook. The houses first appear on Tompson's parish map of 1804.

Immediately to the north of Cook's Row St Pancras Vestry Hall was built in 1847 by the Vestry's surveyor, Mr Bond. He omitted stairs to the first floor and steps had to be added outside. The building was replaced by a new Vestry Hall by H H Bridgman in April 1875. George Bernard Shaw attended Vestry meetings here. It became St Pancras Town Hall in 1900. It had been designed for 30 staff but by the 1920s over 100 were squeezed in. It was superseded by the Town Hall on Euston Road in 1937 and demolished a decade later.

In the mid-19th century the poor seeking outdoor parish relief had to wait outside the Vestry Hall from the early hours of the morning without shelter. Up to 900 people might gather. It could be 8pm before relief was given, in the 'Black Hole', a basement room with foul air and disgusting conditions. At the time, the St Pancras Vestry shared the widely held utilitarian belief that poverty was immoral.

Directly ahead, are red and yellow brick **Goldington Buildings**, set around a courtyard behind a monumental archway guarded by massive security gates. Note the large scrolled gables. Designed by K D Young and opened in June 1904 this was the first of many blocks of flats to be erected by St Pancras Council, providing 'housing for the working classes', as the foundation stone attests. Councillor G B Shaw is said to have been among those who campaigned for their construction. The new Borough Council had inherited from St Pancras Vestry some of the worst housing in the capital; St Pancras was described by *Reynolds's News* in 1899 as the 'foulest parish in all London'.

An early resident, in flat 17B, was Ethel Le Neve, the secretary and mistress of the dentist Dr Crippen. Camden-born, she lived there with her parents at the time of her ill-fated affair with the wife-poisoner – midway between their New Oxford Street workplace and the Crippens' home in Hilldrop Crescent (off Camden Road), where the poisoning took place in 1910.

The flats were refurbished in 2011 and larger living spaces created. The block stands partly on the site of the Elephant and Castle pub (see below) and a timber yard; the River Fleet flowed between them. The timber-yard was acquired in 1825 by the builder Thomas Cubitt, but seemingly never developed at the time for housing, perhaps for fear of flooding. Facing and named after Goldington Crescent (p 123), but with a Royal College Street postal address, the U-shaped block also extends to the right along **ST PANCRAS WAY**, up which we now turn.

St Pancras Way was originally part of Gray's Inn Lane that led from Holborn to Kentish Town. By the 1820s it was here known as King's Road. The numbering along it was changed in 1885 to odds and evens, retained when it was given its present name in 1938.

Its winding route follows an ancient track running in part alongside the River Fleet. The river still flows but is now enclosed in a storm-relief drain below ground. Lining the east side of the road in the early 19th century was a long row of poplars, depicted in King's *Panorama*, that extended from Cook's Row (p 38) to the grounds of William Agar (p 42). Still shown on an 1834 map, the trees were cut down when some of the first houses of Agar Town were built in 1840.

The public house once standing on the west side of King's Road at its south end was originally called the George and Falcon, and run in 1693 by a certain Thomas George. Across the road was a meadow called George Field. In the early 18th century the inn was renamed the Elephant & Castle after the supposed discovery in 1714 of an elephant tusk near the River Fleet. This find was attributed to the antiquarian Thomas Conyers (who had died in 1694), but the accounts are contradictory and probably relate to an earlier discovery made by him nearer the City. Alternatively, the renaming may have referred to the arms of the Cutler Company. The Elephant & Castle was often used by the Vestry for meetings, and many inquests were held there. It was licensed as a theatre from 1854-91 and remained in business until Goldington Buildings were erected. During WWI its surviving premises was used as the HQ of the National Reserve (St Pancras Battalion).

Opposite the site today is **St Pancras Hospital**, formerly St Pancras Workhouse **[9]**. Previously in Camden Town, the parish workhouse moved in 1809 into new functional buildings erected on George Field; the architect was Thomas Hardwick. By the mid-century it was hopelessly overcrowded, with patients in its infirmary having to be placed on the floor. The number of inmates varied from 1,500 to 1,900, of whom some 1,000 were elderly and infirm. Children as young as eight were sent away to cotton mills in the North. The ventilation of the buildings was so poor that both patients and staff complained of sickness brought on by the fetid air. Dysentery was rife.

After critical articles in *The Lancet* and the *Illustrated London News* the Board of

9 Dinner time in St Pancras Workhouse, 1911

Guardians decided to build a new St Pancras North Infirmary on Highgate Hill, opened in 1869; the one in the Workhouse became St Pancras South Infirmary. In 1881 H H Bridgman drew up a plan for a new workhouse, after land was acquired at Cook's Terrace, but development was piecemeal. Only his South Wing (p 38) was built. In 1890-96 a number of blocks designed by A & C Harston were erected; the dormitory blocks we saw from St Pancras Gardens survive. In 1899 separate chapels for Anglicans and Roman Catholics were built. The Anglican building stands on the right and is now a multi-faith centre called 'The Well'; the Roman Catholic chapel lies at right angles behind it.

Workhouse births – usually registered as at 'No.4 King's Road' to spare blushes - included in 1861 the 'Original Pearly King' , Henry Croft (p 105), who also died here, and in 1919 both the boxer Tommy Lowne, who represented England many times, and Beatrice, later Baroness, Serota, the politician and social reformer.

In 1929 Boards of Guardians were abolished and the London County Council took over management of the Workhouse (renamed the St Pancras Institution). The infirmary had since 1920 been known as St Pancras Hospital and by the end of the decade it had subsumed the whole site. When the NHS was formed in 1948 it became part of University College Hospital. From 1951-98 it also housed the Hospital for Tropical Diseases. It now specialises in psychiatry and care of the elderly. The novelist Sir Kingsley Amis died here in 1995.

Opposite the hospital entrance at **No.7** is a 2-storey Victorian stable block with a painted sign 'South Stables'. The block was built about 1870, with a 1-storey block behind a few years later, for the MR who had larger stables just a little to the north. It remained in railway use for 100 years. From 1971 to the end of the century a scrap metal dealer was based here but it has since been converted into offices. Alongside it is a detached house, **No.9**, dating from the 1860s and also once owned by the MR. On the 1901 census it is called Burton House, the home of a Bass Company clerk who worked at the nearby Granary, of which more shortly. It became a night shelter in 1974 and is now a St Mungo hostel, for adults with drink or drug problems. A row of dwellings these buildings supplanted, here at the start of the 19th century, was known as Elephant Row from the adjoining pub (p 39); it can be seen on the 1830 Greenwood map.

The hospital grounds stretch to **GRANARY STREET**. Begun as Oxford Row, Agar Town in 1840, the road ran alongside the workhouse wall. At the far end was the workhouse's first infirmary block, built in 1848-49, while at this junction were the female oakum-picking rooms. In 1885 the road was renamed as part of Cambridge Street (p 47), some 20 years after that street's course had been diverted due to the MR's works which destroyed all the residential properties here. The works included an extensive goods yard north of the Regent's Canal. When the yard closed down in the 1970s, Cambridge Street (by then Camley Street) was extended across the canal, and the road here was given its current name after a huge warehouse that stood on its northern side.

This was the MR's Granary (not to be confused with its more famous namesake in what is now King's Cross Central). On its site from 1840 had been cottages known as Oxford Terrace, built alongside the main road, and behind them Oxford Crescent, from which led Oxford Street, Agar Town. Many were put up by the prolific local builder Thomas Want, who also built the first Vestry Hall. No.1 Oxford Crescent was the home of Anthony Portington, the Agars' land agent, who was found drowned in the nearby canal in 1845, with the Agars' rents in his pockets. Many of the buildings were cleared in 1853 when the New Bridge (p 45) was built over the canal to carry a road that was projected across Agar Fields to meet up with the new Queen's Road (p 64). The land and the surviving buildings were sold to the MR in 1860.

The immense Granary was then erected. Opened in 1865, it was designed to house 100,000 barrels of beer from Burton-on-Trent and was often known as Bass's Ale Stores. The beer arrived by train at the north of the building via a two-track bridge over the canal. Trade was not as good as expected, and the warehouse was soon also being used to store grain. From 1920 the Granary was Woolworths' London depot. It burned down in 1978 in a massive fire, in which one fireman died. The next year Rupert Murdoch bid unsuccessfully to develop the 3-acre site as the base for News International, before settling in Wapping.

In 1980-81 the present large, brown-panelled building was erected by the Post Office. It served as the Royal Mail North West District office until 1995 but now houses No.6 and No.6A. The latter is known as the Ugly Brown Building and has a hoarding featuring a lobster at its entrance; it is the HQ of the fashion brand Ted Baker plc, which now owns the freehold. In 2017 it was proposed to demolish the building and erect five 11-storey mixed-use blocks but it was still standing in early 2020.

Opposite, lining **ST PANCRAS WAY** is a large block of student flats opened in 2014 and run by Unite Students. At ground floor level is an extensive builders' merchant's yard (Travis Perkins), first created in 1982. This had been the site of the MR's main stables, which included a forge. In the 1960s the stables were rebuilt as a GPO Engineering Depot.

Beyond the student block is a small turning known as **College Grove**, which leads to Royal College Street to the west. It follows an old footpath that ran across the grounds of the Royal Veterinary College, and sloped steeply down to the River Fleet along the western side of King's Road. There were two little bridges here on a map of 1825, when the Fleet was enclosed. With an entrance in College Grove, at No.35A King's Road, in the 1870s & 1880s was H Schweitzer and Co. manufacturers of cocoatina, 'the highest class of soluble cocoa or chocolate'.

On the northern side of College Grove is **Beaumont Court**, also run by Unite Students. The Gestalt Centre which provides psychotherapy training occupies its lower floors. The flats cover the site of the Prince of Wales pub, here for a century from the mid-1800s. Alongside it was once the immense Camden Works of Charles Goodall & Son, playing card makers and stationers, begun in Royal College Street during the 1830s and expanded towards King's Road as it began producing most of the playing card sets sold in the UK. Goodall's distinctive court card pattern was copied around the world. The firm was merged with its rival De La Rue in 1922. The buildings survived until they were bought by the Post Office in the 1970s.

On the pavement beyond Beaumont Court is a hexagonal Penfold-designed pillar box; it is Listed and dates from about 1872. We now pass the extensive yard of Parcel Force, stretching along St Pancras Way to the next turning left, Pratt Street. Parcel Force's premises is on the site of the Idris mineral water factory, opened in 1891, whose main entrance was on Pratt Street, the next turning left. Along St Pancras Way was its Syphon & Seltzogene Department. Idris closed in 1965, its factory having been sold to the Post Office.

Here once stood the Stereotype Printing Office run by Andrew Wilson, who in 1811 was awarded a gold medal by the Society of Arts for helping to introduce and perfect stereotype printing in England. His extensive works shut down in 1821 and the factory and grounds were auctioned off for building the following year. The grounds were then developed with houses set in big gardens. After 1870 industrial concerns sprang up, fronting the main road. At No.33 was The Viking Food & Essence Ltd from the 1890s until WWI; they dealt in beef extracts and competed with

Bovril. During WWI Glaxo & Co. produced their once famous infant food at Nos.45-47. It was made from dried milk and sales rocketed at the time. Icilma, manufacturers of toilet preparations, including face cream and shampoo, had a factory at Nos.37-41 from 1911 until 1938.

On the corner of Pratt Street is a postmodern block of flats, **No.49**, built in 1993. The block stands on the site of Camden Town Fire Station opened in 1888 and in use until 1968. The fire station was at first encircled by a narrow passage called Acre (later Waite's) Place entered from both King's Road and Pratt Street. Initially the alley ran past eight small dwellings and ended at the Avenue Baptist Chapel and school, but all were demolished in 1891 for the Idris works. Idris paid for a replacement Baptist Chapel on Pratt Street that opened in 1892; it was converted in 1912 into the short-lived Avenue Cinema.

Just behind the buildings on the east side of St Pancras Way runs the Regent's Canal. Two large wharves for coal and lime – Pratt Wharf and Star Wharf – were constructed to the north of some of the houses of Agar Town that lined the street after 1840. Industrial concerns slowly took over. These included from 1855 to 1879 the Steam Harmonium Works of James Hillier, who began as a piano maker but switched to organs. He produced an ornate 'orchestrophone' (a mixture of organ and harmonium) which received an honourable mention at the Paris International Exhibition of 1878. Before and during WWI Nos.18-20 was the factory of James Coxeter & Sons, surgical instrument makers, who were the chief suppliers of University College Hospital.

Today, the industry has gone. Facing the Parcel Force yard is a row of recent apartment blocks of various size and shape. **Nos.8-14** are the offices and flats of Canal Side Studios. Here is the London office of Cartwright Pickard architects. **Nos.22&24** (Somerston House) are metal-faced flats, which replaced Superchrome House, itself of moulded corrugated iron. **No.38** is Knowles Wharf, built in 2007 and named after John Knowles & Co., makers of fireclay goods who were based at this address for many years and took over both Star Wharf and Pratt Wharf. **No.40**, Star Wharf flats, also date from 2007.

Opposite the last is a long brick wall, the back of the St Pancras Commercial Centre in Pratt Street. This marks the site of a refuse destructor plant built in 1895 over residential buildings. It doubled as an underground V1 rocket factory in the film *Operation Crossbow* (1965).

On the north corner of Pratt Street was the Fortune of War pub. There sand gatherers once sold the sand they had brought from Hampstead Heath to poor housewives as a substitute floor covering for carpets and rugs. The pub was demolished about 1905 as the electricity generating station (built in Pratt Street in 1894 by the recently founded St Pancras Borough Electricity and Public Lighting Department) expanded. Fuelled by incinerated refuse, the station was known as the King's Road Power House and was supplied with water from the canal until the 1930s. It closed in 1968.

We now climb up to **Gray's Inn Bridge**. Opened in 1897 by William Henry Matthews, Chairman of the Vestry (as the foundation plaque states), this replaced an earlier brick-built bridge named at a time when many still regarded King's Road as a continuation of Gray's Inn Lane. The plaque bears an image of St Pancras, with a halo and a palm frond to signify his martyrdom. It was a cast-iron structure until the 1980s, when the bridge was modernised; the iron panels were lost but a view of the canal was gained.

After it opened in 1820 the Regent's Canal was a vibrant artery of commerce bringing trade and life to the area. Its construction had however been delayed by the actions of the local landowner, William Agar (1767-1838), who was a lawyer in the Court of Chancery. Called to the Bar in 1791 he was later made a King's Counsellor, and is often referred to as

Counsellor, or more confusingly Councillor, Agar. He had purchased the lease of St Pancras manor house and grounds at auction in 1810 and formally took over the lease of the whole prebendal manor of 72 acres from the prebend Rev. William Beloe in 1816. For many years he fought a battle - which literally came to blows - against the Regent's Canal Company to prevent the canal traversing his land. In 1815 the company's surveyor, James Morgan, gave notice that he intended to survey the land and ignored Agar's letter of protest. Agar ordered his gardeners and servants to barricade the gateway. Morgan's men used barrows and planks to force an entry, then started digging. Bow Street officers were called the next day. In 1818 Agar received compensation of over £15,000, but he continued to complain and it was not until 1832 that matters were finally settled after nearly 20 years of litigation.

The canal was nevertheless opened on 1 August 1820. Over eight miles long, traffic quickly built up and new industries, such as the Imperial Gas Light & Coke Company (p 24), were attracted to it. Yet the canal was to lose out to railways, and later to roads. The last commercial barge was towed by horse along the canal in 1956. Now it is given over mainly to pleasure craft, and walkers and cyclists along the towpath; Camden completed its path in 1974, the year that the Regent's Canal was declared a Conservation Area.

Abutting the bridge is the **Constitution** pub, earmarked for refurbishment in 2020. This could be said to be the last remnant of Agar Town (see p 47), survivor of the few buildings which the MR left standing along the east side of what was then King's Road. It was built by the developer Thomas Bolton, who gave his name to Bolton Street, Agar Town, on a plot of land on which he had taken a 99-year lease from 5 March 1853. In the same year Bolton also laid out the now-demolished Lodge Terrace, north of the pub beyond the then entrance way to the Agar family's residence, Elm Lodge **[10]**.

10 Elm Lodge (drawing by Henry Guest RA, 1850s)

On the west side of King's Road, Tompson's parish map of 1801 map shows a field bordered by the River Fleet and called Bowling House Field. Local historian John Richardson has conjectured that on this stretch of St Pancras Way stood the medieval manor house of Cantelowes Manor, later taken over for the earliest parish workhouse (but cf. p 66).

By the 1820s a row of terraced houses had been built. This was St Paul's Terrace, its name reflecting the centuries-old connection between St Pancras and St Paul's Cathedral. The engraver Robert Simpson lived at No.20 in the mid-1840s. The terrace was renumbered as part of King's Road in 1885. Beyond the railway bridge a remnant of the terrace survives at Nos.111-121 (p 67), but the houses to the south were lost in the building of canalside Reachview Close, entered from Baynes Street ahead and completed in 1982. Today, along St Pancras Way, are two housing blocks: small **Pegasus Court** (at No.105), completed in 2013, faces the street, while **Caulfield Court** beyond has its back to it. The latter, initially run by an Irish housing association, was opened in 1995 by the Irish President Mary Robinson. It now provides independent living for single people.

Facing it is an imposing red-brick building with a sloping wall. It was built by the MR in the 1880s for one of its customers, George Skey & Co., brick, pipe and tile maker of Wilnecote, Staffordshire as the company's London depot, and housed 3-storey stables. Its water tank served locomotives on the adjacent North London railway line. Skey & Co were taken over by Doultons in 1935. The building is now home to the **Camden Garden Centre**, which moved here from Kentish Town in 1990. All the Centre's profits are donated to a charitable trust which helps to employ, educate and train disadvantaged people, including ex-offenders and the homeless.

Its entrance is round the corner in **BARKER DRIVE**. Tom Barker was the socialist Mayor of St Pancras (1958-59), who once famously hoisted the Red Flag above the (Euston Road) Town Hall. Barker Drive lies over the former entrance to Elm Lodge and then to the Midland Goods Yard, developed from 1861-65 over the Agar family grounds and northern parts of Agar Town. The MR had purchased the land from the Ecclesiastical Commissioners, who had become freeholder of prebendal St Pancras manor after the last prebend, Arthur Robinson Chauvel, died in 1847, and who had bought out the Agars' leasehold interest.

The Goods Yard opened in stages but fully from January 1865, handling mainly coal and beer. Its site was sold to the London Borough of Camden in 1974, and in September 1975 the Council gave approval for six acres to form a new estate, intended to house nearly 3,000 local residents. These early plans came to naught and there were complaints in the press of vandalism and fly-tipping in the area. In 1980 the Department of Environment refused a loan sanction for council housing. Much of the site was subsequently sold for a mixed development of housing association and private housing to designs by Peter Mishcon: the present-day **Elm Village**, whose name recalls Elm Lodge and its grounds. The Estate won an award from the Housing Centre Trust in 1984 for outstanding housing achievement.

Bear right into **ROSSENDALE WAY**, with a hidden street sign with Hampstead-style black tiling. The road skirts the canal, over which there is viewing platform, but we continue straight ahead into leafy and tranquil **BERGHOLT MEWS**. Note the Soane-like surrounds to the doors. Reaching a semicircular lawn in front of a curving terrace, turn left and shortly left again across a car parking area fronting **BLAKENEY CLOSE**. At the end is a triangular area, transformed into allotments in 2010 but now, sadly, locked. This is the site of Elm Lodge.

William Agar (p 42) built Elm Lodge for himself and his wife Louisa, niece of the Earl of Shrewsbury, after he first purchased the lease of St Pancras manor in 1810. Drawings of the house with its rounded bays show it

11 Pancras Bridge (drawing by Henry Guest RA, 1850s), St Pancras Workhouse in the background

was a late Georgian building, surrounded by a lawn, an orchard and a park full of mulberry trees. It was built on or near the site of the medieval St Pancras manor house, which had been owned by the London vintner William Belasyse in 1561, when he was married at St Pancras Church. The 1861 census shows the Agars' daughter Louisa was still living here but in November that year the contents of the house were auctioned off, as it became marooned within the MR's goods yard. It was used as railway offices until the 1880s and then demolished.

Retrace your steps and turn left to regain Barker Drive. Turn right and then, leaving the Elm Village Estate proper, turn right into winding **WEAVERS WAY**, one of a number of streets developed in the early 1990s and recalling rural occupations. After a few minutes pass round a barrier, where some old cobblestones from the MR goods yard remain. At the T-junction turn right into **PLOUGHMANS CLOSE**, and bear left reaching the canalside wall that once enclosed the yard. Walk left along the footpath fronting **REAPERS CLOSE**.

There is a good view over the canal and on the opposite bank the old Royal Mail building in St Pancras Way, on the site of which once stood the MR's Granary building (p 41). A bridge was built in the 1860s to carry sidings across the canal to the warehouse. Before that there had been two bridges in close proximity, a little to the south. Pancras Bridge **[11]** was erected when the canal was first constructed in 1819 and later carried Oxford Street, one of Agar Town's main thoroughfares. The New Bridge was put up in 1853 to carry a road across fields to link up with Queen's Road (p 64). Both bridges were demolished when the MR's goods yard was laid out.

At the end of the path stands a red-brick industrial building. To operate cranes and capstans in the goods yard a hydraulic pumping station was built, which housed steam engines that pumped water at pressure into a mains system. As part of Camden's celebration of the Queen's Silver Jubilee in 1977, it was converted to house the Jubilee Waterside Centre, which provided kayaking and canoeing and a large climbing wall. The centre closed in August 2007. In 2010 the Frank Barnes School for Deaf Children moved here from Swiss Cottage, before leaving for the Plimsoll Building (p 54) in 2015. The present temporary occupant is the Abacus Belsize Primary School, which wishes to relocate to the redeveloped Hampstead Police Station on Rosslyn Hill, a move at present blocked by Camden Council. Its current address is oddly No.105 Camley Street but that reflects the emptiness of the area before the Estate was completed.

Continue along the road and turn right into **CROFTERS WAY**. Follow it down into **CAMLEY STREET**. This northern part of Camley Street was laid out in the 1970s after the goods yard closed, although before that was built Salisbury Street in Agar Town had followed its course. The first permanent church of St Thomas (p 65) was begun opposite us in 1859 to designs by S S Teulon **[12]**, but the MR acquired the site in 1860 and it was never completed. An adjoining church school building, opened in 1857 and used as a place of worship while the church was being built, was also demolished.

12 Agar Town Church and School (from The Builder, 5 June 1858)

North of this point – under the present-day **CEDAR WAY** industrial estate – several streets were developed on 99-year leases from 1856, under the auspices of the freeholder, the Ecclesiastical Commissioners: Kingston, Bolton and Chichester Streets and Durham Terrace. This better part of Agar Town was demolished in 1862-63 to form part of the MR's goods yard.

Beyond the car park of the Booker cash and carry at **No.106 CAMLEY STREET** you may spot a tall log fence. Behind this the **Alara Permaculture Forest Garden** has been formed on waste land on the industrial estate. Planting began in 2006. There is an orchard, a vineyard and raised beds. A free communal compost heap is maintained just off Camley

Street, where Alara Wholefoods has its premises at **Nos.110-112**.

Camden Council owns the freehold of the industrial estate, which faces redevelopment. The businesses have joined together with the inhabitants of the Elm Village Estate to form the Camley Street Sustainability Zone. It has proposed community-led development here, an alternative to ubiquitous luxury flats.

Turn right and soon pass No.103, **Urbanest St Pancras**. Its inner courtyard leads onto the canal towpath. Designed by AHMM architects and opened in 2016, it replaced two railway offices put up in the early 1980s fronting a yard with a depot by the canal. The new buildings provide a wide range of student accommodation and also house Collective Base KX, a co-working space that offers young people in the creative industries desks and meeting rooms.

Opposite, at Nos.98-102, is **King's Cross Onyx**, a high-rise apartment block by Glenn Howells Architects. It is separated from similar King's Cross Central developments by the railway tracks but together with No.103 and No.101 (p 48) forms a 'strategic gateway link' between King's Cross Central and Camden Town.

It stands on the site of Salisbury Crescent, Agar Town, a collection of individual cottages built in the 1840s alongside the canal. Pulled down by the MR the area became the southernmost tip of the MR's goods yard, full of sidings. After the yard closed, a warehouse stood here before being demolished for the current scheme.

Pause at **Oblique Bridge** for a view over the canal and towards the St Pancras skyline. The bridge is a concrete and steel replica, dating from the mid-1980s, of the original cast-iron structure, first built in 1819-20 (as Skew Bridge) to carry a driveway to Elm Lodge. It later connected the central thoroughfare of Agar Town, Cambridge Street (renamed Camley Street in 1937) with Salisbury Street, north of the canal.

Agar Town was an area developed from 1840 onwards, mainly by working men. Small plots of land on 21-year leases were offered by the landowners Mrs Agar, widow of William Agar, and their son William Talbot Agar. The traditional view of Agar Town is that it was a squalid slum, housing many poor Irish who had been squeezed out of more central districts such as St. Giles. Much of this stems from an influential article in Dickens' *Household Words* which depicted Agar Town as a suburban Irish shanty town. A different picture emerges from study of records such as deeds, Vestry minutes, and census and poor law records, and the interested reader is referred to *Agar Town: The life and death of a Victorian 'Slum'* (CHS Occasional Paper 1).

Agar Town's poor image meant that it fell easy prey to the Midland Railway, who obtained Parliamentary powers and swiftly tore down the area in building their line into St Pancras Station. Inhabitants were left to find other accommodation wherever they could. The MR's metropolitan extensions demolished 4,000 houses in Camden, Somers and Agar Towns, displacing perhaps as many as 32,000 people. The MR's treatment of the dead in the nearby churchyard aroused fury; the plight of the living was met with indifference, even plaudits for the removal of a blight on the face of London.

Cambridge Street once ran in a straight line but when the railway line was built the road was diverted. The bending course of present-day Camley Street under the railway tracks more or less follows the line of former Cambridge Crescent. In the 1851 *Household Words* article this was described as full of shopkeepers 'the poorest exhibiting in their rag-patched windows a few apples and red-herrings'. However, that year's census shows that majority of the single-occupancy houses were headed by bricklayers or bricklayers' labourers. On the corner of Cambridge Crescent's southern junction with Cambridge Street an iron chapel, later faced in brick, was opened in 1847 but not well maintained. After ten years it was so dilapidated that the Ecclesiastical Commissioners provided a site for a new school and church (p 46). A Temperance Society met in the chapel. Facing it was a pub called the Talbot Arms, with tea-gardens and skittle-ground; William Agar's widow was related to the Talbot Earls of Shrewsbury. Her daughter Louisa paid for an Infants School at the northern egress into Cambridge Crescent.

Continue along Camley Street past the site of former MR offices, latterly a large warehouse that was demolished for a mixed-use development by KSR Architects at **No.101**. As at No.103 there will be so-called Enterprise Incubator facilities: commercial floorspace for small and medium-sized concerns.

Cross Granary Street (p 40) and look along the 19th-century wall which bounded the Workhouse. It gave access in the 20th century to public washing facilities and slipper baths. The tall concrete water tower, built for St Pancras Hospital in 1939, is prominent.

Passing the mortuary (p 36) and the rear entrance to Pancras churchyard, created in 1883, pass under the railway tracks, which were considerably widened by the CTRL works. The MR's original tracks here destroyed an Agar Town cul-de-sac called Canterbury Terrace. We emerge by the gated entrance to the St Pancras Cruising Club (p 55).

Note on high the **Victorian Waterpoint** of 1872. It has fine Gothic detailing, designed at the office of Sir George Gilbert Scott. It once stood next to the railway tracks just outside St Pancras Station to provide water to steam locomotives. Threatened with demolition during CTRL works in 2001, it was saved by English Heritage but had to be moved. The building was sliced into three using a huge circular saw. The lower storey was demolished and reconstructed here, but the top two original sections including the former 2,400 cubic ft water tank (now a viewing platform, still with its ballcock) were re-erected, having made the 700m journey along Camley Street by specialist transporter. The Waterpoint now contains the cruising club's bar and has great views from the top.

Pass Somers Town Bridge (p 55) leading to King's Cross Central and arrive at the impressive entrance to the **Camley Street Natural Park**. After Agar Town was demolished, coal drops or shoots were built on both sides of the road. The MR's were on the west, facing those of the Great Northern Railway Company (GNR). The latter were the brainchild of Samuel Plimsoll (1824-98), coal merchant and MP, who became famous for his 'Plimsoll Line' to help the safety of merchant shipping (and to prevent it undercutting his railway interests by deliberate overloading). He had patented a coal drop, which minimised the level of breakages, first successfully tried out within the GNR Goods Yard on the opposite bank of the canal. The yard's boundaries were extended in 1865 when houses, stables and canalside wharves fronting Cambridge Street were cleared and a viaduct on iron girders built across the canal by Plimsoll. Below the railway line was a series of bays, which after the GNR bought the coal drops from Plimsoll's heirs in 1891 were each rented by a different coal merchant. Wagons were pulled over the correct bay on a traverser propelled by a capstan. Coal was then tipped down a chute for bagging up below, loaded onto a cart and taken off for distribution; until 1895 it was also loaded onto barges here.

With the post-WWII decline in the demand for coal, the two coal drops were shut down. That formerly belonging to the MR was pulled down in the 1960s and the land used as the King's Cross Waste Transfer Station until St Pancras International was built.

The GNR coal drops survived until 1977 but the ground was also used as a tip, although unofficially, and was largely colonised by wild flowers. The Greater London Council (GLC) eventually stepped in. After discarding plans for a coach park it began the creation of Camley Street Natural Park in 1983. It was opened on 7 May 1985, as a London Wildlife Trust nature reserve. On its first anniversary

Ken Livingstone, then GLC Leader, unveiled its fine wrought-iron gates which had formerly stood at the MR goods depot in Somers Town (p 69). In clearing the site, the Trust discovered many fragments of Victorian pottery and oyster shells, evidence of earlier occupation when this was part of Agar Town.

Take time if you can to explore the Natural Park, a two-acre wildlife haven with year-round activities. The park contains a pond, viewing points over the canal, a man-made hill and shaded, bark-strewn walks. The original visitor centre, housed in a wooden former cricket pavilion was demolished in 2018. Work began in 2019 (complete in early 2020) on a new one boasting super-insulated walls and roof and water-source heat pumps extracting solar energy from the canal, and the creation of an outdoor learning centre by Somers Town Bridge.

Continue along Camley Street. Off its west side (now covered by the CTRL tracks) some of the first buildings of Agar Town were built, described on the 1841 census as 'cottages near or opposite Spann's Buildings'. These cottages appear to have been built by working men in their spare time, especially on Sundays, on leased plots typically of 32ft by 72ft. Like most of Agar Town the small streets here – Canterbury Place and York Place – remained unpaved and unlit until the late 1850s. In early 1860 the Imperial Gas Company, having bought the freehold and leases cheaply, cleared the site and constructed gasholders. These were telescoped and given large decorative guide frames in 1880: the Listed Gasholder triplet (p 54) now re-erected in King's Cross Central.

We explore this new district in the next chapter. For now, regain Goods Way and retrace your steps to the Underground station for your onward journey.

King's Cross Central and Agar Grove

Linear walk from King's Cross St Pancras Underground Station to Camden Road Overground Station

This is a walk of two halves, linked by regeneration. We walk first through the old Railway Lands being spectacularly reborn as King's Cross Central, and then through an area of social housing to the north also in the throes of rebuilding.

From the northern concourse of King's Cross St Pancras Underground Station take the exit marked 'Pancras Square and Granary Square'. This leads through the 'Light Tunnel', featuring an 'art wall' made from LED lights that is used to showcase artistic commissions. Emerge by the office blocks of Pancras Square (p 24). This is part of the King's Cross Central development, of which more shortly. Turn up King's Boulevard and then cross Goods Way and pause on the Regent's Canal Bridge (p 58).

The land to the north of the canal previously formed the Goods Yard of the Great Northern Railway (GNR). Before this, it had been held for centuries by St Bartholomew's Hospital and was known as Allensbury, otherwise Elm Friars or Alkichesbury. This last name was recorded during a Visitation by the Church in 1249-50, when the estate consisted of 60 acres, with a grange, a garden and two villeins; it had been demised by William de Belmeis, canon of St Paul's, to Stephen Albus of the Priory of St Bartholomew's by a deed c.1168-81. By the early 19th century the land, bordered to the east by Maiden Lane **[13]**, was farmed by the Rhodes family, who also ploughed nine acres along the eastern side of the canal, shown on an 1840 map as Agar's farm. In the late 1830s they converted the latter to a brickfield and constructed a brick kiln. In September 1842 four young boys died in the kiln; they had climbed into it at night to roast potatoes but had been suffocated by fumes.

In 1846 St Bart's sold its estate to the GNR for £50,000. It was discovered during discussion of the future of the Goods Yard site in the 1980s that the hospital had a residual claim to repurchase the land at 19th-century prices should it cease to be used for railway purposes; a settlement was reached in the High Court. In 1849 the GNR also purchased Agar's farm.

The GNR's Goods Yard covered 59 acres and was walled off from the outside world and guarded like a naval dockyard. The GNR's consulting engineer was Sir William Cubitt and the architect who designed its larger buildings was Lewis Cubitt (no close relation). In 1850 it was the biggest goods station of the period and one of the most important of its kind.

The GNR revolutionised the supply of key commodities into London. It served rich farmland along its route, and helped eliminate regional variations in food prices through rapid, regular and cheap delivery. It was also keen to wrest control of the coal trade to London from the sea-borne carriers, hence the coal drops it built in the yard. Originally the yard provided for smooth transfer of goods from railway to canal and vice versa; there were two canal basins, both long filled in.

The Goods Yard was still in full swing when London and North Eastern Railway (LNER) took over the site in 1923, having absorbed the GNR. Over the next decade LNER made a number of alterations, demolishing redundant buildings.

In June 1931 the architect Charles Glover publicised in the *Illustrated London News* his unusual plan for a Central Airport for London. He proposed erecting across the whole site tall rail cargo warehouses that would support a pinwheel arrangement of half-mile concrete runways. The spoke design allowed take-offs and landings in eight directions, but at £5m it was too costly. Four decades later the idea

13 A View of Maiden Lane (watercolour 1835 by E H Dixon), looking north from the Regent's Canal. The site of King's Cross Central is on the left. In the medium distance on the right dark smoke billows from Belle Isle (p 61).

million price tag. Four decades later the idea of siting an airport here was revived: a government feasibility study in 1971 suggested the Goods Yard as one of four possible sites for a 'Vertiport', for use by vertical-takeoff aircraft. Acting together eleven local societies loudly objected to the proposal, mainly on the grounds of noise, and it was soon abandoned. Another use for the Goods Yard seriously explored during the 1950s and 1960s was as a location for Covent Garden fruit and vegetable market, before Garden fruit and vegetable market, before Nine Elms was eventually chosen. After WWII, transport of freight by rail rapidly declined, losing out to road haulage. In the 1980s most of the rail lines in the southern part of the Goods Yard were removed and the area was used by lorries.

In 1987 British Rail announced its intention to develop the site, linked to a plan for a low-level terminal of the Channel Tunnel Railway at King's Cross Station. Sir Norman Foster won a competition the following year with a design for an office city, with 7.5 million sq. ft of floor space and including two 44-storey towers, which was to be developed by the London Regeneration Consortium. The scheme was thwarted by recession and some very active local campaigning. A revised plan including a massively enlarged terminus at St Pancras Station was enshrined in the Channel Tunnel Rail Link (CTRL) Act of 1996 with certain safeguards for the local community. London and Continental Railways (LCR), the promoters, declared bankruptcy within two years but the Government brokered a rescue.

In 2000 Argent was selected as the developer by the landowners LCR and Exel (now DHL) and subsequently formed the King's Cross Central Limited Partnership. Argent created a framework scheme which was submitted to the London Borough of Camden, which granted outline planning permission in March 2006. Work started in 2008 once the CTRL works were complete. The recession slowed development but building continued. The site has been owned and controlled by the King's Cross Central Limited Partnership, with Argent as the overall developer and funded through pre-lets and Argent's pension fund backers; since 2015 AustralianSuper has had a major stake. The master planners were Allies and Morrison; Demetri Porphyrios; and Townshend Landscape Architects. The aim was to create a mixed-use high density development, with some 26 acres dedicated to new public routes and open spaces. King's Cross Central, as the development has become called, has several new streets and its own postcode: N1C. Work should be complete by 2022.

Continue ahead into **GRANARY SQUARE**, designed by Townshend Landscape Architects and opened in 2012. It is named after the building which dominates the space. In front of it was once a large canal basin, with four short canal docks within the Granary for transshipment of goods. The basin was filled in during and after WWI. The watery connection is now provided by over 1,000 choreographed fountains, each individually controlled and lit, and popular with children in hot weather. One of the original rail turntables was restored and topped with a glass panel.

More than 400 mature trees have been used in the development. Over to the left is a Parisian-looking patch of lime trees, with metal chairs beneath. Inscribed in the ground are words from local poet Aidan Dun's *The Brill*: 'Kings Cross, dense with angels and histories. There are cities beneath your pavements. Cities behind your skies. Let me see!'

Close by was an engine house with the original hydraulic accumulator and pumping engines; hydraulic pressure was used throughout the Goods Yard. The boilers were removed in 1927, when electric pumps were introduced and the tall chimney, prominent in photographs, was taken down. Alongside was the Horse Provender Store, later converted into stables.

The Granary was brought into use in 1851 and was sufficiently impressive for its architect Lewis Cubitt to display a watercolour of his design at the Royal Academy. Six floors high, with a prominent cornice hiding a double-hipped roof, it has an internal frame of cast-iron columns and beams with timber joists and floors. Sacks of grain could be transferred from the top floor to the ground floor by a series of chutes; some 60,000 sacks could be stored in the building. The top floor originally contained a 150,000-gallon tank used in a low pressure hydraulic power system for operating hoists.

The central building was flanked by two 580-ft-long transit sheds designed for transshipment of goods between rail, road and canal, with stabling for the GNR's horses beneath. Behind the Granary was a huge space full of railway tracks and called the Train Assembly Shed. Here were put together loaded or empty wagons released from the transit sheds on either side. In the late 20th century the buildings were used by the road transport company Pickfords, but the Train Assembly Shed was home (from 1994) to Raceway, then Europe's longest indoor go-karting circuit.

The buildings were transformed by architects Stanton Williams. Since 2011 they have been home to Central Saint Martins, the art and design college, now part of University of the Arts, London (UAL). The Western Transit Shed has been converted into offices with shops and restaurants at street level.

Walk through the ground floor of the Granary, with a high ceiling for handling goods. On the right there is access to the **Lethaby Gallery**, which is dedicated to promoting work by UAL students and holds regular public exhibitions.

The cavernous glazed space beyond, leading to the security barriers for the college, affords a fine view of the rear of the Granary where the outline of the roofs of the transit sheds is clearly visible. The space contains table tennis tables, evidence of the agreement struck with Camden Council that free sporting facilities would be provided across the development. The space is now known as **The Crossing** and often hosts exhibitions and other events.

Turn left and out onto **STABLE STREET**, which runs atop the former stables beneath the transit shed; there were also stables underneath the viaduct leading from the Coal Office, ventilated from openings in the canalside wall. These were not the best conditions and a large new stables was built in 1897 offsite in Blundell Street, off the Islington side of York Way. It is estimated that by 1900 the GNR yard as a whole used 1,300 horses on carting, delivery or shunting duties. Far from reducing the need for horse labour, the railways increased it. There was even a horse infirmary in the northwest corner of the Goods Yard, since there was always a proportion of the equine workforce that was sick or injured. After the LNER took over the Goods Yard it began removing horses; they had all gone by 1930.

On the right at **No.5** is Dishoom, a very popular Indian restaurant, outside which long queues form each evening. It preserves much of the historic fabric of the transit shed inside. At **Nos.9&10** is Spiritland, an all-day café with a unique sound system that hosts DJ sets and events, and also has a radio production suite. **No.11** houses the **King's Cross Visitor Centre**, with displays and books about the area's history and a large model by Pipers of the new development. It also offers free tours.

Along the west side of Stable Street is Coal Drops Yard (p 55). We reach **LEWIS CUBITT SQUARE**, opened in 2015. It's a place to linger ... but watch out for the arching water jets.

In the last century the scene north of here was one of countless railway sidings. Over on the west side were several large engine sheds forming the Locomotive Depot, later known as Top Shed. Incorporating the GNR's original, crescent-shaped locomotive shed, the depot initially carried out heavy repairs and locomotive overhaul, but this work switched to Doncaster in the early 20th century; thereafter it carried out more routine repairs and stabled some big express passenger locomotives, such as the famous *Flying Scotsman* **[14]**. The sheds were all demolished in 1963 when the age of steam ended. Surviving until recently was the Locomotive Superintendent's House on Wharf Road to the north of the sheds, which the 1870 OS map shows had its own garden alongside the main line of the rival Midland Railway (MR). It was pulled down during the CTRL works.

The square is surrounded by large modern buildings: the white block on the right is the Aga Khan Centre (p 58) while over to the left is an office block designed by Mossessian Architecture and clad in dark volcanic lava stone from Armenia. It has been pre-let to Google and Nike will move in to a similar block being built alongside. Both will back onto a small Keskidee Square, named after the Afro-Caribbean arts centre that flourished in Gifford Street, off Caledonian Road, from 1971-91. Its founder was the Guyanese architect Oscar Abrams (d.1996), and a kiskedee (sic) is a species of flycatcher native to Guyana.

Behind the present large hoarding another block is rising, designed by Allford Hall Monaghan Morris (AHMM) which will house a cultural centre with theatre and Facebook's offices from 2021. Now walk across the square and along a pedestrian access route passing on our left the entrance to Coal Drops Yard. We will see this later but here is a good view of its so-called kissing roof (p 55), below which Samsung have opened a major showcase.

Continuing we reach on the left **Gasholders London** – address No.1 Lewis Cubitt Square – 145 chic apartments formed within the

14 *Flying Scotsman* at Doncaster (photo by Rich@rd)

Gasholder Triplet that was moved here from the Pancras Gasworks site at the south end of Camley Street (p 49). Each flat has grey sliding panels for shutters. Completed in 2018, the designer was Wilkinson Eyre Architects and Dan Pearson Studio landscaped the gardens. Originally belonging to gasholders Nos.10, 11 & 12, the guide frames comprise three tiers of hollow cylindrical cast-iron columns, cast-iron capitals in correct architectural order and three tiers of wrought-iron riveted lattice girders. Sharing a common spine, they were once nicknamed the 'Siamese Triplets'. Oval plaques on each column record their erection in the 1860s, and the 'telescoping' of the internal gas tanks in 1880. The three gasholders were decommissioned and purged of gas in 2000, and restored by a specialist engineering firm in Yorkshire.

Gasholders London stands on the site of a coal and stone-handling canal basin. In the second half of the 19th century, as London house building expanded, large quantities of York stone and bricks from Bedfordshire were unloaded here. The basin was filled in and the Western Goods Shed built over it in 1897-99, following a major reorganisation in the handling of goods in the Yard. The Shed was first used entirely for outward goods traffic and offices were provided on the western side. It was demolished to build Gasholders London.

Running to the right is **WOLLSTONECRAFT STREET**. As new streets and parks are laid out they have been given names from a final shortlist of 30, arising from a naming competition launched by King's Cross Central Ltd Partnership in March 2013. There were over 10,000 entries. Recalling proto-feminist Mary Wollstonecraft (p 108), this was the first street to be allocated one of the shortlisted names.

On its western side is the **Plimsoll Building**. Completed in 2015 and named after Samuel Plimsoll (p 48) this is a mixed-use cluster of towers arranged around a communal garden and including a community hall. The 13-storey building was designed by David Morley Architects and the second-floor residents' garden by Dan Pearson Studio. On the far corner is the original Everyman King's Cross cinema, kept as a one-screen annexe to its new main venue in Handyside Street and renamed 'Everyman on the Corner'.

Contained within the Plimsoll Building, at **No.4** is the King's Cross Academy, a nursery and primary school which opened in 2015. It is co-located with the Frank Barnes School for Deaf Children, which moved here after five years at the Jubilee Waterside Centre (p 46). Academy pupils learn sign language from nursery age, a skill they can put into practice at lunchtime when children from both schools sit together.

Continuing, follow the roadway over Goods Yard land that was latterly used for concrete crushing and waste transfer. It leads to **Gasholder Park**. This was landscaped by Bell Phillips Architects within Gasholder No.8, which had remained in use at Pancras Gasworks until 1999. The 25m-high frame consists of 16 hollow cylindrical columns in two tiers and has an internal diameter of over 35m. It was taken down in 2011 and refurbished by the same company that refurbished the Gasholder triplet before its re-erection here for the opening of the park in 2015. A sculpted and reflective glass canopy with seating surrounds the circular lawn.

The terracotta building overlooking the park and canal, and at the foot of **CANAL REACH**, is **Tapestry**, a collection of apartments, townhouses and penthouses designed by Niall McLaughlin Architects. It has a roof garden, a free indoor public sports pitch and a multi-storey car park. The latter is built over the **Energy Centre** with its Combined Heat and Power Plant (CHP), which contains huge, gas-powered Jenbacher engines generating electricity. The heat from the engines is captured and used to provide 99% of the heating and hot water for the whole development through a hot water distribution network, one of the biggest in the country. The CHP cools the buildings too.

The western edge of Tapestry lies on the site of Winchester Terrace, the easternmost street of Agar Town (see Route 2), developed in the mid 1840s. When first built the diminutive terrace looked out onto fields but in just a few years the GNR built its Goods Yard, surrounded by a huge wall, which marched north from this point, and against which was said to run a deep, evil-smelling ditch. Winchester Terrace and the streets behind were pulled down in the 1860s by the MR, who built a complex of sidings here. The site has been included in King's Cross Central, although most if it lies under the CTRL tracks.

From Gasholder Park walk down to the canal. On the other side is **St Pancras Basin**. This was excavated in 1867-68 and opened in 1870 as a coal wharf for the MR. Iron girders projecting from the west wall of the basin are the remnants of the coal staithes which used to run above the basin. It was also used for unloading ash from MR locomotives into barges which were taken up the canal to tips at Cowley, Oxfordshire. The coal wharf was re-opened on 6 October 1958 as the St Pancras Basin to provide moorings for 60 pleasure craft. The St Pancras Cruising Club (SPCC) grew out of informal mooring here; in 1964 the SPCC helped form the Association of Waterways Cruising Clubs, which provides self-help and emergency aid on Britain's canal network. The SPCC's club house is behind the basin and the impressive Victorian Waterpoint (p 48), on its grounds since 2001, houses a bar.

South of the basin is **St Pancras Lock**. The original lock-keeper's house had stood on the east side of the canal. The present cottage opposite was built in 1898 and served as a pumping station to return water to the head of the lock.

Where the path divides leave the canal and walk left up to a footbridge completed in 2017. By Moxon Architects, working with engineers Arup and called **Somers Town Bridge**, it links King's Cross Central with Camley Street Natural Park (p 48). The park is on the site of coal drops, once reached by a railway viaduct featured in the Michael Caine movie *Alfie* (1966). From the bridge there is a fine view north over St Pancras Lock, Gasholders London and Gasholder Park.

Turning back walk ahead onto the upper deck of the redeveloped **Coal Drops Yard**, which opened in October 2018. It provides a new retail quarter akin to Covent Garden, housing boutiques, restaurants, galleries and music venues, while the cobbled yard plays host to markets and street festivals. The traditional gabled roofs of the two coal drop buildings have been linked together in a 'kissing roof', designed by Heatherwick Studio (p 29). It has been covered in over 80,000 dark blue grey slate tiles, from the same seam in the same quarry in North Wales as those used on the original roofs.

The Western Coal Drops on our left were built in 1859-60 and four decades later converted to a general goods transit shed. Its Loading Bay canopy was supported by steel cantilevered beams and ornate cast-iron brackets. At the other side of the cobbled yard – used in the late 20th century by Charles Wells brewers – are the earlier-built Eastern Coal drops of 1851.

These at first carried four high-level railway tracks, from which wagons discharged coal into storage bins on a mezzanine floor above cart-loading bays. The distribution of coal from South Yorkshire was a very important part of the GNR's goods traffic. When first built it was predicted that these drops would be capable of handling a thousand tons a day. The northern section was badly damaged by fire in 1985. The southern section had been converted in the mid-1870s into warehouses, including a unit taken by Yorkshire-based bottle makers and glass merchants Bagley and Co. From 1991 this housed the eponymous Bagley's nightclub. Here some 2,000 people squeezed in to enjoy raves and DJ parties. In 2003 the club was renamed Canvas and a dance-club The Key was opened alongside. Both had to close in 2008 as redevelopment works commenced.

Now return to the footpath overlooking the canal, turning left along it. This is **BAGLEY WALK**, an elevated green route created in 2017, which bends round to pass a collection of brick buildings forming the **Coal Office** at No.1. Originally known as the Fish and Coal Buildings these were constructed in several phases from 1851 for clerks who monitored the flow of freight through the Goods Yard. 'Coal Office' is painted prominently in white on the side brickwork of the far end wall. The buildings were gutted by fire in 1983, but permission to demolish them was refused two years later after a public inquiry. From 1993 six arches below were host to The Cross nightclub; redevelopment work forced its closure in early 2008.

The floors and roofs of the buildings have been rebuilt and the whole restored for offices, studios and restaurants. The Jamie Oliver Group was to be the occupant but withdrew in January 2017 when it announced its business would be slimmed down amidst Brexit fears. The designer Tom Dixon moved his HQ here in 2018, with a flagship shop, showroom, office, restaurant and cafe.

Beyond the **Coal Office** alongside the canal are **Canalside Steps**, covered in the warmer months in artificial grass. No trace remains of the railway bridge at this point which carried coal to the Pancras Gasworks opposite, nor of Somers Bridge, built in 1819, which later provided road access to the Goods Yard. It was taken down and replaced by a concrete bridge further east in 1921. When works began in 2008 a massive crane was used to remove that heavy bridge; **Regent's Canal Bridge** which we crossed earlier was then constructed. Designed by Knight Architects and opened in 2012 it carries within it services pipes across to the offices in Pancras Square. The old canalside wall has been removed.

Bear left diagonally across **GRANARY SQUARE** with, to your right, **The Lighterman** pub and dining room, designed by Stanton Williams, and past The Granary, towards a 3-storey 5-bay building. This was erected in 1850 to Lewis Cubitt's designs as the main Goods Yard offices, at a time when such purpose-built examples were rare. It had large windows and a convenient plan. The building suffered extensive wartime bomb damage in November 1940 and had to be rebuilt. It was renovated again in the late 1980s and renamed Regeneration House, as the HQ of the London Regeneration Consortium. Redeveloped by John McAslan & Partners, and now known as **Two Granary Square**, it houses both the Arts Fund and the House of Illustration, the world's first public gallery and education space dedicated to the art of illustration, which opened in 2014. This was the brainchild of cartoonist (Sir) Quentin Blake, first Children's Laureate but best known for his drawings for Roald Dahl's books.

Continue left into the large covered space roofed by the **West Handyside Canopy**, built in 1888 by the civil engineering firm of ironmaster Andrew Handyside. It provided cover for unloading fish and other perishable goods for onward distribution around London. Fish was sold here on Sundays when Billingsgate Market was shut. Railway traffic ceased in the 1970s but the area remained in use for deliveries and parking. The canopy has been reglazed and restored and this area is now an event space and host to the weekly Canopy Market.

Over to the right is Waitrose supermarket housed in the former **Midland Goods Shed**. This was built in 1850 as a carriage shed for its Maiden Lane terminus by the GNR, who agreed in 1858 that the MR could use it for its goods. The MR soon afterwards completed its own goods yard in Agar Town, but the Midland name stuck. The building has been altered perhaps a dozen times over the years. In 1869 the southern part was leased to Kilner Bros, makers of the eponymous jar, as their London base before the Shed was adapted for inwards goods traffic during WWI. Kilners moved to the Eastern Coal Drops (p 54) in 1915, remaining there until their bankruptcy in 1937. Before redevelopment the Shed was being used for vehicle hire and as a mini-cab office.

Wheel round to the right (under the canopy) past tables and chairs and walk alongside a 7-bay 3-storey office block which was added to the Shed. This faces the east side of Two Granary Square, here with the entrance to the House of Illustration. The green space ahead is known as **Wharf Road Gardens**, designed by Townshend Landscape Architects (TLA) with support from Dan Pearson Studio. The name comes from the former roadway which encircled the Goods Yard. It was bizarrely configured; having crossed the canal at Somers Bridge (p 56) it split two ways, becoming the Goods Yard's internal perimeter road. One branch did a sharp U-turn and continued along the yard's west and north sides, emerging into York Way ¾ mile northward, while the other ran east to an exit in York Way, here beside the canal. This exit has now become a new **WHARF ROAD**, which gives a postal address both to the ice cream parlour on our left, and to Waitrose with its main entrance and outdoor seating area just beyond. Here also is the Waitrose Cookery School which provides day courses in preparing and cooking food for both adults and children.

This side of Waitrose abuts **Handyside Gardens**, opened in December 2013, to the designs of Dan Pearson. These were laid out over old railway sidings, which are reflected in the network of hedges. The plant beds are raised because they sit above railway tunnels (including the original Gas Works Tunnel, built using cut and cover. The planting is inspired by growth found on railway embankments. The gardens are flanked over to the right by the ArtHouse apartment blocks designed by architects dRMM. At ground floor level along York Way there are units for shops and studios.

Here was the site of the temporary passenger terminus of 1850, which preceded King's Cross and was known as Maiden Lane Station, set just off Maiden Lane (now York Way). It opened on 7 August 1850 and before its closure on 14 October 1852 had to cater with both the huge crowds that came for the Great Exhibition, and at least one royal departure for the North. Indeed at one time the GNR directors considered making this their permanent terminus, since the canal was a major and expensive obstacle.

Once King's Cross terminus opened, the GNR abandoned Maiden Lane Station. Within three days it was converted into a wholesale Potato Market **[15]**, which was successively enlarged and adapted. Potatoes from Yorkshire were one of the company's most important commodities and the potato market quickly became established as the leading one in London, with nearly 1,000 tons sold each week in the mid 1860s. The Goods Yard was convenient for traders and the supply was always regular, unlike the sea carriers on whom the traditional centre at Tooley Street depended. The potato trade reached a peak after WWI and continued into the 1970s when the southern part of the market was demolished; the northern part came down in 1988.

The eastern side of the Midland Goods Shed (Waitrose) is covered by a curved, gabled roof

15 Potato Market, 1864

supported on trusses attached to brackets. This is the **East Handyside Canopy**. It was added in 1888 so that the potato dealers could unload their wares under cover. This was in response to the MR's recent opening of its own potato market in Somers Town. More warehousing was added, bringing the total number of traders to 39. It also helped the growth of the trade here in home-grown fruit and vegetables.

The canopy, which to the north was linked to the West Handyside Canopy, is now behind curtain walling added by Bennetts Associates when they remodelled the Midland Goods Shed. It can however be admired by popping into the supermarket, where the spandrels of the 1850 temporary passenger station can also be seen. The northern section of the Canopy (not visible) provides offices for New Day, a financial services provider. A key feature inside its offices is the preserved hydraulic accumulator vessel, the machinery of a tower added to the Shed in 1878, when increased operations in the yard meant that the capstans needed more hydraulic power.

Walk through the gardens and pause at the gate at the end of the children's playground. The land to the north of here, bordering **YORK WAY**, was a coal stacking ground but in the 1990s became central London's only full-length golf driving range. The King's Cross Sports Hall is under construction. With the Gasworks Tunnel running just 2.5m below, it is lightweight timber structure, clad in black zinc. It has been designed by Bennetts Associates for a dual purpose, to also provide a temporary home for the King's Cross Construction Skills Centre (p 61). Since 2004 this has offered training and apprenticeships to local people with a view to their working on the King's Cross development.

Northward along York Way will be a small open space named Gatti Park, after Carlo Gatti, the 19th-century ice merchant and ice-cream maker, who had several ice wells along the Regent's Canal.

West of the sports centre site, is **WILBERFORCE STREET**, named after the little old lady in *The Ladykillers* movie. Still embryonic in 2020, the street will eventually become L-shaped, bearing left to meet Tapper Walk (p 59).

Turn left along **HANDYSIDE STREET**, flanked by tall blocks on its northern side. **Nos.14-18**, the block clad in pink metal panels, was designed by Duggan Morris. Offices occupy its upper floors, while its ground floor houses a large, 7m-high entrance lobby, a public space from which visitors can access a 3-screen cinema, the Everyman King's Cross. The building faces the back of the University of the Arts London, of which **Platform Theatre**, the performance venue here, is a part.

The names earmarked for two proposed short streets behind Nos.14-18 are Peppercorn Lane, after Arthur Peppercorn, last Chief Mechanical Engineer of the LNER and designer of many of its top-link steam locomotives; and Harrier Yard, recalling the 1969 visit of a certain Harrier jump-jet to 'RAF St Pancras' (p 24). Pass a short walkway leading nowhere, the future south end of an extended Beaconsfield Street (p 60).

The ten-storey block beyond, faced in white limestone and rounding the corner ahead, is the **Aga Khan Centre,** opened by the Prince of Wales in June 2018. It is home to the UK institutions of the Aga Khan Development Network (AKDN) that works to increase understanding of Muslim civilizations and improve the quality of life of the world's most disadvantaged communities. A series of roof gardens, terraces and courtyards showcase the diversity of Muslim cultures through landscape architecture. The building, designed by Japanese architects Maki & Associates and their first in London, has a huge central atrium with a lattice work sculpture by Rasheed Araeen. It also houses the Aga Khan Library with many rare books and manuscripts.

We reach **Lewis Cubitt Park**, a wide grassy

area forming the main green space at King's Cross Central, completed in 2015. Along both sides runs **LEWIS CUBITT WALK**, dominated by tall blocks. At the foot of No.1 on the west side is the Little Creatures Brewery, while on the east side beyond the Aga Khan Centre the Luma apartments at No.6 (under construction at time of writing) are by architects Squire & Partners with interior designers, Conran & Partners. Next, at No.5 is **Fenman House**, high-rise apartments designed by Maccreanor Lavington Architects, featuring hand-set brickwork and completed in 2017. To the east both these blocks will overlook **Jellicoe Gardens**, a tranquil spot inspired by Persian gardens.

Past Fenman House the pathway becomes **TAPPER WALK**, which probably takes its name from the wheeltappers who, in the steam age, would hit train wheels with a long hammer in order to detect cracks; a cracked wheel would not ring true. At **No.1**, Roseberry Mansions contains 'extra care' apartments designed for the active elderly and run by One Housing Group above office space. It was also designed by Maccreanor Lavington and opened in 2013.

16 Lewis Cubitt Park with swimming pond, April 2016 (photo by Andrew H)

The block faces the northern part of Lewis Cubitt Park, here once home to the UK's first ever, man-made natural swimming pond **[16]**. The chemical free pond was created in 2015 by Ooze Architects and artist Marjetica Potrč as an experiential art installation, before it was grassed over the following year.

The park will terminate at Cadence, a cluster of arcaded blocks, surrounding an inner courtyard, designed by Alison Brooks. The interiors are designed by Conran & Partners. The apartments are being constructed on the sites of a Viewing Platform and of the Skip Garden, which closed in September 2019. Begun as a moveable vegetable garden built in skips it became a community project run by the charity Global Generation, which provides all kinds of opportunities for local young people. Everything was built using recycled materials – mostly from the construction site. Many of the structures were designed by students from the Bartlett School of Architecture. Some of these have been moved to another temporary home at the Story Garden by the British Library (p 73).

Walk over to the left to emerge in **CANAL REACH**. To your left, the road leads down to Tapestry (p 54) by the Regent's Canal, and will be lined with tall office blocks, including further Facebook offices at Nos.11-21. Facing you at No.25 is the student accommodation called **Victoria Hall**, part of the AKDN campus and designed by Stanton Williams and opened in 2016.

It stands on the site of the Midland Roundhouse (or 'Derby Shed'), built by the GNR in 1859 to stable locomotives of the rival MR during its decade-long intrusion into King's Cross. Numerous tracks ran into the polygonal building which had a 40-ft diameter turntable. When the MR left, it was used it as a carriage and wagon shop by the GNR, but later the LNER decided it had to go. In 1931 it was spectacularly demolished. Ripped apart by two steam locomotives hitched to it and tugging in different directions, it vanished in a cloud of black dust.

Turn right along Canal Reach. On the corner of York Way is King's Cross Central's tallest building, **Urbanest King's Cross**, by Glenn Howells Architects. Completed in 2013, it provides further student accommodation. Outside is a graphic sculpture by Simon Hitchens called *Unity*. Weighing 6 tons, and suggestive of two large redundant cogwheels, it alludes to the heavy engineering involved in the Goods Yard's industrial past. The granite symbolises the robust building materials used there, and the blue resin hints at the Regent's Canal. The sculpture can also be seen as a stylised letter 'X' (or Cross).

Between the two student halls is the entrance to a service road aptly named **CHILL LANE**. Running (out of sight) alongside the CTRL tracks, it passes the **Cooling Pod**, 120m-long and with folded metal fins, designed by Allies and Morrison. The cooling network harnesses excess heat generated at the nearby Energy Centre (p 54) and converts it into low-carbon cooling which is distributed to selected buildings across King's Cross Central.

We emerge into **YORK WAY** and turn right (and south) past another block designed by Maccreanor Lavington at **No.5**. This is Saxon Court, an affordable residential scheme delivered for One Housing Group in 2013. The architects' three buildings form a cluster inspired by Chicago Modernism.

Cross **BEACONSFIELD STREET**. The street's name derives from Beaconsfield Buildings, which stood off the opposite (Islington) side of York Way until pulled down in 1970. Latterly nicknamed 'The Crumbles', the three tenement blocks had been erected in 1879 by the Victoria Dwellings Association, of which Benjamin Disraeli, Earl of Beaconsfield, was the patron. Crumbles Castle Adventure Playground was opened on its site. Along on the left is **Tile House** (No.1), a community unit providing supported accommodation for 15 residents with severe mental illness. It is run by One Housing Group in partnership with Camden & Islington NHS Foundation Trust.

At **No.3 YORK WAY** is 10- to 15-storey **Rubicon Court**, one of the earliest developments at King's Cross Central, completed in 2012 and designed by PRP Architects. It is also run by One Housing Group and has a large roof garden planted by Global Generation. There are retail and office areas on the ground floor of the buildings. In Unit 1 is the Finnish Institute in London which aims to increase awareness of Finnish culture and society in the UK and Ireland. The potato market (p 57) once stretched to this point and the 1894 OS map shows cattle pens alongside the main road. In 2020 an edible community garden was opened to the public at Rubicon Court.

On the Islington side, on the brow of the rise, is the abandoned York Road Underground Station. Opened in December 1906, it was one of three little-used Piccadilly Line stations that were closed in 1932. It is a fine example of the work of architect Leslie Green, with his familiar ox-blood tiles. Although renovated in 1989, it is unlikely to be re-opened, given the costs of extending the old platforms.

An Old Bailey trial in November 1907 highlighted the problem of 'riotous behaviour' along York Road, where it was said that each week there was fighting between rival gangs of youths, armed with guns. The stretch here was badly lit at the time.

Turn round and walk back north. Hereabouts, before the CTRL arrived, York Way passed over a long, multi-arch brick viaduct, spanning the tracks which led to the vast expanse of sidings that fanned out across the Goods Yard. As part of the CTRL works, the viaduct was demolished in 2005 and the road was slewed westward to dip beneath the CTRL tracks. The borough boundary, which had followed the line of the viaduct, remained unaltered, so that a small sliver of Camden was suddenly marooned on the 'wrong' side of York Way.

No.180 was the former home from 2004-20 of the King's Cross Construction Skills Centre (p 58). Designed by David Morley Architects, and an RIBA Award winner in 2009, the dramatic building was intended as a 'lesson in construction' for the trainees. It is being demolished and this and a triangular site behind (in Islington) will see the creation by 2022 of three mixed-use blocks centred around an ecology garden with a focus on education and community engagement, managed by Global Generation, all to a master plan by David Morley.

At the CTRL bridge we leave King's Cross Central and enter the second half of the Route. There are bus stops close by for those who might wish to split the Route into two separate walks.

Intersecting from the left just past the CTRL bridge is **FREIGHT LANE**. Following the line of the northern arm of former Wharf Road, this is now a long and very dusty cul-de-sac leading to cement works. Formerly home to British Rail's Freightliner Terminal, it now also leads to a bus maintenance yard and to a Council transport depot, whose address is **No.7 YORK WAY**.

Beyond, York Way climbs and goes under another railway bridge that carries the Richmond-Stratford Overground line. A railway line from Camden Town to the docks at Blackwall had been authorised by an Act of Parliament in 1846, but the line ran at first into Fenchurch Street and so built up what proved to be valuable passenger traffic. The railway opened to the Docks in 1852 as the East & West India Docks & Birmingham Junction Railway, and was able to compete successfully for goods traffic with the Regent's Canal. It was, however, as the commuter North London Railway that it was best known. Its Maiden Lane passenger station stood here from 1887 until 1916, when it was hit by an enemy bomb. It closed on New Year's Day 1917 and was never replaced. A bricked-up doorway remains on the far side of the bridge.

Opposite, in Islington, is Vale Royal, home to the studio of the sculptor Antony Gormley. The land here was from 1299 owned by the monks of Vale Royal Abbey in Cheshire. *Vale Royal* is the title of Aidan Dun's 1995 epic poem based on the mysteries of King's Cross. The locality's 19th-century name was Belle Isle. Far from beautiful, it was then a collection of ramshackle industrial buildings with tall chimneys devoted to boiling bones, blood and carrion; varnish making; and the manufacture of artificial manure. Here horses that had finished their useful working life were slaughtered, many in the yard of John (Jack) Atcheler; he was later buried in Highgate Cemetery. An 1856 leading article in *The Metropolitan* states that 'the nuisance makers of Belle Isle are still permitted to affect their neighbours with nausea, sickness, diarrhoea, dysentery and cholera to any extent they please for their own private advantage'. The St Pancras Vestry minutes record several petitions about the noxious odours from Belle Isle. James Greenwood in 1874 described the noisome conditions of the adjoining cottages in ironically-named Pleasant Grove, where 'poor, patient little boys and girls ... are kept in ignorance and doomed to work through their young lives in dirt and squalor and the very shadow of death'. The whole district was compulsory purchased by the LCC in 1959 and declared an industrial improvement area in 1980.

Further north off the west side of present York Way was the coal, vegetable and cattle depot of the London & North Western Railway (LNWR), which arrived here by way of Kentish and Camden Towns. Sheep and cattle pens had been relocated from Camden Town ready for the opening in 1855 of the new Metropolitan Cattle Market (once a few hundred metres up on the right; livestock trading continued there until WWII). Imagine herds of livestock unloaded from trucks from Shropshire and driven to the market **[17]**. Replacing the 'live meat' market at Smithfield, it had been built over Copenhagen House and Fields, a favourite tea garden and meeting place of Londoners in Georgian times.

On the west side we pass a tall tower and a long row of Modernist buildings with balconies, the **XY Apartments**, so called for their location 'on the XY coordinates between King's Cross and Camden stations'. They were completed in 2017 replacing a small industrial area. They flank entrances into the Maiden Lane Estate (p 63), of which they technically are a part and whose concrete aesthetic inspired the architects PRP.

Next are **Nos.11-15**, a short row of mid-Victorian houses with stucco window surrounds, known in the 19th century as New Market Terrace. At the corner with Agar Grove at No.17 is the **Newmarket Ale House**, until recently the New Market Inn; it is now a gastropub and hotel. It was licensed as a theatre from 1867 to 1871, when its proprietor was Charles Buckhurst. He owned the pub, its stables and sheds and a triangular portion of land behind, on which in 1876 he opened a roller skating rink (p 63).

At the traffic lights turn up **AGAR GROVE**, which was St Paul's Road until renamed in 1938. We have now crossed over the boundary of Allensbury, the land once belonging to St Bart's and have entered the former manor of Cantelowes. The boundary ran behind the gardens of the houses on this south side. Both sides of the road belong to the Camden Square development, which began at the far (western) end of St Paul's Road in 1846, and was largely

17 Cattle arriving at the Metropolitan Cattle Market (*Illustrated London News*, 1865)

complete by 1860. The numbering originally ran consecutively along the south side, but was changed from 1864, with odds on the north side and evens on the south. Note that the windows of the tall houses – many of them semi-detached villas - have margin glazing bars, a mid-century feature, and some have original ironwork surrounds.

St Paul's Road at first enjoyed a good reputation, its inhabitants featuring in the Court Guides. By the 1890s however most of the houses were let out as apartments and lodgings. In 1897 Ernest Aves, who was updating Booth's Poverty Map, reported that the Police Inspector who accompanied him thought the road had 'gone down' and that only three families now kept servants. The demi-monde reputation of Camden Town in the Edwardian period was reinforced by the notorious murder of Emily 'Phyllis' Dimmock at No.29 (see *Streets of Camden Town*, which describes the northern side of the road.)

The Irish TV presenter Anna Nolan lived for several years from 1998 in a flat at **No.136**.

Take the first left turn into **ST PAUL'S CRESCENT**. The street was renumbered in 1879. There are charming mid-Victorian cottages (of 2 storeys plus basement) on both sides. **No.25** was the family home of Edith Underwood before her unhappy marriage to George Gissing in 1891. In his novel *New Grub Street* he describes the crescent as 'a quiet by-way, consisting of small decent houses'.

On the left is the gated development of **ST PAUL'S MEWS** (1987-91), designed by the CZWG Partnership. One can peer through to see the double-curving sweep of town houses whose construction caused something of an outcry because of a perceived lack of consultation. Camden Skating Rink, an indoor roller skating rink, was here from 1876 to 1900, when Joseph Thornley (who had lived at No.122 St Paul's Road) ceased to be the ratepayer. He had been the proprietor for several years, and had given a deposition at the inquest in August 1890 of 15-year-old Charles George who collapsed and died at the rink (verdict: 'syncope whilst suffering from heart disease'). The Mews became a builders' yard in the 20th century and before redevelopment housed a cable works.

Beyond, **No.33** was in 1963 the home of Betty Ambatielos, a tireless campaigner for the release of political prisoners in Greece, including her own husband. That year she achieved notoriety when she confronted Queen Frederica of Greece outside Buckingham Palace; it was reported she had slapped her. At **No.37** Cecil Hepworth (c.1874-1953), the film pioneer, lived when a child. His father was a magic lantern expert, described as a 'scientific lecturer' on the 1881 census.

There is a turning opposite St Paul's Mews marked **No.44**, which is shown on the 1870 OS map as a house in its own park. This was described as pleasure gardens when sold in 1891, after which factories and workshops were built there. From the early 1890s until WWI the turning led to the works of George Cording, waterproofer to the Prince of Wales and then to the King, when the Prince became Edward VII. After Cording's death in 1912 the company was caught up in a legal battle over naming rights with another but longer-established waterproofing firm, preferred by the new King George V and called J C Cording Ltd. A decision in favour of the latter was made in the House of Lords in 1916. From 1900 the ARC lamp lighting company also had a factory in the yard. After WWII it housed a pickle factory and a machine tool works. In more recent years the units have been converted to gated, residential use.

Continuing, we reach the **Maiden Lane Estate**. Begun in 1976 and finished by 1983, it lies on the site of the LNWR's coal, vegetable and cattle depot, which had been purchased by Camden Council in 1972. The first tenants moved in in 1980 but after only a few months there were many complaints about design faults and constructional failings (for example, dust carts could not get into the estate and drainage was inadequate on the stepped houses). Designed by Gordon Benson and Alan Forsyth, then employed by Camden Council and also responsible for the redevelopment of Gospel Oak, the Maiden Lane Estate is mainly low-rise with west-facing terraces above garages. It suffered from a very poor image for years, until major refurbishment works began in 2015. 273 new flats have been built, the majority for sale (including the XY Apartments), reflecting the current wisdom that private capital must be harnessed to finance the regeneration and expansion of social housing.

Parallel to the street to our left, and at a higher level, are two residential walkways: **Rosebank Walk** and **Linkwood Walk**. The street ends at **Maiden Lane Community Centre**, which includes a squash court and hosts a playgroup, a youth club and various classes. Running off to the left is one of three small streets on the estate whose names recall the history of the area. The first is **MAIDEN LANE**, which turns into a crescent behind York Way, encircling **St Thomas' Place**. The other two are **BROADFIELD LANE** and **ALLENSBURY PLACE** (off which is **Elm Friars Walk**). The northernmost field of Allensbury (p 50) was called Broadfield.

In front of the Community Centre and to our right is an almost concealed short flight of steps. Walk down them and then ascend another flight of steps above the Centre to reach a patio area with views over the railway line towards King's Cross Central. To the right a ramp leads down to another paved area. Just past a St Paul's Crescent sign, turn left and walk along a passageway passing front doors, with views right over the Estate towards **St James Gate**, leading from which are **Bowmore Walk** and **Springbank Walk**.

Descend past a fenced playground and then turn right along a wide path by the side of the main railway line. A Dissenters chapel once occupied the ground where trees and an adventure playground now stand. It was opened in June 1867, the congregation presided over by Alderman Sydney Waterlow (commemorated by the Highgate park). It was used in the 1870s for a branch of the Free Christian Church, whose HQ was in Clarence Road, Kentish Town. The minister of the chapel in 1874 was Moncure Conway, at the time also pastor of South Place Unitarian Chapel, Finsbury and who is remembered in Conway Hall, Red Lion Square, the present home of the South Place Ethical Society. The temporary chapel was later used by Wesleyans before it was pulled down by the MR, who took over the site in the 1890s.

The MR's main line had obliterated Queen's Road, a turning off St Paul's Road which stretched south as far as the North London Line. Two roads led off it to the west: Elm Road and Wrotham Road (whose junction with Queen's Road by the NLR was called Wrotham Square). The first leases were granted in 1852, when the new streets collectively were called Agar New Town; it was planned to link Queen's Road with King's Road (p 40) across Agar Fields.

At No. 1 Queen's Road was the Camden Congregational Chapel and the house of its minister Rev. George Hogben. His son, George Hogben (1853-1920) later emigrated to New Zealand where he became an important educationalist. No.3 was home to the engraver Charles Henry Jeens (1827-77), who moved to No.67 St Paul's Road when the street was demolished. The botanist Arthur Henfrey was living at No.4 in 1856, when his younger son was born. His elder son Henry William became a numismatist. Harold Copping, an illustrator of Biblical scenes, was born in 1863 at No.13, the son of journalist and writer Edward Copping and Rosa, daughter of the painter John Skinner Prout. At No.27 the weatherman George James Symons was living in the late 1850s, when he was meteorological observer to the Registrar General. He later founded the British Rainfall Association and kept meticulous precipitation records, assisted by an army of volunteers.

Walk past a tall wall, over to the right,

behind which are the former factories and workshops off St Paul's Crescent. This follows the ancient boundary of St Pancras Prebendal Manor and enclosed the LNWR's coal, vegetable and cattle depot.

Regain **AGAR GROVE**. To the right, in the corner house at **No.76**, the photographer Edgar Prout (son of John Skinner Prout) ran a studio from 1888 until his death in 1900. **No.82** was the home from 1881-91 of William Aumonier, who set up a successful firm of architectural sculptors and carvers in Tottenham Court Road, assisted by his son William junior. Next door, at the then No.41, the church architect George Low resided in the early 1860s. **No.98** was the home until his death in 2013 of the Holborn librarian Malcolm Campbell MBE; his son, classical singer Colin Campbell, was raised here. At **No.102** (on the corner of St Paul's Crescent) the singer Miss Mina Poole was living in retirement before her death there in a fire in December 1899 (in which her sister Christine also perished).

Turn left over the railway bridge and having passed a cycle path that leads to Camley Street (p 46), turn left again into the **Agar Grove Estate**. This was completed in 1969, on the site of Elm Road and most of Wrotham Road. The street down which we turn was built in 1865 as a replacement for Queen's Road, but with just four houses along it. By 1870 it was called Lomond Street, although it is shown as Loman Street on the first OS map. In 1886 it was renamed as part of Wrotham Road (Nos.41-45).

Bear right where the roadway bends towards the centrepiece of the Estate, the tower block called **Lulworth**. Built in 1965, the tower had an unenviable reputation for crime until the tenants took over its management in 1996. Most of the blocks we walk past are due for demolition over the next few years as the Estate is regenerated but Lulworth is to be retained and given a makeover.

It covers the site of No.30 St Paul's Road, a large detached house built in the late 1840s as St Paul's Lodge by the builder Richard Richardson, who lived here for some years. It was set back behind the houses along the roadway and abutted the Agars' land. St Paul's Lodge was home in 1881 to George Cruikshank, a watercolour artist, almost certainly related to his more famous caricaturist namesake. Near neighbours in houses along St Paul's Road included at No.26 the artist and female suffragist, Charlotte Elizabeth Babb, and at No.34A Frederick Selby Meakin, an architect in partnership with his father, William Fountain Meakin (d.1888). On the 1901 census the householder of No.38 was William H Seymour, for 20 years stage manager for the D'Oyly Carte Opera Company at the Opera Comique and the Savoy. His 17-year-old daughter, named aptly perhaps Patience, is described as a vocalist. She appeared in the chorus at Gilbert and Sullivan operas. No.27 (original numbering) was the marital home of the popular Victorian actress and mezzo-soprano Elizabeth Poole, whose surgeon husband Samuel Bacon died there in 1856; his namesake Frederick Bacon (1803-87), artist and engraver lived next door at the original No.28.

By the tower block, look left at **Agar Grove Children's Centre**, which in 2008 replaced a community nursery opened in 1993. It stands on the site of the church of St Thomas, Wrotham Road (also known as St Thomas, Agar Town). This was built in 1862-63 partly from £6,000 supplied by the MR for the erection of a church, school and parsonage to replace the one it had torn down in Agar Town (p 47). It was consecrated on 19 June 1863, with Robert Clemenger (p 123) as its first Vicar. The new church, by Samuel Sanders Teulon (also architect of St Stephen's, Hampstead), had diapered brickwork, a pyramidal roof and an unusually large unsupported span. Pevsner described it as 'immensely coarse'. From 1870 to 1884 the organist was John Baptiste Calkin, known as a composer of sacred music. In 1948 the benefice was placed under the charge of the Vicar of St Michael, Camden Town and the two parishes were united in 1954. By then derelict, St Thomas' was demolished and the site was sold in 1955. In front of the church was a towering 50-ft sycamore, known locally as the Ghost Tree of St Pancras, under which many newlyweds were photographed. The tree mysteriously died when plans to develop the area into an Estate were made public.

In Elm Road (also covered by the Estate) was the vicarage of St Thomas', where Rev. Clemenger died in December 1878. At No.3, next door, lived Henry George Luff (1843-1905), having been forced to move from his home in the demolished Queen's Road. A fellow architect, Henry John Wadling, was boarding with him at the time of the 1871 census.

Keeping the tower block to your left walk around it to emerge in the remaining stump of **WROTHAM ROAD**. Recently constructed apartments in dark grey brick at **Nos.14&16** lead us out of the Estate and to the corner (right) of **AGAR PLACE**, a short road, which we shall not traverse, lined by three Victorian terraced houses. It leads back to Agar Grove and continues across it. The road began as mews behind the early-19th-century villas called Camden Cottages that lined what is now St Pancras Way, and which was known before 1949 as Rochester Place. By its intersection with Agar Grove was the former No.6 St Paul's Road, where the architect Henry Tanner, who became principal surveyor to the Office of Works, was living in the early 1880s. Later in the decade it was home to Mabel K Haynes, an actress who was in the first performance of Ibsen's *A Doll's House* in 1889.

We continue ahead to the end of **WROTHAM ROAD**. On the north side two large stuccoed houses were converted into flats by Camden Council at the start of the 1980s. They face three houses, **Nos.8-12**, part of a terrace which once stretched east to the MR main line. They back on to what is now the London Overground.

The street was given odd and even numbering in 1871. No.36 was the first marital home from 1867-1875 of the ornithologist Richard Bowdler Sharpe. While there he became the first librarian of the Zoological Society of London, before beginning in 1872 his long career at the British Museum, where he produced its mammoth *Catalogue of Birds*. At No.52 the artist William Gillies Gair lived in the 1870s. The Carl Rosa Opera Company, taken over by the director Walter van Noorden in 1900, was based at Nos.14&14A in the years before his sudden death in 1916. This was their scenery stores and Head Office; it was converted in the mid-1920s into a church hall for St Thomas'.

St Thomas Court, a block of flats built in 2003, replacing industrial buildings, rounds the corner of **ST PANCRAS WAY**. On the opposite corner is a pair of quite fine early-19th-century stuccoed villas, **No.56** and **No.58**. The latter and the now demolished villa next door (replaced by post-war **Linton Court**) were part of a row of semi-detached and detached villas dating from the 1820s and called Camden Cottages, which fronted the road to Kentish Town. In 1885 they were numbered as part of King's Road, as St Pancras Way was then called (p 38). At No.23 Camden Cottages (on the site of Linton Court), the engraver Frederick Marshall was living 1861-1873, but the building had become a common lodging house by 1898 when Booth's researcher Edward Aves visited to update the poverty map.

In this area was the original St Pancras Workhouse, opened in 1731. Its exact location is unclear. In 1772 the workhouse building was declared unsafe and the Vestry subsequently took over the Mother Black Cap (then on the site of Camden Town Underground station), although the inmates did not move in there until 1778. This second building soon became overcrowded and the workhouse moved again in 1809 to new purpose-built accommodation, at the southern

3 William Bruges, Garter King of Arms, in a manuscript lumination from c.1430. Bruges is shown kneeling efore St George.

end of King's Road. The original workhouse building hereabouts was left to decay. In a case at the Old Bailey on 10 April 1782 it was said to harbour footpads who robbed people on the local highways. James King's *Kentish Town Panorama* shows a ruin on the east side of what is now St Pancras Way abutting the wall of the Agars' lands, roughly where St Thomas Court now stands. He records it as the remains of a workhouse. It may also be what was left of an ancient house in which a local magistrate William Woodhouse lived at the start of the 18th century. Woodhouse wrote that this had been the home of William Bruges **[18]**, first Garter King of Arms, where the Holy Roman Emperor, Sigismund, was entertained in lavish style in 1416. Bruges' house could well have been built as near as possible to the most important house in St Pancras manor, the manor house, which stood nearby (p 43). However, others believe Bruges lived in what is now Kentish Town Road.

Opposite stands a row of early-19th-century terraced houses. These formed the north end of St Paul's Terrace (p 44). **Nos.111-121** are now Listed. The balustraded building on the corner of Baynes Street opposite has replaced a shabby one-storey building that was known in the 1980s as the King's Road Forge.

The wide railway bridge above it was built for the North London Railway. On one side it now carries the London Overground line, but the other side (currently without tracks) is planned to become part of the Camden High Line. This projected 1.2 km green walking route between Camley Street and Camden Gardens is intended to link the tourist hotspots of King's Cross Central and Camden Market.

Our walk ends at this point. An onward short stroll along Baynes Street, beneath the railway bridge, then turning right up Royal College Street, will lead you to Camden Road and its Overground station.

Eastern Somers Town and Euston Road

A walk from King's Cross St Pancras Underground Station, through eastern Somers Town via the British Library and the Francis Crick Institute, and then via Euston Road to Euston Station

Here we make a circuit of the vast site mostly occupied by the British Library, before striking westward along the north side of Euston Road, Somers Town's southern boundary. Leave the Underground station by its 'Euston Road (North Side)' exit. Turn right and walk west along the north side of **EUSTON ROAD** beside the frontage of the St Pancras Renaissance Hotel.

Carefully cross Midland Road, and very shortly veer right into the **British Library** (BL). Promptly turn left and make for the western end of the library's Piazza. Standing here, 12ft high, is the 1999 bronze statue of Isaac Newton by Sir Eduardo Paolozzi, who was inspired by William Blake's 1796 print of Newton at Tate Britain. The statue was funded through a subscription to the Foundation for Sport & the Arts by Vernons football pools. From here, there is a good view across to the library building.

The original plans in the late 1960s to build the BL in Bloomsbury were thwarted by much local opposition. It was not until 1975 that the government paid £8 million for the St Pancras site. The architect Professor Sir Colin St John ('Sandy') Wilson **[19]**, involved in the BL project from the outset, described the library's protracted genesis as 'The Thirty Years War'. The co-designer of the new building was M J (Mary Jane) Long, Wilson's American wife who, while bringing up two small children, became the principal architect partner on the site. When she died in 2018, aged 79, she was hailed as 'the brains behind' the scheme.

The English Free Style building was designed in red brick and slate to harmonise with the neighbouring former Midland Grand Hotel. Budgetary constraints led to it being built in phases; the completed building was much smaller than intended. The BL's four basements, said to be the deepest in London, house 300km of shelving for 12 million books, maps and manuscripts assembled from 18 different buildings, including the BL's previous main location in the British Museum. The huge quantities of waste produced in their construction were used to create, *inter alia*, a ski slope at Beckton in east London. Formally opened by the Queen in 1998, the library was Grade-I Listed in 2015 for its 'outstanding architectural and historic interest'.

Descend into the eastern part of the Piazza. On your right is Poets Circle, a small amphitheatre intended for outdoor performances. Encircling it are eight boulders incised with human forms, a 2002 sculpture entitled *Planets* by Antony Gormley. He stated that it celebrates 'the dependency of the body on the material world in this library, which is

19 Bust of Colin St John Wilson in the foyer of the British Library. Photo, 2011, by Fæ

the repository of the fruits of the mind'. Beyond the Circle, but rather inconspicuous, is Anne Frank's Tree, planted in 1998 to commemorate the teenage diarist who died in Bergen-Belsen concentration camp in 1945, and all children killed in war or conflict in the 20th century. In front of the library entrance is another work by Gormley, his *Witness* (2011), commissioned by English PEN to mark their 90th anniversary and in the form of an empty chair, a symbol used by the association to represent imprisoned writers worldwide.

Subject only to a bag check, and apart from the reading rooms, the British Library is open to all. An information leaflet may be picked up at the desk. The free exhibition galleries display such treasures as Magna Carta and the Lindisfarne Gospels. Beside the shop is a larger gallery for special major exhibitions, where an admission charge applies. From the café one can contemplate the home created by M J Long for the King's Library. The 65,000 volumes collected by George III and given to the nation by George IV, are contained in a 6-storey glass and bronze tower with their spines facing outwards, their binding forming a rich tapestry of subtle leathers and gold tooling. The books are actually available to readers, mobile shelving and internal lifts facilitating their retrieval by staff. At the back of the lower ground floor (turn left beyond the cloakroom) is a very small display about the St Pancras Housing Association, featuring 3 finials sculpted by Gilbert Bayes, salvaged from the clothes-line posts of Somers Town, and including the carpenter's tool-bag from St Anne's Flats (p 91).

Back outside, the Piazza, with its Last Word coffee shop, is a good place to sit and enjoy a drink in fine weather, or indeed to absorb something of the BL site's complex history. Its frontage along the New (later Euston) Road was once lined by a terrace of houses named Judd Place West (see p 78). Like the terrace, half of the courtyard area lay on the northern edge of the Skinners' estate (p 79). Once running diagonally across the piazza site, off Euston Road and along the estate's western boundary was West Street; and bisecting the triangle so formed was a shorter James Street, running east to Skinner Street (now Midland Road, p 79). The County Ale Brewery was at No.2 West Street from the 1830s to 1850s. A decade later, the street had gone down considerably: a brothel was recorded there in 1862, and an inquest in 1865 recorded the death of a child of 2 from 'pneumonia accelerated by want'.

In 1874 the Midland Railway (MR) acquired all the land northward as far as today's Brill Place (p101) as the site for its Somers Town Goods Depot. Designed by engineer John Underwood, the depot was built in 1883-87 on two levels, the upper one formed of wrought iron plates and girders supported on 400 cast iron columns. Covering 14 acres, the depot could accommodate several thousand wagons. After crossing the canal to the north, and then passing over Pancras Road, trains ran onto the upper level. Powerful hydraulic hoists lowered wagons to the lower level, for onward transport of their cargoes by road. Coal, and perishables such as potatoes, milk and fish were among the miscellaneous freight for which the depot was used between its opening for traffic on 1 November 1887 and its closure in 1968. The depot was then dismantled, and the flattened site subsequently became an al fresco coach park, grandiosely named as the London Coach Station of British Coachways, before its eventual acquisition for the BL.

Passing between the library and the coffee shop, emerge into **OSSULSTON STREET**. This southern stretch was known until 1867 as Wilsted Street – sometimes spelt 'Wilstead', although the Bedfordshire village of that name had no apparent connection with any of the players in the development of Somers Town. This new self-contained community, north of the then New Road, was developed from the late 18th century on the Brill Farm property of Lord Somers. Along with parallel Chalton Street (p 94), Wilsted Street was one of the earliest streets; house building was well advanced here by 1787. Noteworthy residents were the radical politician John Gale Jones (p 119) who, on withdrawing from politics in the 1820s, returned to his former profession of surgeon and apothecary, setting up practice in Wilsted Street, where he died. In the 1830s and '40s the watch and clock maker Louis de Fontaine had his premises at No.18.

Though erected very rapidly by small builders, under contract to Jacob Leroux (p 102), the area's earliest houses were of a reasonable size and had quite generous back gardens. Many of these were later built over, and 'every interstice filled' with inferior housing. Somers Town was to deteriorate into a notorious slum.

Across the road is the east end of unlabelled, and once unhealthy, **WEIR'S PASSAGE**. Originally called Denny's or Dennis Passage, it was apparently renamed around 1800 after Alexander Weir, a local paving commissioner, at a time when the alleyway was lined with shops. Standing on its south side by mid-century was the hall of the 'St Pancras Auxiliary' of the British & Foreign Society for the Suppression of Intemperance. The well-known topographical artist Thomas Hosmer Shepherd drew a delightful vignette of this temperance hall and 'occasional chapel' in 1855, late in his career. Some members of the Shepherd family of artists chose to live locally in Somers Town, although not Hosmer who seemed to have preferred Islington.

By the later 19th century Weir's Passage had acquired an unenviable reputation for squalor. Booth's researcher in 1898 called it a 'gloomy looking place' with several shops, one of which was a suspected brothel. A former resident, born c.1920 in the adjacent People's Hall (p 99), described it as 'an alley festering on both sides with filthy hovels where no policeman would venture, although the Sisters attached to the mission were allowed to go unmolested'.

The Housing & Town Planning Act 1909 empowered local authorities to oblige owners of slum properties to take action to improve the living conditions of their tenants. Among the recommendations of the St Pancras Medical Officer of Health was the demolition of Nos.2-10 Weir's Passage, to 'open up and bring considerably more light and air into this passage and to Wilstead (sic) Cottages' (see below). No.5 Ossulston Street was also to be pulled down and its site left open surrounded by boundary posts. The MR, who owned the properties, was slow to comply but eventually largely did so, though later maps suggest that only one or two houses were actually pulled down here and show No.5 as still standing. Required to be kept open 'for all time', the present empty grassed area protected by bollards seems to have been a 1930s creation.

Turn north up **OSSULSTON STREET**. Today, the west side is lined by the east side of the LCC's interwar Ossulston Estate (p 96). On its site, running along the back of the original houses here, and approached by a flight of steps from Weir's Passage, was a range of dwellings known initially as Dennis Row, and later as Wilsted Cottages. A little to the north, a covered entry off Wilsted Street gave alternative access to them via a diminutive Wilsted Court. Booth's researcher in 1898 described the inhabitants of these 2-storey cottages as 'quiet'. He also noted that one of the largest houses in neighbouring Ossulston Street, No.45, had been home to Frederick Purchese (p 119) before his recent move to Platt Street. When he left, it briefly became a brothel.

Lining the opposite side of Ossulston Street today is the colonnaded west face of the British Library. There is now no trace of the perimeter wall, ¾ mile long, which once surrounded the Goods Depot. Its brickwork was much admired for its craftsmanship and praised by Pevsner for its excellent detailing. Liking to use materials that were the products of its home territory, the MR here used unusually small bricks imported from Leicestershire, and blue bricks from Staffordshire that offered excellent damp-proofing. The general approach to the lower yard was through large gateways on the west side along Ossulston Street. Openings on the outer wall along Euston Road were filled with artistically designed grilles of hammered iron and a pair of the impressive wrought iron-gates was salvaged for re-use at the Camley Street Natural Park (p 48).

Swept away in the 1870s to make room for the Goods Depot was a bewildering maze of narrow streets, courts and cul-de-sacs, with rows of small cottages fronting onto even narrower pathways, and often accessed through covered entries or tunnels. In this densely populated area 10,000 people lost their homes. Many of those made homeless moved elsewhere: Charles Booth wrote of a 'whole colony of very rough people' from Somers Town who 'settled in badly built streets near Junction Road, Archway'. Others remained locally, thronging into the already overcrowded surviving streets of Somers Town. The MR did nothing to alleviate the situation until 1894 when it built Polygon Buildings (p 107), but even then the new flats were let mainly to railway staff.

From south to north, the first turning eastward off Ossulston Street was a cul-de-sac originally called Providence Place but soon renamed Isaac's Place. Here, in 1868 at No.15, the one-year-old daughter of a labourer died of 'choleriac diarrhoea'. Next came Phillips Buildings, running east to meet Brill Row (p 76) and subsuming an early Northam's Buildings on the way, with a tiny Northam's Square off its south side.

Off the north side of Phillips Buildings there were a number of yet smaller turnings – a cul-de-sac called North Place; Marson Street, leading into the original Brill Place (p 76); and two tiny courts called John's Place and Beale's Place, both with tunnel entrances. Off the east side of Marson Street another tunnel led into Caroline Place, while off the west side were the three cottages of Cromer Place. On the southwest corner of Marson Street stood a pub called the Cheshire Cheese. In 1817 the landlord was convicted of having allowed illegal gaming in his premises on at least two occasions. In 1844 the Somers Town Victim Committee organised here a 'harmonic meeting' (or concert), admission 2d, for the benefit of Chartists deemed to have been wrongly arrested.

Pause by the northernmost arched entrance to Levita House. Here former Chapel Street (also p 97) intersected. A building on the southeast corner at the crossroads was home for a while to the Agar Town Ragged School (p 32) on its displacement by the MR. On the southwest corner, at No.37 Wilsted Street (later No.69 Ossulston Street) was the African Chief public house, with a tiny Africa Place alongside it at one time. The Price family ran the pub for 50 years before selling it in 1864; it remained in business until 1923. As advertised in the *Teetotaler* newspaper in 1841, confronting the demon drink two doors south of the pub, in its temperance hall at No.39 Wilsted Street, was the Metropolitan Roman Catholic Total Abstinence Association.

Chapel Street was known until the mid-1820s as Chapel Path. Off its south side, east of Ossulston Street, was the place of worship from which it took its name. An Anglican chapel had been functioning here as early as 1798, but it failed to flourish, and from 1802 two quite distinct Baptist congregations successively occupied the building. The first of these remained for half a century, naming it Beulah Chapel, rebuilding it in 1821 after a fire (they were uninsured), and opening there a British Society 'Lancasterian' school (see p 75). In 1852 they departed for the new Zion Chapel in Goldington Crescent (p 123). A second flock of Baptists then moved into the Chapel Street building which became the Bethel Chapel; but *they* stayed only briefly, leaving again in 1856. The premises were then reclaimed by the Anglicans, serving as the mission hall of nearby Christ Church (p 96).

North of Chapel Street in its early days, and aligned north-south, were Suter's Buildings, Named after George Suter, a local bricklayer, the street later evolved into a very narrow Phoenix Place, with tunnel entries at both ends.

Chapel Street was a busy thoroughfare, full of shops and the venue for a thriving local market. Known for the male and female costermongers and wood cutters who traded there, it was also famous for its many 'marine stores', which sold very cheap goods. One observer remarked that their presence here was suggestive not so much of thrift as of extreme poverty. The 1865 directory lists only six businesses of a more respectable nature in Chapel Street, those of a hosier, bootmaker, clothier, hardwareman, fishmonger and pork butcher. The market moved to Chalton Street (p 97) in the 1880s, when the eastern end of Chapel Street was pulled down by the MR.

The original market had spread north along Middlesex Street, known likewise for its cheap shops. The peripatetic James Peller Malcolm (p 95) was living here in 1797. And the Scottish veterinary surgeon William Dick stayed here at No.27 from 1817, while enrolled at the London Veterinary College. He went on to found the Edinburgh Veterinary College, which was incorporated into the University of Edinburgh in 1951; the university court instituted three new chairs named after him. A serious fire occurred in Middlesex Street in December 1856 on Mr Hedge's premises. He was a timber merchant and a cowkeeper and, sadly, both his wood and his cows were consumed.

John Arnott (1799-1868), sometime General Secretary of the National Charter Association, and a cordwainer (shoemaker) by trade, lived with his family at a succession of local addresses – in Suter's Buildings in 1841, at No.8 Middlesex Street by 1846 and at No.11 Middlesex Place by 1848. A 'moral force' Chartist, he wrote a letter to *The Times* on 3 April that year, saying it was the 'firm determination of the committee that the demonstration shall be peaceable, orderly, and a moral display of the unenfranchised toiling masses'. The poetry Arnott wrote for the Chartist press caused him to be known as 'The Somers Town Chartist Rhymer'. He died locally after suffering a stroke in nearby Equity Buildings (p 101).

On the west side of Middlesex Street, at No.56, was a King's Head pub. Close by was the Somers Town Institute, housing both a British Society day school and the Presbyterians' Middlesex Mission. It was founded in 1843, in rooms above a stable, by Dr James Hamilton of the Regent Square Church. The Institute's 'plain and neat' building contained two ground-floor classrooms with a large hall above, and the windows were protected against vandalism by wire guards. A leading light of the mission was Rev. Zephaniah Banks Woffendale. Mancunian by birth but educated by Quakers in Kendal, he had come to London at the age of 14 to work in the Railway Clearing House (p 115). He later took to street-corner preaching in Somers Town, and was eventually ordained. In 1874 the mission's activities were transferred to the Zion Chapel at Goldington Crescent (p 123).

Tucked away behind the Institute was a small cul-de-sac containing the six cottages of Holwell (or Holywell) Place and three houses known as Nos.1-3 Old Romney Place. Off the east side of Middlesex Street, and parallel to it, were Denton's Buildings (Samuel Denton having been Clerk to the local paving commissioners); and bounding the Buildings was a very narrow, L-shaped Middlesex Place.

Walk on along **OSSULSTON STREET**. This stretch, north of erstwhile Chapel Street, was marked as Ossulston Buildings on a map of 1801. Ossulston was one of the 'hundreds' of the county of Middlesex, of which St Pancras was a part, and whose ancient meeting-place had been by Oswulf's Stone near what is now Marble Arch. The Somers Town street received its present name in 1807, when the politician Lord Ossulston was serving in the 'Ministry of All the Talents' under prime minister Lord Grenville.

In the street's more affluent days, the engraver Benjamin Smith lived, worked and died in 1833 at the original No.65. He worked mainly in stipple, producing portrait illustrations, and allegorical and biblical images after prominent artists of the day. Earlier still, before moving to Latham Place. (p 88), the Georgian satirist John Wolcot (*alias* Peter Pindar) lived in Ossulston Street, 'where he buried his old and faithful servant, Nell, upon whom he wrote an epitaph too indecent' to appear in print.

On the west side today is post-WWII **Hadstock House**, built on the site of the war-damaged former Christ Church National Schools (p 97). Opposite was the northern half of the former goods depot **[20]**. Though its site was earmarked for the British Library, the project ran out of cash, and only a third of the original scheme was actually built. After the BL's opening in 1998, the land here lay vacant for some years. For a while it contained an assemblage of portakabins housing offices for the Channel Tunnel Rail Link. In 2011 work started on the 5-year-long construction of the Francis Crick Institute ('the Crick', p 74), the massive structure looming ahead. The empty space to the south of it was in 2017 a haven for wild flowers, including some handsome purple toadflax.

Here the temporary Story Garden opened in July 2019, run by the charity Global Generation, who have moved planters and other structures from the Skip Garden at King's Cross (p 59). The local community are being encouraged to plant and cook together and the project is part of the British Library's wider community engagement work. Local views have been sought on the BL's plans, in partnership with Stanhope, to develop the 2.8 acre site for additional facilities for the Library and a permanent home for the Alan Turing Institute (for data science), founded in 2015. Building work is likely to commence in 2021.

Continue as far as the junction with Phoenix Road and Brill Place. On the southwest corner is interwar Chamberlain House (p 96). Previously on its site, and with a tunnel entrance off Ossulston Street, was another enclave of slum housing comprised of Ossulston Place (originally York Place) and Eastnor Place (once Tucker's Rents). Booth's researcher in 1898 called the former 'the very home of squalor' and the latter neglected and 'very rough and drunken'. Eastnor Place was

20 Somers Town Goods Depot, junction of Ossulston Street and Phoenix Street (now Road), 1927

a further beneficiary of the improvements made in the wake of the 1909 Housing & Town Planning Act; here some 15 houses were pulled down to 'open up' those remaining.

The garden now flourishing opposite, near the Brill Place corner, is lovingly cared for by local volunteers. Adjacent is the entrance of the St Pancras & Somers Town **Living Centre**, a community space provided by the Crick for the local population. Local people were fully involved in defining its aims and objectives: 'to bring the community together' and 'to boost people's physical and mental health and well-being'. Visitors are welcome to look round the large entrance hall, where one can discover the events and activities that take place here.

Backtracking slightly, turn east along **DANGOOR WALK**, which runs between the Crick and the Story Garden. Sir Naim Eliahou Dangoor, CBE (1914-2015) was a British-naturalised, Iraqi-born Jewish entrepreneur and philanthropist. Having studied engineering in London, he returned to his homeland, where he built up a business empire, bottling Coca-Cola and manufacturing furniture and matches. Anti-Semitic persecution in Iraq forced him to flee with his wife to England in the 1960s. Dangoor Walk, a new route for pedestrians and cyclists opened in 2017, was named in recognition of the Dangoor family's generous support of the Crick Foundation (and of the BL).

We are here near what was the northwest corner of the Somers Town Goods Depot. Hereabouts stood the entrance to its Milk & Fish Depot, and the steam engines and accumulators that provided hydraulic power to the complex. On the 'Crick' site to the left were the raised sidings of the yard's coal depot, which lined the length of present-day Brill Place (p 101).

After the closure of the Goods Depot in 1968, the northern end of its upper level played host to a short-lived, but official, airbase called RAF St Pancras. Both opened and closed in May 1969, it was installed here in connection with the Trans-Atlantic Air Race sponsored by the *Daily Mail* to celebrate the 50th anniversary of the first crossing of the ocean by Alcock and Brown. The race was between the top of the Post Office (now BT) Tower in Fitzrovia to the top of the Empire State Building in New York, and competitors had to use some form of air transport. There were 21 prizes in different categories. Clement Freud won the prize for travel with a commercial airline and Sir Billy Butlin for his use of a private jet. The £6,000 prize for the overall fastest time, of 6 hours 11 minutes, was won by Squadron Leader Tom Lecky-Thompson, who on 5 May took off in his RAF Harrier jump-jet from the abandoned Purchese Street coal depot just to the north (see p126).

Reaching the far end of Dangoor Walk, emerge into **MIDLAND ROAD** and bear left. The **Francis Crick Institute**, named after Francis Crick (1916-2004), co-discoverer of the structure of DNA, is one of the largest bio-medical research establishments in Europe. Opened in 2016, it is a partnership between the Medical Research Council, Cancer Research UK, The Wellcome Trust and three colleges of London University – UCL, King's and Imperial.

Designed by US engineers/architects HOK with London-based PLP Architecture, the huge building consists of two blocks housing 30 laboratories, with space for 1300 scientists to work on cancer, heart disease, stroke and infectious and neurodegenerative diseases. Linking the two blocks is a soaring atrium, a notable feature of which is a scattering of little informal meeting places, encouraging the cross- fertilisation of ideas through scientists from different disciplines mingling to discuss and critique each other's research. On the ground floor, open to the public from Wednesday to Saturday, is an exhibition space and small café. Beside this is another example of the Crick's educational and community outreach work, a lab for use by local schoolchildren.

The wide pavement outside is dominated by a 14-metre-high sculpture. A twisting stack of weathered steel tetrahedra that grow in size, this is *Paradigm* by Conrad Shawcross. He said 'it is inspired by science and the ideas of science and the potential to grow, to take risks, to be bold and brave'. Scientific advance does not progress seamlessly but through 'paradigm shifts' - radical changes in underlying beliefs that lead to breakthroughs, and this informs the ethos of the Crick.

Opposite, the northern part of Midland Road is lined by the elevated platforms built to accommodate East Midland train services on their exile from the main St Pancras train shed; together with an entrance to the International and Thameslink stations.

This part of Midland Road began life as Brewer Street, developed after 1811 at the southern end of the Brewers' Company's estate (p 125). When the MR arrived in the late 1860s, the street's houses and shops were demolished to enable construction of the MR's underground link to the Metropolitan line (p 21), and the roadway was widened.

Still surviving at the time, to the west of Brewer Street, was the rump of the mostly demolished Perry Street (p 21). Off its south side was a triangular Brill Mews, facing which, on the site of the Crick, there was a much humbler academic institution. A nonconformist school, this had been founded in 1819 by the 'Bloomsbury & Pancras School Society', to give instruction to the poor on the plan of the Lancasterian System, promoted by Joseph Lancaster (1778-1838) and also known as the Monitorial System. Older pupils taught the younger ones, so enabling a small number of adult masters to educate large numbers of children at low cost. In 1836, an illiterate teenager called Thomas Bennett, who had attended the 'free Perry Street school' for 18 months, complained that 'they never larnt me nothing. They sets a parcel of boys to teach you. They are always playing or talking. Then, if you complains to the master, they take care to be always having you up for everything, and gets you a hiding.' The establishment continued to function as a British School for

21 'Brill Inn' (anonymous watercolour, c.1830)

boys and girls until around 1870; it appears on the OS map surveyed in 1871.

South of Perry Street at No.8 Brewer Street was the shop of Thomas Fielder, master baker. He was fined in October 1838 for selling a loaf before 9 am on a Sunday morning. The informant, one Stowell, received half of the ten shillings fine. Stowell was a regular informant against bakers, telling the court he did this 'for the benefit of the public'. Fielder himself was bankrupt by 1843.

Walk south past Dangoor Walk, into what was once the heart of The Brill. The name is now taken to derive from an old French word for a park or wood stocked with beasts of the chase. According to Rev. Dr William Stukeley (1687-1765), an antiquarian noted for his eccentric theories, the name indicated the site of one of Julius Caesar's encampments. He even drew a detailed map of his imagined 'Caesar's Camp', extending astride the River Fleet all the way north to Fig Lane, now Crowndale Road (p 122).

At The Brill was the farmhouse of the 50-acre Brill Farm owned by Lord Somers, on whose fields Somers Town was developed. A Brill Tavern or Inn **[21**,p 75**]** was recorded here as early as 1690, and in the 18th century it was a popular place of resort for Londoners, who would walk there across the fields for an evening tipple. The pond outside was also popular with would-be suicides. The publisher and bookseller Samuel Bagster recalled how, as a child in the 1780s, he visited his uncle who lived in a prosperous hamlet called The Brill and who owned a brick, tile and chimney-pot factory there.

By 1820, Brill Row had struck northwest along the line of the old Brill Path (p 119). A Bee Hive pub traded there at No.55, at the south end of east-facing Brill Crescent, out of which Phoenix Street (p 102) led west. In 1831, at the Tiger Brewery in Brill Row, the pugilist Thomas Morgan fell asleep whilst sitting next to a copper of boiling beer into which he fell; he died of his injuries. A *Times* editorial in 1845 criticised the magistrate who sent a poor boy to gaol for five days for selling apples on the pavement of Brill Row. The boy's crime was 'obstructing pedestrians' although he told the court he had sold fruit from the same spot for 7 years without hindrance. In June 1873 various local businesses were fined for Sunday trading.

Off the southern end of Brill Row, a narrow *original* Brill Place snaked westward, with a branch running north to meet Chapel Street, and off that an even smaller Cottage Place. Brill Place ended alongside a row of poor cottages called Spann's Place erected by the eponymous builder (p 32). In 1827, Mrs Mary Wittenback of No.28 Brill Place was found guilty of murdering her husband by lacing his suet pudding with arsenic.

Near the eastern entrance to Brill Place was a tiny court called Stevens Place and a short terrace called Garden Gate where, at No.6 in 1798, the Abbé Louis-Luc Chantrel, a French émigré priest, opened a small Catholic chapel. This forerunner of St Aloysius Church (p 104), charmingly dedicated to Our Lady of the Garden Gate, stood close to the site of today's Midland Road gateway into the delivery and parking area behind the BL.

In the angle of the forked junction of Brill Row and Brewer Street, and replacing the rustic Brill tavern, Benjamin Perry (p 21) built an urban gin palace he called Brill House; it was later known simply as The Brill.

A vibrant street market grew up around the junction **[22]** and spread to join up with the markets in Chapel and Middlesex Streets. Brill Market started on a Saturday evening and continued on Sunday. It was so large and so well known that some of the customers would have walked from 5 or 6 miles away. Visitors were greeted with 'unnaturally loud cries of men and women, boys and girls anxious to sell edibles and drinkables and the necessities of life'. It can only have been a tremendous blow to the working classes when in 1858 the market was closed because of rowdyism. The Brill pub was demolished in 1865.

The southern half of Midland Road superseded Skinner Street, which was begun in the late 1790s on the Skinners' Company's Sandhills estate (p 18). Besides the usual mix of houses and shops, there was a pub named the Triumph at No.36. When the site for the MR's Goods Depot was cleared in the 1870s, Skinner Street was doubled in width and combined with the already widened Brewer Street to form Midland Road. Along the west side, large stores for the depot's vegetable and potato traffic were built in the 1880s, now superseded by the BL. Behind, a drive-through testing facility for NHS staff opened during the Covid-19 pandemic of 2020.

22 Brill House and Market on a Sunday morning (drawing, c.1860)

Look across to St Pancras International. This west side has been entirely reconstructed. Here the MR had laid out sidings leading to coal drops and a parcel station. These were built partly on a brick viaduct and partly on retained fill, with Gothic arches below and a multi-arched parapet above, which screened the trains from view. In 1892 the MR revamped this with a much larger roofed area for delivery of goods. By the late 20th century this side of the station was in a sorry state. The majority of the buildings here were derelict at upper-floor level, while the street-level arched vaults provided a location for marginal businesses.

It was decided all this should go, because a new cut-and-cover subsurface station was required for Thameslink trains (p 21). During its construction Midland Road was closed for two years. English Heritage demanded that replacement works should be in a Gothic style. A new side building houses mechanical plant and hides the ventilation shaft rising from the station below.

Beyond rises the modern wing of St Pancras Renaissance Hotel (p16), designed by RHWL Architects and built on rubber pads to minimise vibration from Thameslink trains. The public rooms of the Hotel are in the building that terminates the west side of the

23 The splendid staircase of the former Midland Grand Hotel designed by George Gilbert Scott (photo, 2011, by Helen Simonsson)

street, the original Midland Grand Hotel, whose magnificent staircase **[23]** is lit by the huge Decorated windows so prominent on the elevation.

Regaining **EUSTON ROAD**, turn right along its north side, with a sense of déjà vu. This time walk straight ahead along the BL's frontage. Here, before the advent of the goods depot, and as noted previously, was a New Road terrace called Judd Place West. It was numbered from east to west, originally as Nos.1-16, but before long as Nos.17-32 (treated for numbering purposes as a continuation of Judd Place East). Unlike most of the New Road houses, those here did not have a long front garden, but instead faced onto a very wide pavement; their short gardens were at the rear.

The judge Sir George Hayes (1805-69) was born at No.7 Judd Place West, the second son of Sheedy Hayes, an owner of land in the West Indies. No.8 was the last known address of Thomas Kirk (1765-97), a noted artist, book illustrator and engraver who exhibited at the RA. In 1796, the more famous Mary Wollstonecraft was living at No.16 with her 2-year-old daughter Fanny Imlay, while involved in a premarital affair with her future husband, William Godwin, who was residing in Chalton Street (p 98) at the time.

The actor William Barrymore (born Bluett, and no relation to the later acting dynasty) lived at No.20 for at least five years from 1796, when he appeared as *Hamlet* at the Theatre Royal, Haymarket. He had been a regular at Drury Lane from the mid-1780s. His son William became a stage manager and a playwright during the Regency period and throughout the 1820s. Benjamin Smith, an engraver who lived at No.21 Judd Place West, was gaoled in 1813 for debt; he later moved to Ossulston Street (p 73). Thomas Fryer Ranson, a fellow engraver resident by 1816 next door at No.22, was likewise gaoled, wrongly imprisoned two years later at the behest of the Bank of England for possessing an allegedly forged £1 note eventually proved in court to be genuine.

In 1846 the Private Spinal Institution moved to No.26 Judd Place West, from No.31 Queen Square, and changed its name to the Hospital for Spinal and Other Deformities. It had been set up by Joseph Amesbury, who had founded the Spinal and General Orthopaedic Association to treat spinal disease with machines he had patented. The medical staff was paid for by the sufferers themselves. The building was up for sale in 1856, advertised as a 'large and commanding premises with a plate glass front'.

Judd Place West was renumbered as Nos.62-96 Euston Road in 1857. In the 1860s No.70 was the photographic studio of William Henry Sinclair. Another photographer, J Ward, was at No.78. He was commissioned by the MR to record the construction of St Pancras Station in 1867-68 and his photographs survive at the National Railway Museum. The itinerant New York-born black actor Ira Aldridge, who made his name in tragedies, lived at No.76 for six months in 1860. Contemporaries dubbed him 'the African Roscius'.

Past the British Library's portico – designed by stonecutter Lida Cardozo and typographer David Kindersley, and framing Isaac Newton's statue within – reach the corner of Ossulston Street, where a public house called the Crown and Anchor was in business until 1880.

Cross over to the entrance, at No.100 Euston Road, of the **Pullman London St Pancras Hotel**. The building's lower four floors were formerly occupied by St Pancras Library, designed by Elinor Davies and opened in 1971 by Princess Anne. As well as catering for the local community, it included a splendid reference section on two levels, and served as the headquarters of Camden's then world-renowned library service. In 1993 a cash-strapped, rate-capped Camden Council closed the library, relocating its lending section along the road to the ground floor of the then Town Hall Extension. No.100 was converted into the present 312-bedroom hotel, initially named the Shaw Park Plaza.

Behind the hotel is the **Shaw Theatre,** named after George Bernard Shaw, playwright and sometime St Pancras vestryman and councillor. Opened along with the library in 1971, it was run by Camden Council for many years. It served as the main venue for the lively annual Camden (Arts) Festival and until 1984 was the base of the National Youth Theatre. Countless well-known actors, musicians, singers and comedians have performed over time at the Shaw. Refurbished in 1998, the theatre boasts 446 seats with cinema-style seating, and is nowadays managed as a hire venue by the hotel.

Outside the theatre entrance stands a large sculpture called *St Joan*. Created in 1971 by Keith Grant, an artist better known as a painter, it takes its title from the play thought by many to be one of Shaw's finest works. The abstract forms represent a knight's armour and the longbows and lances of the warring French and English. Relocated from the library entrance and modified by the artist in 2002, the sculpture still glows red and blue at night.

The theatre entrance marks the site of the Eliza Doolittle pub, the 1971 successor (at No.3 Ossulston Street) to the Somers Arms public house and hotel, which had stood here for at least 120 years (initially as No.69 Wilsted Street).

Originally known as Wilsted Place and lined on both sides by 4-storey houses, this southernmost part of Ossulston Street has always been unusually wide. In Victorian times it was a welcome space in a very congested area. It was furnished with a cab rank, presumably for the use of Somers Arms hotel patrons and passers-by on the main road. Most Somers Town folk were too poor to ever use a cab. Provided here for their benefit were a drinking fountain and a urinal.

Now continue west beside the Euston Road frontage of the Pullman hotel. The original houses built here in the 1780s, along the New Road, began life as Nos.23-13 Somers Place East, numbered from west to east as a continuation of Somers Place West (see later).

In 1788 the Royal Masonic School for Girls was established in Somers Place East by Chevalier Bartholomew Ruspini, a philanthropic Italian-born dentist surgeon. At first known as the Royal Cumberland Freemasons' School for Female Objects, it was intended to support '15 daughters of distressed or deceased Freemasons'. After seven years the growing school moved to larger premises in St George's Fields south of the Thames; today it is in Rickmansworth.

Living in 1800 at No.22 Somers Place East was the ubiquitous engraver and topographer James Peller Malcolm (p 95). No.16 was home in 1832-34 to Nathaniel Whittock, lithographer to Oxford University, who is remembered for his topographical views of London and other cities, and for his depiction of Frankenstein's monster as portrayed in an 1823 stage adaptation of Mary Shelley's novel. Augustus Finlaison, an insolvent debtor in 1859, and 'late of No.17 Somers Place East', was described as being both a photographic artist and a dealer in guano. At No.15 in 1822 lived the surgeon W B Diamond, father of Hugh Welch Diamond (p 18), then seeking mentally deranged gentlemen for his asylum. Resident at No.14 in 1836 was the mezzotint engraver Henry Cousins, younger brother of the better-known Samuel, and noted for his engravings of portraits and works by such artists as Romney and Landseer.

In 1857, when all the New Road terraces were renumbered as part of Euston Road, Somers Place East became Nos.98-118.

During and after WWII, a former Lyons' café at No.102 was stacked with books to serve as the South East branch of St Pancras Public Libraries, a somewhat makeshift but welcome facility for locals in those dreary days of austerity, and a modest predecessor of the prestigious library later built on the site.

When back in 1898, Booth's researcher visited Euston Road, he noted that No.108 had become the Cecil Reading Club, which he suspected was a front for betting. When police raided it in 1900, they discovered a game of *chemin de fer* in progress, as well as a bar and billiard table, a telephone, and a telegraphic ticker-tape bearing the names of racehorses. Arrested and taken to court, the gambling den's proprietor and customers were given the choice of imprisonment or a fine; the limited company that owned the 'club' was soon dissolved. The premises were then home to Motor Mart Ltd, a publishing company whose managing director was one Alfred Dunhill. He was already running a store selling 'motorities' (motoring accessories) at Nos.359-361 (see *Streets of Fitzrovia*) before branching out into the tobacco business.

The long, narrow properties along the New Road in the 18th century observed the contemporary regulation that houses must be set back at least 50ft from the highway. When in the next century the road became increasingly commercialised, many of their long front gardens were built over with single-storey extensions, mostly serving as shops. Others were turned into stone yards by the numerous monumental masons who colonised Euston Road; for example listed in 1870 at No.112 was statuary Richard Ryland.

Nos.110-116 were acquired by the Metropolitan Railway, whose line, running beneath the length of Euston Road, had opened in 1863. In the forecourt of Nos.110&112 they first installed a tunnel ventilation shaft and then later, after the electrification of the line in 1905, an electricity substation. To the rear by that time was the factory of Charles Wells, a maker of blinds.

This stretch of Euston Road was once popular with makers of keyboard instruments. Having previously been based at No.76 throughout the 1870s, demolition by the MR forced pianoforte maker Charles Cullum to move, to No.98. He was there from 1882-84, then at No.108 until 1897. Back in 1861, John Fincham (p 83) was recorded as a maker of organ pipes, employing one man and a boy at No.110. By Edwardian times, organ builder Charles Allen was at No.114. Piano manufacturers John Strong and Sons had a factory behind Nos.114&116, and an odd-looking showroom with a barrel-vaulted roof, at No.118 on the corner of Chalton Street. This had earlier served for many years as the showroom of Biddlecombe's, a carriage manufacturer. The tall former office block there today, built as part of the St Pancras Library complex and once occupied by British Petroleum, now forms part of the Pullman hotel.

The Rocket pub opposite, at Nos.120-122 Euston Road, was long known as the Rising Sun. Its old name may still be seen in the decorative red brickwork, together with an image of a sunrise and the date of the pub's rebuilding by Shoebridge & Rising in 1899. The original house at No.122 was retained and is still extant, although the pub now occupies its long forecourt. Added during the pub's rebuilding was its 2-storey extension along Chalton Street, described at the time as a hotel. The Grade-II-Listed building was renamed the Friar and Firkin in 1992 and more recently as the Rocket. The present pub sign depicts Robert Stephenson's pioneering steam locomotive of that name. A public house of Somers Town, when the neighbourhood was still separated from London's built-up area by many acres of farmland. According to the memoir of Thomas Uwins (see below) by his widow Sarah (herself born and raised in Somers Town), the fields were so dangerous after dark that the inhabitants would pay a man to blow a horn every half hour near the Rising Sun, at which signal those who wished to cross would assemble and proceed in a body for mutual protection.

Walk on past the pub. At **No.124**, an early cinema flourished from 1910-14. Run by Gale and Co., and named the Gale Cinematograph Hall, it had been converted from premises earlier used successively by a cab builder, a carriage dealer and the Euston Motor Company. After WWI the building housed the Association of People's Palaces, formed in 1915 to address problem wartime drinking by encouraging the provision of workplace canteens, and public 'palaces' and bars selling non-alcoholic refreshments. Now occupied by the China Travel Centre, No.124 is a surviving example of the front extensions built over the gardens of the original New Road houses, which as mentioned above survive at No.122, and (slightly adapted) behind No.124.

The houses were first known as Nos.12-1 Somers Place West (later Nos.120-144 Euston Road). At No.9, which became No.126, was the (St Pancras and) Northern Dispensary, founded in 1810 as a non-provident dispensary to provide medical assistance to the 'deserving poor'. Among its subscribers was the legal reformer Sir Samuel Romilly, and its first consulting physician, offering his services free of charge, was his nephew Dr Peter Mark Roget. Born in Soho, the son of a Swiss Huguenot clergyman, Roget was a man of wide-ranging interests, for 21 years Secretary of the Royal Society and one of the founders of the University of London, but is now best remembered for the *Thesaurus* he compiled in later life. By the 1840s the dispensary had become partly provident, so allowing working-class members to make contributions when they could afford it and draw on services such as midwifery and home visits when needed. The Northern Dispensary remained at No.126 until 1912, when it moved to Oakley Square (p 132).

Also located in 'Sommers Place' was an earlier Ossulston Dispensary, instituted in 1787 for the 'administering of advice and medicines in all cases of physic, surgery and midwifery', with Lord Dacre as President and Jacob Leroux (p 102) among the subscribers. It stayed here only for four years, before moving to what is now Museum Street, Bloomsbury, 'in the Vicinity of which more Objects of real Distress are to be found' – presumably an allusion to the nearby slums of St Giles.

At the west end of the terrace, No.1 Somers Place West was home to the painter Thomas Uwins RA (1782–1857), Surveyor of Pictures to Queen Victoria and in 1847 appointed Keeper of the National Gallery. A genre painter, best known for once popular scenes of Italian peasants, he also produced fashion plates for Ackermann and wrote for the weekly *Repository* under the nom-de-plume 'Arbiter Elegantarium'.

Covering the sites of Nos.128-144 Euston Road today at No.130 is the main building of the **UNISON Centre**, the headquarters of Unison, the public service union. Designed by Squire and Partners, the 9-storey tower with an internal atrium was completed in 2011; 4,600m² of limestone was used in its construction. With 3 other towers erected out

24 Elizabeth Garrett Anderson painted in 1900 by Reginald Grenville Eves

of sight to the rear, the Centre both wraps round and incorporates the Victorian building ahead on the corner of Churchway (p 88) – the former Elizabeth Garrett Anderson Hospital.

Elizabeth Garrett Anderson (1836-1917) was the first woman in England to qualify in medicine and surgery – though she had to go to Paris to do so. In 1866, in Marylebone, she opened her first dispensary (for women and children only), and then in 1872 a 10-bed ward. Her New Hospital for Women relocated two years later to Marylebone Road, and then again in 1890 to a purpose-built building here at No.144 Euston Road. Its design, by the London Scottish architect John Brydon, harked back to the English Baroque in a style that he dubbed 'Wrenaissance'. Incidentally, he had trained Elizabeth's sister Agnes and her cousin Rhoda Garrett, who together set up the first interior design company in Britain to be run by women. Agnes designed the fireplace in the hospital entrance.

The hospital's new location not only had the advantage of excellent transport links, but was also chosen because of the appalling levels of child mortality in Somers Town, where nearly 1 in 5 babies died before their first birthday. The slums of Somers Town offered plenty of work for Dr Anderson, who felt great concern for the health of working-class women. Her hospital was the first to be run for and by women. No male was allowed on the staff – not even a tomcat! One of the country's first women surgeons worked here and one of the wards was named after her – Louisa Brandreth Aldrich-Blake, whose monument can be seen in nearby Tavistock Square.

Anderson **[24]** was a redoubtable feminist, who at her wedding refused to promise obedience and who wrote that she 'married without millinery and almost without cookery'. After her retirement from medicine, Elizabeth returned to her family home in Aldeburgh where in 1908, aged 70, she became England's first woman mayor. In the same year she became an active supporter Mrs Pankhurst's Women's Social and Political Union, but when the suffragettes turned to arson, she transferred her allegiance to the suffrage movement's less militant, suffragist wing.

The New Hospital for Women was renamed after Dr Anderson in 1918. Queen Mary, wife of George V, opened a new wing bearing her name in 1929. Then in 1937 a 7-storey block facing Euston Road and rather dwarfing the original building was opened by the Duchess of Kent. Containing a Nurses' Home and a Preliminary Training School for Nurses, its entrance hall was designed as a memorial to the overseas nurses who had lost their lives during WWI. On the foundation of the NHS in 1948 the EGA became part of the Royal Free group of teaching hospitals. Recommended for closure in 1976, it was saved by a public campaign and a change of Government (Margaret Thatcher declared her 'staunch support' for the hospital). However, from 1992 it only treated outpatients and in 1999 it merged with the Obstetric Department of University College Hospital (UCH) and moved to Huntley Street.

After lying empty for several years, the Grade-II-Listed Euston Road building was bought in 2006 by UNISON, who magnificently restored it, along with its original boundary walls and railings. Inside the old EGA building, but accessed from No.130, there is a lasting memorial to the hospital and its founder in the Elizabeth Garrett Anderson Gallery, open to the public from Wednesday to Friday. The exterior sculpture on the corner – 6 steel rings by Wendy Taylor CBE, called *Unity* – links UNISON, who commissioned it in 2010, with the work of pioneering women everywhere, including Dr Anderson, who is also remembered in the naming of the new maternity wing at UCH along the road.

The building lies over the site of No.136, home in the late 1850s to the optician Thomas Slater who held séances here with his friends Lord Brougham and Robert Owen. The latter said he would come back as a spirit and in 1872 Slater, then fascinated by spirit photography, claimed to have captured an image of the dead Owen.

Cross Churchway and pause in front of the 16-storey glass-clad block now known as **Evergreen House**. Opened in 1970, it was one of only three 'hung' structures in Britain at the time, with a light curtain wall suspended from a steel umbrella at the top of the building, devised by the structural engineer Harold Waterman. Present occupants include Evergreen Marine, a global Taiwanese sea freight company, and the Taiwanese airline EVA Air. The block has rejoiced under various names: as Unicorn House around 1990 when it served as a temporary HQ of the Wellcome Foundation; previously as Univac House (after the computer firm), and originally as Hearts of Oak House.

One solitary rusticated granite pillar is all that remains of a row of pillars which, topped with urns, punctuated the railings in front of the former headquarters of the Hearts of Oak Benefit Society. Formed in 1842 in an upper room of the Bird in Hand tavern in Long Acre, the society had prospered and had built a grand new classical-style headquarters here, opened in 1906 by Edward VII and Queen Alexandra. Outside was a 7-ft bronze statue of the King in full regalia on an 8-ft granite plinth, which when the building was demolished was moved to Broadstairs (where it still stands outside a former Hearts of Oak convalescent home).

Evergreen House covers the site of several former buildings, including **No.164** Euston Road, where the Jews' Deaf and Dumb School was based in the late 1860s and during the 1870s. It was one of the few institutions at the time to offer speech training to deaf people. By 1881 it was home to the artist Charles Gogin. Also based on the site then was John Fincham, who from the making of organ pipes at No.110 (p 80), had progressed to manufacturing complete instruments at Nos.148-150, along with his son Henry.

The original New Road terrace here, developed during the Regency, was called Seymour Place. The landscape and figure engraver Charles Heath was at No.6 Seymour Place from at least 1816. He was one of the most active and influential figures in British book production in the first half of the 19th century, and among the first to grasp the commercial advantage of steel over copper plates. The family business branched out into security engraving for banknotes, and in 1840 Charles and his son Frederick Augustus were responsible for engraving the world's first postage stamp, the 'Penny Black'. After Charles' death in 1848 the house became the London Female Dormitory, set up in 1850 'for the rescue of destitute and fallen women'. Its work was taken over from 1857 by the London Female Preventive and Reformatory Institution (p 154).

No.4 was the early base of the opticians (Hugh) Powell and (Peter) Lealand, in business together from 1841, who produced high-quality microscopes (see also p 112). Hugh Powell died at the house (renumbered No.170 Euston Road) in 1883. By then installed at No.172 were piano manufacturers Jules Gautier and Co. The 11th Marqués de Valparaíso, José Eusebio Bernuy y Valda, a Spanish grandee, died at No.2 Seymour Place in 1856.

Two houses which had formed part of Seymour Place at Nos.182-184 Euston Road were converted in 1861 into one of Britain's first Turkish baths. They remained open until the end of the Victorian period.

On their site today is **Euston Fire Station**, an early London County Council (LCC) station built in 1901-02. It uses the provincial red brick much favoured by the Council – bricks whose importation from outside London was made possible by railway transport. The station is a notable Arts and Crafts building, most probably designed by Charles Canning Winmill, head of the section of the LCC Architects' Department devoted to fire stations. Pevsner rated the quirky design one of their most inventive, enjoying its 'romantic composition of gables and chimneys'. Sir John Betjeman, on a visit to Euston in 1962 to try to save the Euston Arch (p 161), was so impressed with the fire station that he helped it to become Grade-II-Listed.

Note the delicate ornamentation on the Portland stone on its façade. The two large entrances opened from the shed housing the appliances: in 1902 one horse-drawn and one 'steamer'. The large plane tree partly shading the forecourt was carefully included in the architect's plans.

There was an earlier history of fire service on this site. An 1867 map marks an 'escape station' here; such stations were set up by the Royal Society for the Protection of Life from Fire to locate supplementary escapes or ladders. Actual fire stations (the nearest then being at Great Portland Street) were concerned at that time with saving property rather than human lives. Two watchmen were employed to man the ladders and a little box was provided for them to shelter in while on duty. To this day a stint of duty answering 999 calls is known as being 'in the box'.

Cross ahead at the lights and turn north, beside its Gardens, along the east side of **EUSTON SQUARE**. Note opposite, on the west side of the fire station, the fanciful little balcony at 5th-floor level leading from the upper-floor flat, once the quarters of the Divisional Officer North and occupied in 1925-33 by the aptly-named Commander Sir Aylmer Firebrace RN, later Chief Officer of the London Fire Brigade. Below it are gates leading to a now bricked-in archway, the exit for the commander's car; the high round window marks the shaft which housed the connecting lift. Balancing this to the left, the square bay with louvred openings housed the hoist which raised the used hoses to hang up to dry in the days before new materials rendered this unnecessary.

To the left, with a quite imposing entrance, is **Nos.70&71**. Typically Regency and once wholly stuccoed, although now only partly so, this is the only original building still remaining in Euston Square. It began life as two private houses; No.70 was home to Richard Gilbert, printer and editor of reference works, particularly for the clergy, who died here in 1852. By 1870 the two houses had been knocked into one as a 'Clerical Hotel' – one of the myriad hotels of all sizes which once surrounded Euston Station. By the end of the century it had been renamed the London Temperance Hotel. In 1951 the building became St Philomena's Convent, a hostel for young female students run by the Poor Servants of the Mother of God; the nuns later added a substantial extension round the corner in Grafton Place, to be encountered in Route 5 (p 88).

Carefully crossing the bus station entrance, turn immediately left to enter Euston Station for your transport home. You will pass the **Doric Arch** pub (formerly the Head of Steam); on display there are various railway memorabilia and, behind the bar, one recovered stone from Euston Station's demolished Propylaeum (p 161). Alternatively, continue straight ahead along Eversholt Street to the stepped station exit where Route 5 begins.

Western Somers Town

Sinuous walk from Euston Station through southwest Somers Town to Chalton Street, via Churchway, Doric Way and Drummond Crescent

If arriving at Euston by Tube turn left and follow the lime-green signage for the 'Wellbeing Walk' (part of which we will traverse in Route 6).

Descend steps to emerge in a section of **EVERSHOLT STREET** known before 1938 as Seymour Street. Only later do we reach Somers Town proper. The land here was historically not Lord Somers' property but lay in the southeast corner of the Grafton-Southampton estate, and several streets hereabouts were therefore given names connected with the FitzRoy family. Frances, the second wife of George FitzRoy, 2nd Baron Southampton, was the daughter of Lord Robert Seymour. The present Eversholt Street numbering scheme, with even numbers on the east side and odds on the west, dates from 1865 when Seymour Street and Upper Seymour Street (p 105) were combined.

Look across to street's eastern side. The large block to the left is **Euston House**, built in 1934 to designs by W H Hamlyn and A V Heal as the headquarters of the London Midland & Scottish Railway Company, and subsequently the HQ of the British Railways Board. In the 1930s its publicity department opened a film unit here, with a viewing theatre in the basement and two mobile cinemas which travelled the system showing films - numbering about 150 by 1939 - to staff, their families, and the public.

Upon nationalisation in 1948 Euston House became the HQ of the British Transport Commission (from 1963 the British Railways Board). It amalgamated two existing railway film units to form British Transport Films in 1949. The new unit, which produced some celebrated documentaries, was initially based here before its move to Savile Row. After rail privatization in the 1990s Euston House served as a temporary home of the Wellcome Institute for the History of Medicine, a branch of the ubiquitous pharmaceutical giant Glaxo-Wellcome, another dominant presence in the Euston area. Current occupants include the IT training company Learning Tree International. Architecturally, the building's only feature of interest is a relief of railway features at the top – you may need binoculars to see it.

One of the properties demolished to make way for Euston House included one of Euston's two original Underground stations. This little ornamental green-and-white-tiled building, designed by the architect known as S R J 'Tate Gallery' Smith, belonged to the pioneering City & South London Railway, the world's first underground line run by electricity and also the first deep-level true 'tube' railway. It was extended to Euston in 1907, later becoming the Bank branch of the Northern line. Soon lift access was provided, from within the mainline station, to the platforms of both the C&SLR and the 'Hampstead Tube' (whose surface building was in Melton Street, (p 148); the two companies' separate stations were deemed redundant and were closed in September 1914.

Also on the site of Euston House was the original No.11 Seymour Street, the studio from 1840 of the artist Patrick Allan-Fraser, who painted very popular scenes from Walter Scott's novels. He later returned to his native Scotland to become an architect.

The little turning south of Euston House is **LANCING STREET**. Built as a cul-de-sac in the Regency period, and originally known as Southampton Street, it was one of several streets renamed in 1865 after seaside towns. Once lying off its north side was Southampton Crescent, where 'small neat 8-roomed houses' were advertised in 1816. At No.10 In 1820 was Archibald Archer, a history and portrait painter and RA exhibitor 16 times. Installed at

No.5 in the early 1820s were the medal-winning landscape painter Ebenezer Stalker and his son Ebenezer, a mezzotint artist. At the end of the decade the painter W illiam Carse (p 116) lived in the crescent before returning to his native Edinburgh.

Southampton Crescent was pulled down to make way for the Anglican St Pancras National Schools, built in 1837 to a design by Charles Inwood, whose father and brother were the architects of St Pancras New Church (the tower of which can be seen to your right, beyond Euston Road). In their early days the Schools provided 20 boys to lead the singing in the Church. The buildings remained in use until just after WWII, finally closing in 1950. They were not demolished until 1970, when a new square was created on the site, to become the playground visible at the end of the street.

Alongside the schools stood St Pancras Church House, a handsome building of 1833, with a tower staircase, designed by William Teulon, brother of the better-known Samuel Sanders Teulon. It was replaced in 1970 by the present **Church House**, the dark-red-brick building on the south side of Lancing Street, containing flats and two halls. From 1997, the lower hall was home for a while to the 65,000 books of the (Roman) Catholic Central Library, eventually forced by rising costs to relocate to Farnborough. A sign of the times, the vacated space is now occupied by the Euston Foodbank.

Walk south along **EVERSHOLT STREET** beside the 'Podium' and 'Tower' of the block named **One Eversholt Street**; dating from 1980 it houses the headquarters of Network Rail. It covers the site of a mews known as Seymour Row until its 1938 renaming as Eversholt Row. On the corner beyond, at the previous No.1, a Plasterers' Arms pub survived until the 1960s rebuilding of Euston Station.

Opposite, at Nos.8-14, is the **Royal George**, built in 1939-40 to replace a century-old pub and hotel of the same name at No.52 Drummond Street on the mainline station site. The gold eagles on the corners were the symbol of the brewers Truman, Hanbury & Buxton, whose architect A E Sewell designed this remarkably complete example of a 1930s pub. The interior has some fine marquetry panels, contrasting the radios and cocktails of the period with the steam age of a century earlier. There is also a large panel depicting the sailing ship after which the pub is named: in 1782, while lying at anchor off Spithead, HMS Royal George keeled over and sank with the loss of possibly 900 lives. The façade of the Grade-II-Listed pub is meant to resemble the warship's stern.

An earlier building on this site, at No.5 (later No.10) Seymour Street from 1858, was John Lillywhite's Cricket Warehouse. It was run by John Lillywhite (1826-74) **[25]**, son of William, the 'nonpareil bowler', and himself a professional cricketer and umpire. After his death the firm was taken over by other members of the extensive cricketing family, ending up in 1925 in the famous premises on Piccadilly Circus.

Adjacent to the pub is tiny **WELLESLEY PLACE**, all that remains of a short cul-de-sac known as Wellesley Street (no doubt after Arthur Wellesley, Duke of Wellington, the hero of Waterloo – when it was begun in 1812 it had been named Nelson Street after the hero of Trafalgar). The street ended in a beer shop called The Hit or Miss, which had another entrance in narrow Churchway behind (p 88). As early as the 1850s, Wellesley Street had become very rough, dirty and disease-ridden. Booth's researcher said in 1898 it was one of the worst spots in the whole area and looked forward to its impending demolition. In 1901 Wellesley House (p 89) was built on the site.

This in turn is now threatened with destruction under proposals for Crossrail 2, as are the Listed Royal George pub and, on the comer of **GRAFTON PLACE**, the quite recently built **Travelodge** hotel. Crossrail recently advised residents they would safeguard the block. On the Travelodge site, at No.1 (later No.2) Seymour Street, piano maker Richard Edwards was established for four decades from c.1852. The hotel entrance marks thc site of No.72 Euston Square, once the chemist's shop of Richard Farmar.

A frequent visitor was an old friend of the pharmacist, Rev. Harold Davidson (1875-1937), the notorious Rector of Stiffkey in Norfolk. Known as the 'prostitutes' padre', he spent his weekdays (and nights) in London, supposedly 'rescuing fallen women', until in 1932 he was sensationally defrocked for immorality. One of Davidson's many 'lady friends' was Barbara Harris, a prostitute for whom the rector found employment as a receptionist to Farmar's brother Frederick, a dentist who lived and practised above the pharmacy. Barbara, who would sleep there overnight, to the displeasure of the dentist's wife Jessie, said Davidson was a frequent visitor to No.72.

Turn east along Grafton Place. Originally a cul-de-sac off Euston Square, called Seymour Place North, it was renamed after the Duke of Grafton in 1845. Squares built to attract wealthy residents to a new neighbourhood and the streets immediately leading off them, as Grafton Place does from Euston Square, were usually somewhat more genteel than the backstreets. The popular Mancunian, freethinking lecturer Rowland Detrosier lived at No.22 Seymour Place North. A deist, vegetarian and teetotaler, he died here in his mid-thirties in 1834, as a result of riding on an omnibus after speaking in a heated room; his body he left to science. The merchant William Wing Hauxwell died at his home, No.8, in 1841. His widow Elizabeth subsequently married the physician and scientist Thomas Addison (1793-1860). The engraver Charles Heath (p 83) expired suddenly in 1848 in his house at No.24. In 1857 the London Female Preventive and Reformatory Institution was formed from a merger of two earlier agencies helping 'fallen women', one of which was on nearby Seymour Place (p 83). The Institution opened its first home at No.26 Grafton Place before moving within a few months to larger premises at No.200 Euston Road (p 154. In the 1871 census, one Henry Edward Leacock of Grafton Place gave his occupation as 'Quadrille Harpist' (which to us may sound delightful but could have involved nightly drudgery for him).

25 The first English cricket team to tour overseas, on board ship to North America (photo, 1859). John Lillywhite is sitting on the deck on the right.

By the 20th century the street had declined, and the artist Geoffrey Fletcher remembered it as a 'crumbling relic of a vanished London life. The landlord lived in the basement, the gaslight was always on, the hallways were dark and forbidding to normal people, and stank of cabbages and cats; the lino was torn and nailed down in a hundred places....'

On the south side today is **No.2**, built by the Poor Servants of the Mother of God as an extension to their convent round the corner in Euston Square (p 84). It was subsequently taken over by the Depaul Trust as accommodation for the homeless, while the nuns continued to occupy their older building. As Olallo House, the building is now occupied by the St John of God Hospitaller Service with similar aims, to support and house the homeless in London. Opposite is the side of the Travelodge hotel, covering a site that had been left derelict for half a century.

Reaching **CHURCHWAY**, cross over to its east side, here lined by parts of the UNISON Centre (p 81): a limestone-clad 5-storey office block and a towering 9-storey brick-clad apartment block with projecting balconies, both by Squire and Partners (2014). Turn round to be confronted with an unusual building on the corner of Grafton Place – a very forbidding, almost square tower in dark brick. Named **Grafton Chambers**, it was designed around 1927 by E Frazer Tomlin. The 'Chambers' suffix was no doubt meant to attract a professional class of tenant, and the six flats have been home to several women doctors.

Churchway is probably the oldest continuously used thoroughfare in Somers Town. While its name might appear to derive from St Pancras New Church close by, it actually pre-dates the 1819 church, probably by some centuries. The road originated as a footpath from the south through the pastures of Brill Farm to Old St Pancras church ½ mile to the north (p 33). Its slightly winding route contrasts with the grid pattern of the rest of Somers Town. Also known as Church Path, the footway demarcated the boundary between the Grafton-Southampton estate and that of Lord Somers to the east, and also the western edge of early Somers Town.

The earliest development on Churchway's eastern side was a row of small houses known as Latham Place, built by William Latham, with a little Latham Court running off it. One early Latham Place householder was nurseryman Robert Montgomery, whose nursery garden was nearby on the site of Euston Square. His lodger for a while was the famous Georgian satirist John Wolcot, known professionally as Peter Pindar. Born in Devon in 1738, he had trained as a doctor in London. His anti-royalist satires sold in thousands and he became well known as a writer of verse commentating on the mores of contemporary English society. But he was popular and was welcomed in literary and artistic circles. Moving from Ossulston Street (p 73), Wolcot spent his last years in 'Montgomery Cottage', Latham Place. As wrote one of his obituarists, he 'loved the smell of flowers, and the fresh air of the place. ... He received a few select friends, but saw none', as 'a cataract had extinguished the vision in both eyes'. On his death in 1819, he was buried in St Paul's churchyard, Covent Garden.

By 1834 Churchway had become a long, narrow, overcrowded alleyway, one of Somers Town's worst slums. By 1870 entry to it from Euston Road was via a 'ginnel' only 5 ft wide between the houses. In the 1890s the LCC was determined to improve it, widening the street to 40 ft by pulling down properties on either side. Demolished off the east side were Seymour Court, York Buildings (p 99), and Elizabeth Court; off the west side, the Hit or Miss beerhouse vanished, and the 3 cul-de-sacs behind (Lancing Street, Wellesley Street and Grafton Place) were to be turned into thoroughfares. By the time the scheme **[26]** was completed in 1906 Wellesley Buildings (see below) terminated Wellesley Street.

The LCC had been empowered by the 1890 Housing of the Working Classes Act to demolish slums and build new houses for rent. Narrow Churchway, particularly at its northern end, was low-lying and damp, and the ill-ventilated houses were home to people from the section of society labelled by Charles Booth as 'very poor, in chronic want'. Churchway was the first part of Somers Town to be rebuilt, and the LCC's **Churchway Estate** was among the Council's earliest achievements in providing better housing for London's poor. Between 1899 and 1901, fired with the philanthropic ideals of the 1890s and inspired by the Arts and Crafts movement, the Council's team of architects, led by W E Riley, rebuilt most of Churchway in a way which earned the Pevsner seal of approval: 'very pretty for their date and distinguished by their well-proportioned sash windows', was his opinion of the three red-brick blocks designed by E H Parkes.

Erected to house the working classes, they were initially named as 'Buildings'. This nomenclature later became thought of as outdated and degrading, and around 1965 the blocks were renamed as 'Houses'. **Wellesley House**, on your left, still bears its original Wellesley Buildings name, displayed on a well-designed nameplate with Arts and Crafts lettering that puts to shame the later plastic signage nearby.

Born in Flat 13, Seymour Buildings, on the

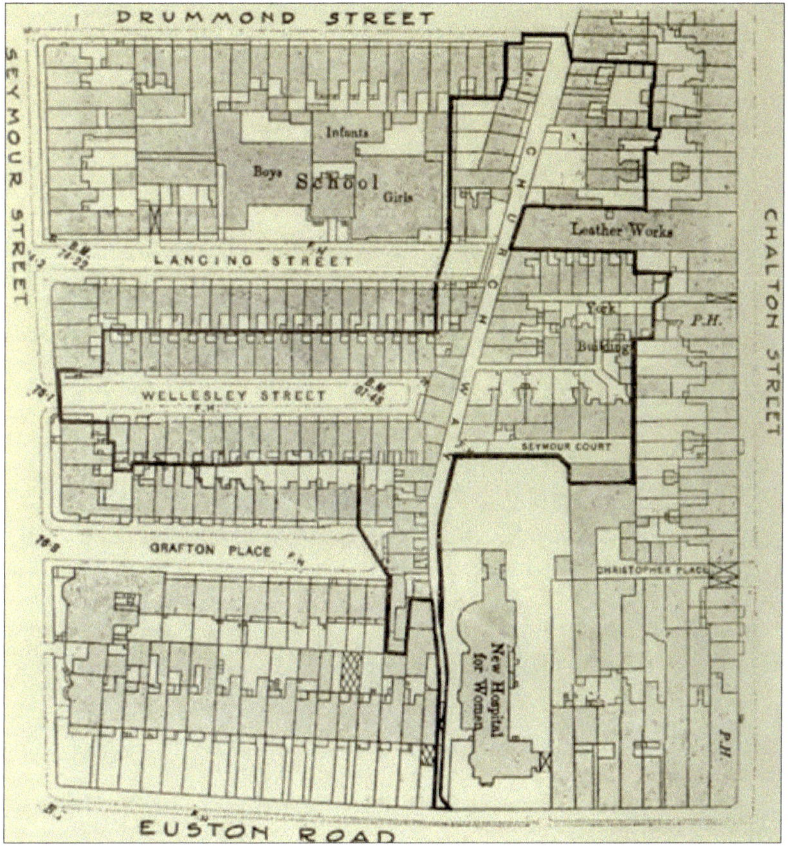

26 Map showing the Churchway improvement scheme. From the Report of the Housing for the Working Classes Committee, London County Council, 1912-13

east side of Churchway, was the geographer Oskar Hermann Khristian Spate (1911-2000), whose later work was to help define the (controversial) border between India and Pakistan. Resident in 1969 in what by then was **Seymour House** was the far-left activist, John Lawrence (1915 -2002), who was leader of St Pancras Council from 1956. He famously raised the Red Flag over the Town Hall on May Day 1958. He was arrested, fined and expelled from Labour and joined the Communist Party. For refusing to implement rent rises, he was surcharged and jailed for three months. The disability rights activist Keith Armstrong (1950-2007) lived for many years in Flat 22, Seymour House. Despite a strong distrust of government, he became an adviser to several London boroughs, including Camden. He continued protesting with the Disabled People's Direct Action Network, whose campaigning led to ramps in buses and improvements to tube and train access, as well as the introduction of the Disability Discrimination Act in 1995.

Ahead is **Winsham House**. Renamed after a Somerset village, it was long known as Somerset Buildings, after Lady Henry Somerset – daughter of the 3rd Earl Somers and freeholder of the site – despite her having withdrawn her original promise of financial support for the LCC improvement scheme.

Between the two blocks, behind railings, is one end of a single-storey rear extension to the former Connollys' leather works in Chalton Street (p 98). Notice how the red brick on the frontages of the adjoining flats is not continued round the sides and back of the buildings, which are in stock brick.

Walk on past the undistinguished block of flats opposite, erected by the LCC in the 1960s. While Horwood's map (1799) shows the area west of Churchway as farmland, by 1804 it was identified on Thompson's map as the Lower Brick Field. Early Somers Town was surrounded by such fields, brickmaking being an important activity of the Rhodes family (p 35), local farmers and tenants of Brill Farm. It was an old St Pancras industry, creating no pleasant environment: Charles Manby Smith in his 1835 article *How London Grows* complained that 'the smell of new-mown hay is superseded by the smell of burning bricks'. By the late 1820s, the Lower Brick Field had been covered with 3-storey terraced houses.

Reach the junction with **DORIC WAY**, and turn left along it. This was originally part of Drummond Street (p 147), which was cut in half by the 1960s rebuilding of Euston Station. This eastern portion was then renamed after the 'Doric arch' that had graced the Drummond Street entrance to the old station (p 154). The street had become very rough by the time Booth's researcher visited it in 1898. Off the north side was a particularly poor mews called Robert's Yard (or Place), reached through a narrow passage and surrounded by tall buildings. The owners of the six back-to-back houses had been taken to court in 1890 for allowing them to be 'unfit for human habitation'.

In the 1919 sale of the Southampton estate, the freehold of the triangular site with Robert's Yard at its centre was acquired by United Dairies. In 1926 they sold it on, for £27,500, to the St Pancras House Improvement Society (SPH).

This had been formed in 1924 by the charismatic Anglo-Catholic priest Basil Jellicoe (1899-1935) **[27]**. He arrived in Somers Town in 1921 as a young missioner for the Magdalen College Oxford Somers Town Mission. This had been active locally since 1908, focused on St Mary's Church, where Jellicoe served as curate, and with a mission room in Oakley Square (p 132). Jellicoe worked tirelessly with his helpers to replace the Somers Town slum houses with pleasing 'housing for the community'. He toured the country in his small car and used his family contacts with the titled and wealthy (the Prince of Wales made a visit) to better his cause. He became ill through overwork and died worn out at the early age of 35, and is remembered still with affection and respect for

27 Father Basil Jellicoe with Mr Tattersall the coalman, c.1926

his inspiring work. Magdalen College now has a new Jellicoe Mission and this time the aim is to 'enable another generation of students to live Jellicoe's convictions'.

The original intention of the body he founded – of buying up and converting existing Somers Town properties – was thwarted by the poor condition of the slum dwellings, and by the impossible task of eliminating the bedbugs and other wildlife with which they were infested. Ian B M Hamilton, the architect of the new flats, took great pains to discourage these vermin by choosing spccial materials and by painting rather than papering the walls. The first flats, here on the **Drummond Estate**, were occupied in 1928, at affordable rents ranging from 9s to 22s 6d (45p–£1.25) per week. The architect shared with Father Jellicoe a belief in the value of art for everyone. To provide decorative elements for the flats, they commissioned the versatile Gilbert Bayes (perhaps best known for his Queen of Time figure holding aloft the clock above Selfridge's main Oxford Street entrance). The subjects chosen point to the religious impulse behind the buildings. On two balconies of **St Anne's Flats** (1932-35), the block facing you, are reliefs of eagles with a fish, both Christian symbols.

The buildings demolished to make way for the new flats had housed many small businesses, and St Anne's Flats incorporated several replacement shops; the semi-basement flats still have their big shop windows. The corner flat, decorated with tiles depicting sealife, rehoused Charles Chapman, whose family's fried fish shop had traded on the site for decades. Beyond are **St Mary's Flats** (1928-29), with a small statue of the Virgin holding a baby, his head now restored after an earlier decapitation. Just visible to the rear, on a west-facing balcony is a Della Robbia-style relief.

Slightly below normal street level is gated **CRACE STREET**. Long known as Little Drummond Street, it was renamed in 1938 after John Gregory Crace (1809–89), a leading furniture maker and decorator, who worked on the Houses of Parliament, and in 1866 designed the ornamentation of St Pancras New Church. Booth's researcher in 1898 said the street had been an evil place, but had become the most respectable spot in the area.

On the west side of Crace Street today, with their rose-filled gardens, are **Edith Neville Cottages** (1954-55 by Hamilton and Chalmers), taking their name from another SPH stalwart, and St Pancras councillor (p 150), who had died in 1951. One of the cottages was the gift of the Brewers' Company as a tribute to Miss Neville's concern for pubs; she shared with Father Jellicoe a belief in the great importance of the pub to the community, especially in poor areas (p 110). Beyond the Crace Street entrance is **Ian Hamilton House,** opened in 1973 by the widow of the SPH architect who had died in 1971.

Regain **EVERSHOLT STREET**. Around 1930, on the left-hand corner, at the then No.34 Seymour Street, was an Express Dairies café, one of several Express branches where the reprobate Rector of Stiffkey (p 87) would often go, in order to 'chat up the birds'. If he bothered the 'girls' too much the manageress,

Mrs Yates, would take him by the scruff of the neck and say, 'Out you go!'

Turn right and walk past an early-19th-century brick terrace with prominent relieving arches to the first floor windows. At **No.48** is the Great Nepalese, a family-run restaurant popular with locals, set up in 1982.

A few doors beyond, **Nos.60-64** (then in Seymour Street) were the base from 1882 of piano maker John Strong, later to decamp to Euston Road (p 80). House Furnishing Ltd opened in 1936 at No.60, in a building rented from SPH. Here families could buy at reasonable prices, as the company operated on just a 5% margin. It was one of several schemes run by Irene Barclay and Evelyn Perry. The two women were respectively the first and second ever female Chartered Surveyors. Barclay and Perry, the partnership they established, took on the management of all SPH property which, much influenced by the Society of Women House Property Managers founded in 1913, they ran on the Octavia Hill System.

Opposite, the monotonous grey side wall of Euston Station was the 1960s replacement for a brick screen wall dating from c.1870, when the station expanded eastward onto Seymour Street. Houses pulled down in the process included the former No.57, where Belfast-born Patrick MacDowell, RA (1799–1870), having been apprenticed to a coach builder but intent on becoming a sculptor, set up a studio in 1826. A year later, the notable line engraver Robert Graves (1798-1873), born in Tottenham Court Road, was living at No.43. Next door at No.44 the physician Golding Bird set up in general practice from 1836, at the same time as giving lectures at Guy's Hospital, which formed the basis of his *Elements of Natural Philosophy*. By mid-century, two piano-making firms were installed alongside each other: John Rhodes & Co. and Thomas Browning & Co., respectively at No.50 and No.49.

Cross Drummond Crescent and pass the Art Deco apartment block, **Regent House**. Sandwiched between it and the **Prince Arthur** pub – for many decades only a beerhouse – is one-storey No.74, which once housed the One World Shop. Owned by the adjacent Roman Catholic church of St Aloysius, and selling Traidcraft goods, the shop was set up by Monsignor Bruce Kent, a priest at the church from 1977 until 1980, when he was released to work full-time for CND. (For the church itself, set back from the road beyond the pub, see p 104; for the remainder of Eversholt Street, pp 105 & 114.)

Now retrace your steps to the corner and turn along **DRUMMOND CRESCENT**, whose course reflects a curve in the old Somers-Southampton estate boundary. On the south side, behind the corner shop, pass a blank white wall with 3 doors. This was No.70A Seymour Street, where in 1930 SPH had an office resembling a 1-storey shop (although headquartered at No.96 at the time). The workshops of electrical engineer T Williamson had previously been located at No.70A.

Beyond are the two **Brereton Cottages** of 1970, named after Colonel F S Brereton who left SPH a £5,000 legacy. A little further on is the gated north end of Crace Street (p 91), offering a closer view of the Edith Neville Cottages (p 91) on its right-hand side. Both sets of cottages, along with nearby properties in Eversholt Street, are threatened with eventual demolition for Crossrail 2. Reach **St Mary's House**, a brick-built SPH block of 1930 with rather small windows, and pause to consider the north side of Drummond Crescent.

The original houses here were numbered from east to west. Musical instrument maker Henry Starck, at No.31 from 1890 to 1927, *claimed* to be the only maker of bagpipes south of the Border. An earlier resident of the originally respectable street, at No.27, was a Mr L Anstey, who in 1825 received 20 guineas and the Silver Vulcan Medal of the future Royal Society of Arts, for his 'Improved Melting Pots for Iron and Brass Founders'.

A covered entry beside No.24 led into a narrow, L-shaped cul-de-sac known as Hayes

Place, containing a handful of dwellings, and stables leased in the1880s to the London & North Western Railway Company, also the owner of many other local properties. Living in 1871, further along at No.15, was cowkeeper Evan Morgan, one of the countless Welsh dairymen who settled in London in Victorian times. His cowmen, and presumably also his cows, were housed behind in a second little offshoot called Perkins Yard.

Erected by 1911, behind the Drummond Crescent houses and covering the site of both cul-de-sacs, was a long, narrow building first occupied by the International Motor Mart Ltd, traders in second-hand cars. In 1926 Drummond Crescent was scheduled by the LCC as 'an insanitary area', and in the 1930s, by then in a parlous state, the houses were pulled down. The motor mart premises expanded onto the Crescent's frontage, eventually lining its whole length. *Evening Standard* vans were initially garaged in the resulting long, red-brick 'depot' at Nos.1-39. During and after WWII (when the area was bombed), it was used by the United Service Transport Co., a road haulage firm; subsequently, Hertz Truck Rental moved in. It was finally taken over in 1984 for use as garages by the Metropolitan Police.

Opened in 2019 was the new building designed by Jestico and Whiles for **Maria Fidelis Catholic School**, similarly long and curved, and faced with red brick. With 1,050 pupils, it brings together on one site both the Upper School (long located in Phoenix Road to the rear, p 103) and the Lower School (displaced by HS2 from North Gower Street, p 143). Controversially, plans for HS2 include a 'temporary' cab rank here (for Euston Station), allowing taxis to line up alongside the school while awaiting custom.

Walk on along the south side of the Drummond Crescent, past **St Joseph's Flats**, to where a red cross on a hanging sign signals entrance to the **Basil Jellicoe Hall**. Both flats and hall were designed by Ian B M Hamilton and opened by the Duchess of York in May 1936. The hall was built with funds raised by the Father Jellicoe Memorial Fund (note the unofficial blue plaque), and was blessed by Father Percy Maryon Wilson, who had taken over from Jellicoe; his important role in the work of SPH during his predecessor's frequent absences and illness deserves greater recognition. The new building had to be strengthened to act as a shelter during WWII. Bunk beds were fitted in 1941. The hall reopened in June 1945. Improvements made in 1954 included a reading and rest room for local people, named the Father Thomas Room. A meeting here in March 2016 saw the birth of a Somers Town History Club ('A Space for Us'), with a successful screening of Pathé Newsreel films.

Just past the hall, through a gateway (often closed), is a former drying yard, furnished with a delightful ring of washing-line posts topped with ceramic doves and surrounding a central post whose finial is a model of a carpenter's bag of tools – alluding to St Joseph, all four Estate blocks being named after the Holy Family. The current finials are replacements, the originals having disappeared, only to turn up later at a fine art auction!

Back in the Crescent, a bollard on the pavement, bearing a George IV monogram, seems to have migrated here from the Crown-owned Regent's Park. On the curved corner beyond is **No.2 Doric Way**, the former Lion and Lamb public house, closed around 2005 and lately remodelled as apartments. A tavern of that name had been trading here since as early as 1831.

Over to your left is the entrance to **Clarendon Grove** (reopened after closure during the construction of the new Maria Fidelis school). On Greenwood's map of 1828 the footway was shown as Lansdown Place. In 1898 Booth's researcher recorded thirteen 2-storey cottages here, most housing two families, but fronted by pretty gardens. There were workshops too: Richard Blizzard, at No.15 in 1871, was a piano small-work maker. At the south end of the Grove by 1871 was the

Phoenix Works, a metal refinery that by the 1930s had become the Euston Forge. At No.10A before WWI was a local branch of the United Irish League, a political party founded in 1898 to campaign for land reform in Ireland. Based at No.5 in the 1920s was a firm called the Underworld Vermin Association, whose rat-catching services must have been much in demand locally at the time. Near the far end of the Grove for many years was the Clarendon Hall (p 96).

We are once again at the north end of **CHURCHWAY**, and facing us is a short Victorian Gothic terrace. **No.62**, on the right and once a fish-and-chip shop, houses a longstanding Muslim travel agent, who organises Haj pilgrimages. The recent restoration of **No.66**, to the left, with its old shop fronts, shows off at their best the mosaic panels above the first-floor windows; the right-hand pair bear the date '1882'.

Cross over and proceed straight ahead. Churchway, having made a right-angled turn here, continues as a narrow alleyway. Once often known as Churchway Passage, this was the first part of street to be built up (by 1790), and is the only part to retain its original width. Today it is the sole reminder of the airless, claustrophobic narrow streets and courts that once pervaded Somers Town. Contributing to the Victorian atmosphere are two (electrified) gas street lamps; the first is not original, but a latter-day replacement for a modern lamp-post standing here in the 1970s.

The near left-hand corner is occupied by **Nos.35-39**, SPH flats built in the 1990s. **No.68**, opposite, where in 1900 a female clog maker sold her wares, now houses the (Bangladeshi) Somers Town Islamic Cultural and Educational Centre, formerly known as the Somers Town Masjid, or Mosque. One of the two doors has delicate patterns of flowers, urns and ribbons.

The light blue door of **No.70** was painted black with red surrounds when the onetime fishmonger's shop housed Mick's Eel Supply. Mick Jenrick's chief interest was the processing of eels –'what I don't know about eels there ain't to know' – though it's not known if he caught the eels himself. He and his workers were an impressive sight, dressed in ankle-length aprons flapping round big rubber boots, and wheeling their great baskets of eels and whelks in the passage area. Sadly, the business declined and the shop closed in the 1980s.

Passing the former No.74, the pre-WWII domain of a cat's meat dealer, emerge into **CHALTON STREET** and pause. Dating from the 1780s, when it was known in part as Chalton Place, this was one of Somers Town's earliest streets. The origin of the street name is unknown. It sometimes appears on early maps, and routinely in parish records too, as *Charlton Street*, reflecting its present local pronunciation. Early houses were of a reasonable size, some with long gardens, and those on the west side looked out for some years over the Lower Brick Field. Still separated at that time from London's built-up area by many acres of open fields, Somers Town was almost a self-contained village community.

Early Chalton Street attracted several notable residents. One such was John Abercrombie, who in spring 1806 died, aged 80, in his home, after falling down some steps and breaking his hip. A successful gardener, with royal and noble clients, he is best known for his manual *The Practical Gardener*. All but one of his 18 offspring predeceased him.

Chalton Street originally ended at Churchway, but was soon extended northward as Evesham Buildings, considered a good address by those who could not afford the houses south of the New Road. (The ground landlord's title was Baron Somers of Evesham.) In 1820 the Buildings were absorbed into Chalton Street, which was then renumbered sequentially, north from the New Road up the east side and then back along the west. A second renumbering in 1938 introduced the present 'Napoleonic' scheme, with odd numbers on the west side and evens opposite.

Walk north along the west side of Chalton Street. Immediately on the left are **Nos.67&69**, once a very early branch of Sainsbury's **[28]**. In 1889 John James Sainsbury bought the dairy that stood here at the then No.87, from Ben Staples, whose daughter Mary Ann he later married. In the 1950s the premises became the Chalton Launderette. Lodging on this site in 1796, at No.2 Evesham Buildings, was James Peller Malcolm (1767-1815), an American-born antiquary, topographical draughtsman and engraver, who was an illustrator for the *Gentleman's Magazine* and whose books included the 3-volume *Anecdotes of the Manners and Customs of London.* Malcolm seems to have had at least 6 different Somers Town addresses and his writings included a detailed account of the district's early history; he eventually died in Gee Street (p 106).

Pass the 'yellow and blue' building at **No.71**, designed for SPH in 1987 by Philip Wharmby Architects; the current Pevsner volume remarks on its 'very perverse railings'.

In 1803 Leigh Hunt, the poet and essayist, and friend of the Romantic Poets, lodged as a young man at No.8 Evesham Buildings. Covering its site is a mixed-use development at Nos.73-85, comprising the 18 flats of **Margaret White House** (named after a long-serving SPH house manager), and below them the **Somers Town Medical Centre**, opened in 1998 by Frank Dobson, the popular local MP. An earlier health facility on this site was the Somers Town Self Supporting Dispensary, originally in Pancras Place (p 23) and located by 1897 at the then No.82, in a former beershop called the Chalton Arms. Two doors away at No.80 was St Mary's Working Men's Club, presumably connected with the eponymous church in Eversholt Street (p 115). At the same address after WWI was the South-East St Pancras Liberal & Radical Association.

Beyond are the flats of **Chalton House**, built in the 1930s by St Pancras Council; recent local news reports have suggested that the building is feeling its age. On this site, in 1797 on his marriage to a pregnant Mary

28 J Sainsbury, Nos.86-87 Chalton Street (photo, 1904)

Wollstonecraft and their move to the Polygon (p 108), William Godwin also took rooms of his own at No.17 Evesham Buildings, which he used until Mary's death as his study. Among his neighbours here was Thomas Whitehorn (p 97), a member of the London Corresponding Society, and a bookseller whose Circulating Library was at No.25. Staying in 1823 in the same house (by then No.63 Chalton Street) was Eliza Macauley, an actress at the time, but subsequently more famous as a lecturer for the London Owenites on subjects as diverse as financial reform, child development, the evils of Christian orthodoxy, and women's right to full social equality.

The former No.65 was later the headquarters of the Christian Men's Union Gospel Mission, an 'unsectarian' body founded in 1862. Behind, at the north end of Clarendon Grove (p 93) was its mission hall. You can walk through to the back of Chalton House to see where it stood. In 1897 the mission advertised: '1,500 free meals given away weekly. Public invited to see the children at dinner at Clarendon Hall'.

Returning to Chalton Street, cross over to its east side and turn back southwards, beside a row of shop units dating from the late 1920s. **No.96** is now occupied by the Chalton Gallery, which showcases contemporary British and Mexican artists, runs art courses and hosts public events. At Nos.**92&94** is Brook Euston, whose advice service to young people, on sexual health and wellbeing, is symbolised in the 48 small colourful mosaics beneath the ground-floor windows; detectable among the varied motifs are the letters 'b r o o k'. Here for four decades from the 1940s was the Somers Town School Treatment Centre, run successively by the LCC and GLC to provide medical and especially dental care to local schoolchildren. At **No.88** is the Dar-al-Hikma bookshop, whose name translates delightfully as 'House of Wisdom.'

On 7 July 1823, a handbill announced the reopening hereabouts, at the then No.57, of 'The Original Sommers Town Academy'. Young Gentlemen could be 'accurately instructed in Greek, Latin, French, English, Geography with the use of Globes, Astronomy, Drawing, Mathematics and other Branches of useful and polite Literature in a lofty, commodious and well-ventilated room'. According to the proprietor, Mr Samuel Maynard, the academy was 'calculated to relieve the incapacity of the Dull, not less than to give full effect to the innate gifts of Genius'.

Above the shop units are the flats of **Chamberlain House**. Its foundation stone was laid by Neville Chamberlain when he was Minister of Health & Housing in 1928, and Edward, Prince of Wales visited the block after families moved in the next year. It was the first block to be completed on the LCC's **Ossulston Estate**. This has been described as 'the most important inner-city estate of the inter war period representing the most considered attempt by the LCC to inject thinking into inner city housing estates'. Its design, by G Topham Forrest assisted by R Minton Taylor and E H Parkes, was influenced by modernist housing schemes in Vienna that Topham Forrest had visited. All the original buildings on the Estate are now Listed Grade II. Next

29 Christ Church, Somers Town, before destruction in 1941 (undated photo)

pass the Estate's children's play area and sports court, with the 'Crick' (p 74) looming in the background. In 1868 the philanthropic lace merchant George Moore provided funds to build a new church on this site to replace the church of St Luke in Euston Road (p 19), which was lost to the MR. The railway company had provided a new church, but in faraway Oseney Crescent, Kentish Town. Designed by Newman and Billing in the Gothic style, with a spire and a 'barn-like' interior, Christ Church **[29]** was consecrated by the Archbishop of Canterbury on 21 December 1868.

Behind the church, also funded by Moore, were the Christ Church National Schools for some 600 boys and girls, which by the 1930s had become the London County School for the Mentally Defective. There was also a parish room, which during WWI housed an Australasian War Club for the wives and mothers of soldiers and sailors, run by women from Australia and New Zealand. All the buildings were destroyed by German bombs in 1941. George Sharp, a local man, made use of the bombsite as a young lad during the war. He has written of his dangerous climbing activities on the three walls and bell tower of the church that were all that was left. It's fitting that the site is still in use for the benefit of the local children.

By 1819, Thomas Whitehorn had moved his bookshop and Circulating Library (p 96) to No.47 Evesham Buildings. That year he was sentenced to one month in prison for seditious libel for selling Richard Carlile's eyewitness account of the Peterloo Massacre. Carlile came to give evidence on his behalf at his trial, but to no avail.

Covering the site of Whitehorn's house today is the northern block of the Ossulston Estate complex built in 1927-31 and named **Levita House**. (Sir Cecil Bingham Levita was LCC Chairman during its construction.) A gated footway, open to pedestrians, leads through to Ossulston Street. Take the opportunity to walk into the courtyard and view some of the inner space of the complex. On your left pass the 2010 'Barn' extension to the **New Horizon Youth Centre**, which works with vulnerable and homeless young people; the designers of the building, with its steeply pitched roof, were Adam Khan Architects.

The pathway is on the line of Chapel Street, which once ran eastward from here across Somers Town. Running off its north side, here at its western end, destroyed in the building of Levita House, was Chapel Mews. Off the south side were Clark's Yard and a row of cottages called Chapel Grove, initially named simply The Grove (though there was probably not a tree in sight). In 1911, the cottages were described as 'shut in by stabling', and their environment, like that of Wilsted Cottages (p 70), was improved at about that time: eight houses were demolished 'to make open paved yards'.

Return to Chalton Street and continue walking south. Rebuilt as part of the Ossulston Estate, the **Somers Town Coffee House** pub at No.60 originally stood a little further south. A coffee house traded here from the late 18th century, when it offered hospitality to the many French refugees who had found sanctuary in the new Somers Town; it was known for serving coffee in the best 'Parisian style'. With its tea garden and skittle ground, it had much to offer the visitor from inner London; it was also a posting house. The coffee house was severely damaged by fire in 1880 and rebuilt. The present building, dating from 1928, was in turn a victim of fire on the evening of 22 June 2018 when, as customers watched a World Cup football match, a blaze ravaged half of the roof and 2nd floor. There were mercifully no casualties.

Past the pub, traffic-calming bollards mark the start of the part of the roadway designated as **Chalton Street Market**. Booth's researcher in 1898 stated that the market had moved here in the 1880s, when railway incursions led to the demolition of the eastern part of Chapel Street (p 71). In late Victorian times, he said, it was held daily and traders came from afar, including Jews from Whitechapel, who sold draperies. Remembered by many in the 1950s, when there were numerous vegetable stalls, the market declined in recent decades and was eventually reduced to a quiet affair on Friday mornings. A crowdfunding appeal launched in 2017 by the Somers Town Community Association, for funds to resuscitate the moribund market, also attracted contributions from local businesses and the Mayor of London. It currently functions on 3 days a week, from Wednesday to Friday, with regular and pop-up stalls selling 'everything from fruit to sarees, rugs to crepes'.

The hornbeam trees that line the wide pavement make for a peaceful atmosphere. This changes every July, when the Somers Town Art Festival of Cultures (START) takes place here. It began in 1997 (see p 129).

As Somers Town's main shopping street, Chalton Street was once lined with dozens of small shops, mostly selling such essentials as clothing or food, and was still blest in 1920 with 8 butchers and 3 milliners. On your left today is a row of replacement Ossulston Estate lock-up shops fronting Levita House, not detracting from the local environment as such shops often do. Six units were taken by Sainsbury's in 1953 when they had outgrown their original premises at Nos.67&69 (p 95).

Southward, the opposite (west) side of the street is lined by a mixed bag of mostly Victorian buildings of varying shapes and sizes, much smartened up as befits their location in the so-called Knowledge Quarter. On the site of **No.61**, a house at the original No.34 was another address of the nomadic James Peller Malcolm (p 106), as also was old No.52 further along. Tall, Gothic **No.57** looks extremely smart; the polychrome banded brickwork shows off the mosaic panels above the 1st-floor windows. From 1984 to 1992 the building housed the British Youth Council.

The three terraced houses at **Nos.47-51** once formed Jack Jones House, named after the leader of the Transport and General Workers Union, who fought for pensioners' rights. He set up the National Pensioners Convention in 1992 and was its president until 2001, when it moved from here. The buildings had earlier been called Family Doctor House when *Family Doctor* was published from here during the 1960s and '70s. Resident in 1822 in a house at No.95 on this site was the eccentric physician Dr Squirrell, author (1798) of *Maxims of Health, or an Essay on Indigestion ... Also Remarks on Sea Bathing* (a copy can be consulted in the Wellcome Library). The Doctor was also resident apothecary to the Smallpox and Inoculation Hospital (p 14). He was rudely, but no doubt aptly, nicknamed by the locals 'Dr Squirt'.

Left of a colonnaded former entrance to Levita House (now disconcertingly closed), the cheese shop at **No.46** marks the site of the original house at No.25 where William Godwin lived from 1792. While here he wrote his 3-volume novel *Caleb Williams*. He had no regular servant, and any guests who came had to help him prepare dinner and then serve themselves. By 1796 he had embarked on a premarital affair with his future wife Mary Wollstonecraft, then living nearby in Judd Place West (p 78). He moved to the Polygon (p 108) shortly before their marriage the next year.

Across the road, the tall, gable-fronted yellow-brick building at **Nos.39&41**, built in 1884, was the HQ and leather works of Connollys; **No.43**, to the right, was a later extension. In 1878, John Joseph and Frederick Connolly, from Ireland, had set up as boot repairers at No.153 Euston Road. They took to making harnesses, and later leather cladding for hansom cabs, hoods for carriages and upholstery for railway coaches. Eventually they were processing 10,000 hides a day in a second factory near Wimbledon, and 'Cowhide, London' was their telegraphic address. As Connolly Brothers (Curriers) Ltd, the firm produced the green leather in the House of Commons (and the red variety in the Lords); upholstery for Rolls Royce and other luxury cars; and for seating in Cunard liners and on

Concorde, in plush West End hotels and in the Royal Festival Hall and British Library. Connollys' Chalton Street works, with a tall chimney behind, stretched back to Churchway. W Heath Robinson, engaged in the 1920s to create humorous adverts for the firm, said on seeing one of Connollys' machines that he himself couldn't have invented anything so 'amazing'. The firm's big trolleys piled high with leather could be seen in Chalton Street until their departure from Somers Town in 1980. Finally located in Ashford, Kent, the firm ceased trading in 2005.

As **Unity House**, No.39 now houses the RMT, the National Union of Rail, Maritime and Transport Workers (previously on the south side of Euston Road but displaced by the Wellcome Trust). Following a very recent refurbishment, Nos.41&43 are now marketed as **The Connolly Works**, and the Disasters Emergency Committee is based here.

Samuel Howitt, a painter and etcher, lived on this site at the former No.103 and died here in 1823. He was a self-taught artist who turned professional when he had financial difficulties and produced sporting and natural history paintings, etchings and illustrations. There are examples of his work in the V & A, the British Museum and the Tate.

A tunnel entry here once led into York Buildings, on the probable site of an early barracks for the Life Guards (later to be housed in Albany Street). In August 1798, 51 young recruits to a regiment of light dragoons arrived at the barracks fresh from Ireland. Some of them set about harassing or assaulting the local populace. To the locals' relief, they were soon marched off to Billingsgate to be shipped to the regimental HQ in Kent. While their ship's departure was delayed, awaiting high tide, they 'began to murmur' and resolved to go ashore and return to Chalton Street. Their riotous behaviour en route led to the St Pancras Association (the newly formed local militia) being summoned to disperse them. The recruits took refuge in the barracks, where they were promptly arrested. Four ringleaders were committed to the House of Correction by Jacob Leroux (p 102), not only a developer but also a local magistrate. The remaining miscreants were marched off again to the Thames, under the watchful eye of the militia. The barracks were subsequently replaced by 'a diminutive square of diminutive habitations', almost certainly York Buildings. (The 'Grand Old' Duke of York was the Army's Commander-in-Chief.) The Buildings, which ran through to Churchway, were swept away in the latter's redevelopment (p 99).

No.37 (once No.106) Chalton Street, now a Sichuan restaurant, was the Victoria (Hotel) pub, from at least 1840 until its closure in the 1980s. The queen's regnal years are prominently displayed beneath the cornice.

Opposite, on the site of the dental practice at **No.30-34,** the poet William Wordsworth lodged briefly in 1795 at erstwhile No.15; while here he paid frequent visits to his neighbour William Godwin ten doors away. Behind the houses at that time were two short cul-de-sacs, Chalton Court and John Court a little to the south. By 1870 their sites had been redeveloped for industrial use. The factory of the Premier Pianoforte Co., behind No.14, was later taken over by piano makers Sandon and Steedman, who moved here from Camden Town in 1884.

Carry on down the street, beside the southernmost Levita House block, with modern apartments of **Avigail House** at No.25 opposite, and pause at the end of unlabelled Weir's Passage (p 70). Once standing on its northwest corner, at Nos.6&7 Chalton Street, was the People's Hall. The castellated building was erected by Lady Somerset, the ground landlord, and leased in 1892 to the Methodists' West London Mission. Among the mission's unpaid social workers, known as Sisters of the People, were the future suffragettes Mary Neal and Emmeline Pethick (-Lawrence). In 1895 they set up the Espérance Club (soon to be based in Cumberland Market), an evening club for

Somers Town 'sewing girls', who worked long hours in the sweated garment industry for £1 a week. Mary introduced them to the joy of music and dance through the medium of morris dancing.

Founded in the Hall in 1907 was the St Pancras School for Mothers. The legend 'Mothers & Babies Welcome' was painted across the façade, so that local women would not be intimidated by the word 'School'. Run by a charity chaired by Mrs Alys Russell (first wife of Bertrand), the pioneering establishment aimed to combat infant mortality, in a borough where 1,000 babies died before their first birthday. It offered cheap or even free meals for expectant mothers and gave classes in 'mothercraft' (a term coined by Dr John F J Sykes, the local Medical Officer of Health). Babies were weighed **[30]** and medically examined, and breastfeeding was encouraged. Cookery classes were provided in the mothers' own homes, using whatever utensils they possessed. The School's Scottish instructress, Florence Petty (1870-1948), became known as the 'Pudding Lady' and would later give cookery talks broadcast on the wireless by the BBC. The 'School' moved along Chalton Street in 1908 to the then No.37, and on again by 1911 to a house with a garden in Ampthill Square (p 142).

With a base in the People's Hall in the 1920s was the Mabys Association for the Care of Young Girls. By then in decline but at one time boasting 1,000 volunteers, it had been founded in the 1870s as the Metropolitan Association for Befriending Young Servants, to provide aftercare for pauper girls leaving a workhouse or Industrial School. In 1943 its activities were taken over by the LCC.

Cross the road with care to the metal gates at **No.13** and look through into **Christopher Place**. The name's origin is unclear. It was first used around 1870 when William Barns, a zinc merchant, was here at the then No.117A Chalton Street. Several Barns family members had Christopher as a middle name, including William Christopher, who became a partner in his father's zinc business in 1877. Later occupants of what became known as the Christopher Works included Charles Kite, whose ventilating, sanitary and heating works were here for many years from the 1880s. As recently as 1980 there was a working blacksmith in the yard.

The pleasing modern building now within, by Troughton McAslan, was built as the UK's first special learning facility for hearing-impaired and speech-delayed children. Opened in 1995, it received a RIBA Award the next year. Audiology facilities were added in a second phase of building and bigger classrooms cater for older age groups. The Speech, Hearing and Language Centre functioned here for 20 years and during that time supported 1,600 children and their parents. Since the centre's closure in July 2015, the charity who ran it has continued as a grant-making trust. The building is now occupied by Blossom Lower School, an independent day school for similarly challenged children.

Continue to the Rocket pub (p 80) on the next corner. To return to our starting-point at Euston Station, turn right along Euston Road, and on reaching the fire station turn right again.

30 The weighing room at the St Pancras School for Mothers

Northern Somers Town

Serpentine walk starting and ending at St Pancras International Station

Leaving the station by its Midland Road exit, cross over and walk north beside the Francis Crick Institute (p 74), then bear left across its forecourt and turn along **BRILL PLACE**. Until the 1990s this was the eastern half of Phoenix Road (p 102). Suggested by Malcolm Holmes, then Borough Archivist, its present name recalls The Brill – its farmland (owned by Lord Somers, and on which most of Somers Town was built); its rustic tavern and tea gardens; and its later bustling street market, are all described in Route 4.

The south side of Brill Place is now lined entirely by the vast premises of the 'Crick'. Off the north side is the south end of the Purchese Street Open Space (p 119). In the face of vociferous local opposition, planning permission was granted in 2016 for the erection here of a 25-storey block of wholly private apartments – in two 'paired micro-towers creating a slim profile and minimal footprint' (to quote dRMM, the architects). Dubbed the Brill Place Tower, the proposed development is part of Camden's Community Investment Programme, and its scheme for 'Central Somers Town'. The Council's income from the sale of the land for the Tower is intended to finance a new primary school, improved community facilities, 'enhanced public open space', and new homes to be built nearby. Critics claiming that the skyscraper will be out of scale with the rest of Somers Town, have been further dismayed by the miserly number of new housing units to be made available at affordable rents.

Lime-green signs on lamp-posts show we are following part of the 'Wellbeing Walk', an Urban Partners initiative promoting a pedestrian route between the local mainline stations, more pleasant than the polluted Euston Road.

Crossing Purchese Street (p 119), note the old brick wall that bounds the open space here, a remnant of the railway coal depot that once stood on the site. Pass **Phoenix Court**, a post-WWII block of offices and 'luxury' flats taken over by Camden Council in 1967. The ground floor has recently been remodelled and now houses the PRCA, the world's largest PR professional body, representing over 30,000 practitioners.

Pausing at the next crossroads, look to the right along the north end of **OSSULSTON STREET**, which we shall not traverse, focusing on its western side. (For its east side see p 70, and for its south end, p 69.) Grade-II-Listed **Walker House**, part of the Ossulston Estate of the London County Council (LCC), was named after Mr H de R Walker, a former councillor for St Pancras South East and chairman of the LCC Housing Committee. Walker House was built in two stages. While its earlier southern end (1929-30) is rendered in the spirit of nearby Levita House (p 97), the later northern end (1936-37) is relatively routine and built in plain stock brick.

The central courtyard of Walker House covers the site of an especially lowly, T-shaped street called Equity Buildings. Edward Aves, while revising Charles Booth's poverty map in 1897, described it as 'a queer little paved cul-de-sac; low one-storey two-roomed cottages with a little wash-house and yard behind; been done up during last year; doors open straight into rooms; many of the houses appeared to be very full of furniture'. On 28 April 1868, in one of these humble dwellings, the former Chartist John Arnott (p 72) suffered a stroke; admitted to St Pancras Workhouse, he died there soon after.

Also on the Walker House site, a house at No.127 Ossulston Street served in 1911 as the offices of the anarchist newspaper, *Freedom*. In the same terrace, at Nos.147-149, was the Marquess of Hastings public house. Thomas Cubitt, the publican in 1863, was not the well-known builder of that name, who had died in the previous decade, although he also was born in Norfolk. Held in the pub was the inquest into the death of local resident George Fleming Richardson, Fellow of the Geological Society, itinerant lecturer and sub-curator at the British Museum. His book *Geology for Beginners* (1842) was initially a great success, but was denounced by a rival geologist as a 'scandalous piracy'. Rumoured to have had expensive habits, and possibly a mistress, he was facing bankruptcy when in the summer of 1848, 'in Somers Town', he took his own life. The inquest verdict was 'insanity'.

Continue ahead along the part of **PHOENIX ROAD** that has kept its traditional name, albeit known as Phoenix *Street* until 1937. Bebbington asserts that the street name derived from a local tavern, but no evidence of the pub's existence has been found. Perhaps the new-built street was seen as having risen, like the mythical bird, 'out of the ashes'– in this case of the dust heaps that once littered the area and whose contents were used for making bricks.

On the south side is the north face of Chamberlain House (p 96), which has a Phoenix Road postal address. Set in the southwest corner of Walker House, opposite, is the **Cock Tavern** at No.23, dating from at least 1826 but relocated by the LCC from the opposite corner when Chamberlain House (on the left) was built. The pub's name may have been a tribute to (or sideswipe at) the Somers family, whose ancestral surname was Cocks. The room upstairs has been used for many years for community meetings, trades union meetings and for many protest and left-wing causes. The Cock was saved from closure in 2014. The Grade-II-Listed building was refurbished in 2017 when the flats above the traditional bar and function room were renovated.

Proceed across Chalton Street and into what before 1938 was one side of Clarendon Square (p 107). On the left, with pleasant oriel windows, is **No.42**, described by Pevsner as 'nicely detailed in a free Regency style'. It was built in 1931 as the Margaret Club and Day Nursery for Fatherless Children, with Princess Alice, Countess of Athlone as its patroness. She opened an extension in 1938. First intended as a safe place for unmarried mothers to leave their children while they went to work, the nursery was later taken over by the LCC, and then eventually by Camden Council. From 1994 the building housed the Hopscotch Asian Women's Centre (now in Hampstead Road, p 137). In early 2018 planning permission was granted, on appeal, to demolish No.42, and replace it with a privately-built 6-storey block of student flats, with a ground-floor community space.

The original building here was a substantial house, built for his own occupation by the area's earliest main developer, architect Jacob Leroux, born in London in 1737 and said to have been of Huguenot extraction; and the next resident was the Catholic priest Abbé Carron (see below). For some 4 years from c.1825, the house **[31]**, as No.56 Clarendon Square, was home to a boy's school, presided over by George Jarrett Lyne, with 'his formidable cane'. Decades later, one of his pupils, George Merry, recalled in a letter to *The Times* that Lyne's Academy had also been

31 Abbé Carron's house, formerly occupied by Jacob Leroux, the developer of early Somers Town

attended 'for a while' by the young Charles Dickens; if Merry's account is correct, this would have been in 1826-27, after Dickens' departure, aged 14, from Wellington House Academy.

A few doors away, the journalist William Henry Wills lived as a boy at No.56 Clarendon Square; in 1819 his father, a wealthy ship owner, had moved his family to London from Plymouth on losing all his money. Young William was put to school 'with a genteel old lady', just opposite in the Polygon (p 107). He was later to serve for some 19 years as sub-editor of Dickens' journals *Household Words* and *All the Year Round*, and as the novelist's confidant was entrusted with the task of forwarding his letters to his mistress Ellen Ternan (p 104).

Beyond the unlabelled narrow tunnel entrance to Clarendon Grove (p 93) is a small fragment of the demolished Phoenix Road premises of **Maria Fidelis Catholic School**. Based here until 2018 was the Upper School, in three adjoining buildings at Nos.34-38, two of Victorian or pre-WWI origin, and the third a modern block. A fragment of the latter has been preserved, adorned by two of the several mosaics created by pupils and staff only in 2010 (with help from specialists Artyface). In late 2018 all three buildings were unceremoniously pulled down and replaced by a blank wall alongside the playground of the new school in Drummond Crescent (p 93).

We are now in what has been a Roman Catholic enclave for over 200 years. The original school was founded by Mme Mary Madeleine Victoire de Bonnault d'Houet, a refugee from the 1830 revolution in France, at the invitation of Abbé John Nerinckx, a long-serving Belgian priest at St Aloysius Church (see below). Built behind the houses on the south side of Clarendon Square, it began as an 'industrial school', funded by charitable appeals and offering girls a very basic education. Gradually expanding onto the Phoenix Road frontage, it evolved to become, first a convent boarding school for girls, and then the non-fee-paying St Aloysius Grammar School. Renamed Maria Fidelis School in 1974, it became a co-educational comprehensive in 2013. Alumnae include the actresses Kathy Burke, Roisin Conaty, Brooke Kinsella and Jane Wymark.

During WWII the main school premises fronting onto the street escaped serious damage, but a high-explosive bomb destroyed the 1830 buildings behind. **No.32** was built in 1972 as a belated replacement for the wrecked St Aloysius Convent. The initials 'FCJ' refer to the Faithful Companions of Jesus, the order of nuns founded along with school by Madame d'Houet. The nuns' home stands on the site of the original St Aloysius Church, which was built to serve a community of French immigrants.

The early development of Somers Town was badly affected by a lack of funds during the Napoleonic wars. What had been planned as a relatively genteel neighbourhood (although the houses were mostly classed only as 3rd or 4th rate) soon found itself, as Dickens put it, 'come down in the world and taken to letting lodgings'. Among those who took advantage of the cheap accommodation were many émigrés escaping the French Revolution, and these included a large contingent of clergymen, banished in 1792 for their refusal to take the oath of allegiance to the French State.

A thousand Frenchmen were said to live in the neighbourhood, earning it the nickname of 'Brittany Bay'. The incomers also included servants of wealthier émigrés and less well-off aristocrats, such as Charles and Louise-Julie Dufayis, whose daughter Caroline was baptised in St Pancras Old Church on 1 January 1794. In 1800 Napoleon issued an edict allowing émigrés to return, and the 6-year-old Caroline travelled to Paris with her by then widowed mother. She later married François Baudelaire; their son Charles, poet of *Les Fleurs du Mal*, was born in 1821. Another émigré (although to Hamburg rather than London) was the Abbé Jacques Delille, known as the poet of the emigration; his 1838 poem

Malheur et Pitié includes the line, 'Salut, ô Sommerstown, abri cher à la France'. It seems that the district was better known abroad than in Britain.

In 1799, coming via Jersey and Fitzroy Square, there arrived in Somers Town the wonderfully named Guy Toussaint Julien Carron de la Carrière (1760-1821). The Abbé Carron brought with him the school he had set up earlier in Fitzrovia and expanded his activities, eventually establishing two hospitals, a seminary and a church, as well as a range of schools for boys and girls, rich and poor. The missionary fervour of the Catholic émigré priests was commented on by prime minister Pitt the Younger. Carron 'had a spiritual audacity that seemed to conjure chapels, schools, hospitals and libraries from the very lap of the angels'; the comparison with Basil Jellicoe (p 90) is interesting.

Following the 1791 Toleration Act, Roman Catholic churches were no longer illegal but were still required to be sited in quiet streets away from any main thoroughfare. Superseding Abbé Chantrel's Garden Gate chapel in Skinner Street (p 76), Abbé Carron's church of St Aloysius was built here in Phoenix Road (then Clarendon Square) in 1808. Carron returned to France in 1814, leaving behind his little church, known to its French congregation as St Louis de Gonzague. With a chapel-like Tuscan façade **[32]** added in 1830, and an elaborately decorated interior with three galleries, St Aloysius' was to play an important part in the Catholic Revival in Britain. In September 1889 a Requiem mass was held there for Pascal Paoli, the exiled Corsican patriot who had died in London in 1807 and was buried in Old St Pancras churchyard. Baroness Burdett-Coutts obtained permission for the exhumation of his body, which was sent home on her private yacht for reburial on his native island.

The church suffered serious bomb damage in WWII, but continued to function, preserving 'like no other Catholic church in London the atmosphere of the age before emancipation' (John Summerson). It was later replaced by a new, larger building that we shall reach very shortly. En route, we pass the low buildings of **St Aloysius Catholic Primary Lower School** (formerly St Aloysius Infants School), the 1952 successor to the likewise bombed elementary school for girls. In 2019 the school was controversially closed for a lack of pupils (cf. the Upper School, p 103).

Ahead is the replacement **St Aloysius**

32 Clarendon Square, 1850: St Aloysius Church and part of the Polygon (from an original sketch)

Church, formally opened in 1968. Designed by A J Newton, it was built on land donated by the FCJ. Elliptical in plan, the church has a clerestory in the form of a brick drum, with abstract stained glass by the Whitefriars studio. The west wall (facing Eversholt Street, ahead) carries a figure of the Risen Christ by D J Purness. Inside is a plaque commemorating the laying of the foundation stone in 1967 by Cardinal Heenan, and a 'history corner', which among other memorabilia features a bust of the Abbé Carron, 'friend of the destitute and unfortunate, comforter of the afflicted'. Sadly, except during services, the church is nowadays kept locked.

Until 1937 this western end of Phoenix Road was named Charles Street, presumably after Charles FitzRoy (Lord Southampton), on the eastern edge of whose estate it lay. Living on the south side at No.1 Charles Street, by 1811 and for at least thirty years, was Cornelius Varley, a landscape painter and inventor of the 'Graphic Microscope and Telescope', which helped artists create images of tiny objects. Born in the same house was Frederick Henry Varley (1842-1916), the youngest of his ten children, who became an electrical engineer, specialising in telegraphy and eventually wireless, and with an interest in spiritualism too: in 1879 he was commissioned to build apparatus to record the weight of mediums during séances.

Living at No.6 in 1821 was the engraver John Romney, with line engraver Robert Graves (p 92) as his apprentice. Mrs Agnes C Hall, who died in 1846 at No.5, was a versatile Scottish writer and translator, whose non-fiction included *Elements of Botany* (1802); she also wrote novels under her pen-name, Rosalia St Clair.

In June 2019, across the road on one-storey **No.17A**, a Heritage Foundation/Camden Council blue plaque was unveiled by a party of London Pearly Kings and Queens. From 1892, No.15 Charles Street, on the site, was the final Somers Town home of Henry Croft. Born in St Pancras Workhouse in 1861 (p 40), he worked as a rat catcher and road sweeper, and in 1875 became London's first Pearly King. Emulating the costermongers, whose clothes were traditionally decorated with pearl buttons, the teenage Croft went one better and created a suit wholly encrusted with them. A true local, he married Lily Newton at Bedford New Town Chapel (p 130) in 1892; they had twelve children. On Henry's death, in the workhouse in 1930, his funeral was attended by 100 Pearly Kings and Queens and a crowd of thousands watched the cortège as it made its way from Charles Street to St Pancras Cemetery (Finchley). Erected there in 1934, and donated by charities he had supported, was a life-sized marble statue of Croft, standing 5ft (1.5m) high, wearing a top hat and 'smother' pearly tail-coat, and holding a cane. Repeatedly vandalised, the statue was restored and in 2002 found a safe home in the crypt of St Martin-in-the-Fields, where the Original Pearly Kings & Queens Society holds its annual harvest festival. Croft's great-granddaughter became a Pearly Queen of Somers Town.

West of No.17A, and opposite the Catholic church, is **St Joan's House**, with a now barely legible white foundation stone laid in 1946 by the (Anglican) Bishop of London. It forms part of the **Eversholt Estate**, whose development by the St Pancras Housing Association (SPH) began in 1939 but was interrupted by the outbreak of WWII and finally completed only 30 years later.

Reaching **EVERSHOLT STREET**, turn right (and north) along a stretch known until 1865 as Upper Seymour Street (USS). Beginning four doors *south* of Charles Street, its numbering ran consecutively up the east side and back down the west. The original buildings on the west side included a Coronation public house at No.125 USS, its name presumably dating from Queen Victoria's crowning in 1838. Resident nearby in the 1830s were the Scottish painter William Denholm Kennedy at No.116 and the engraver James Stephenson at

No.111, both exhibitors at the RA. Subsequently built at No.101 USS (later No.123 Eversholt Street) were the original premises of the Railway Clearing House (see p 115).

On the east side of the street was No.11 USS, where the artist and architect Patrick Allan Fraser, set up a studio in 1840. Now covering its site is **St Richard's House**, built in three stages between 1954 and 1967. A proposal by Ian B M Hamilton, SPH architect, to build a 16-storey block of flats here, had fallen foul of LCC planning policy and been abandoned. High site costs on the Eversholt Street frontage, previously lined by small shops, meant that development would need to include a commercial element. The corner site (now occupied by a car-rental firm) was long a Blue Star petrol station, with an underground garage started before WWII and used as a bomb shelter during it. A little to the north, and above the doorway of **No.102**, is an attractive panel of 1963, carved by the sculptor Alan Collins and representing the life of St Richard, the 13th-century Bishop of Chichester. At **No.110** is the present headquarters of Origin Housing, the latest incarnation of SPH, which was previously based from 1970 at neighbouring **No.90** and **No.114**, and whose original pre-WWI offices were on the St Richard's House site at No.96 Seymour Street.

To the north are the flats of **Hill-Wood House**, opened in 1970 by Wilfred Hill-Wood, then vice-president of SPH. Bridging **POLYGON ROAD**, into which we turn, the block once included the Hillwood Centre, an Age Concern day centre opened in 1971 by *Steptoe & Son* actor Wilfred Brambell. **St Martin's House**, the small SPH block on your right, was opened without ceremony in 1940 on the site of the very first houses ever purchased by the St Pancras House Improvement Society. The adjacent Jubilee pub closed in 2003 and is now offices, but retains its subsequently uncovered 'Cannon Brewery' fascia and a cannon in the gable above. Although the now removed hanging sign showed Queen Victoria boarding a train, a Jubilee pub had existed here since at least 1827, so the jubilee alluded to could not have been hers. On the corner opposite is another small SPH block, **St Margaret's House** (1950).

This end of Polygon Road was originally called Gee Street, presumably after local carpenter-builder William Gee.

James Peller Malcolm, American-born antiquary, topographical draughtsman and engraver, whose books included the 3-volume *Anecdotes of the Manners and Customs of London*, died in Gee Street in 1815, aged 47. Suffering from a debilitating illness, he had latterly been unable to work, and his wife and mother were left destitute.

Here was the last home of one of Somers Town's least known but most colourful characters. Bennet Allen, a rogue Church of England clergyman, was sent to America in 1766 as an agent of Lord Baltimore. Granted a lucrative living in Maryland, he lived there in style with his sister and two black slaves. A self-confessed womaniser and tippler, and unpopular with the locals, on one occasion he suffered a public caning. In 1782, back in England, Allen fought a duel with pistols in Hyde Park, killing his opponent, but thanks to a sympathetic jury served only six months in gaol. For his losses resulting from American independence, he claimed a staggering £90,000 in compensation, but received only £1,100. Despite financial help from several grandees, who had admired his loyalty to the British Crown, Allen died, aged 83 and apparently in poverty, at No.12 Gee Street in April 1819.

A resident in 1836 was the widow of the once eminent clown and rival of Grimaldi, Signor Paulo (real name Paul Redige). He had died the year before and she was living in penury, when their 11-year-old son was abducted; she appealed to the police for help. In early Victorian times, No.10 housed the Training Seminary for Boarders & Day Pupils – 'for the youth of both sexes, upon the plan of the Glasgow Normal Seminary' – where the curriculum included mental arithmetic 'by the method of Pestalozzi'.

Next, turn right along the southern end of **WERRINGTON STREET**. On its west side is red-brick and white-faced **St Augustine's House** (1939), the earliest part of SPH's Eversholt Estate and designed by Hamilton. Swept away in its construction was Clarendon Place, a narrow T-shaped street accessed through covered entrances from three directions. It was not one of the area's poorest streets, being coloured a 'mixed' purple on Booth's 1898 poverty map. His researcher Edward Aves noted 2-storey houses 'with garden fronts' but 'no gardens'.

St Augustine's House faces onto what was, until its renaming in 1938, the west side of Clarendon Square. Begun in the 1790s, its aristocratic name had originally been meant to attract residents of the right class. In its early years the square was home to many professionals, skilled workers such as piano makers, and artists. Among the latter was Samuel De Wilde (1765-1832), an artist of Dutch parentage, who for half a century was the leading theatrical painter of actors and actresses in costume. The engraver James Neagle, a specialist in book illustration, lived at No.39 Clarendon Square in 1816 before emigrating to America. Andrés Bello, the Venezuelan poet, lawmaker, philosopher and educator, resided at the same address before moving to Egremont Place (p 16).

Living at No.40 in 1819 was Rev. Henry Francis Alexander Delafite, a clergyman of French extraction, whose mother had been governess to the daughters of George III. For 30 years he was lecturer at St Paul's, Covent Garden. Noted for his English translation of *Elements of Geology* by the Swiss geologist Jean-André Deluc, he was also a 'very kind friend' of Samuel Wesley (p 139).

Residents who have died in the Square include Thomas Mortimer, writer on trade and finance, who died in 1810; the engraver Edward Scriven at No.46 in 1841 and the Cornish portrait painter John Bryant Lane at No.45 in 1868. Scriven is perhaps the best known. He had lived in the Square since 1813 and was sometime 'Historical Engraver to His Majesty', and in 1810 a prime mover in the founding of the Artists' Annuity Fund, a charity supporting impoverished artists and their families.

Now occupying the middle of Clarendon Square are the red-brick, low-slung flats of **Oakshott Court** (1972-76), named after Bill Oakshott, a Camden alderman and local Labour councillor who died in 1975. Stepped up in an L-shape on two sides of a grassy open space, the flats were so designed, by Peter Tabori, to maximise the number with a south-facing aspect.

Previously on the site were Polygon Buildings, four austere, barrack-like blocks, aligned north-south across the site. Built in 1891 by the Midland Railway (MR), they were some recompense for the great loss of housing caused when it invaded the area, although many of those housed in the flats were railway employees. The porters who looked after the blocks wore MR livery. Booth, on his 1898 poverty map, coloured Polygon Buildings a 'middle class' red!

The Buildings had in turn supplanted the once famous, quasi-circular building called The Polygon. The highpoint of his early Somers Town development, it was begun in 1791-92 by Jacob Leroux, in partnership with a Tottenham Court Road carpenter called Job Hoare. Back in 1768, Leroux had been commissioned to design a similar building in Southampton, which was aborted for lack of money.

Described as an 'experimental building', The Polygon in Somers Town had 16 sides, around which 32 three-storey houses were arranged in pairs, with doorways in the one-storey infill between each pair **[32,** p 104**]** The properties were numbered clockwise from the site's southeast corner. Building work proceeded fitfully and was suspended in 1794. Hoare went bankrupt, and work on the unfinished building resumed only in 1799, the year of Leroux's death.

Among the first residents were some of the French émigrés who settled locally. The Abbé Carron (p 104) moved into No.1 in 1799. A few years earlier, two houses in the still incomplete Polygon had been bought by Charles Goldsmith (b.1737). A younger brother of the poet Oliver, he had spent much of his life as a 'friendless adventurer' in Jamaica, but did marry and, returning to England, settled in one of the houses with his wife and family. He is said to have later died in reduced circumstances 'at humble lodgings in Ossulston Street'.

James Parkinson, who died in 1813 at No.5 Polygon, aged about 83, had been the proprietor of a museum of natural history and ethnography south of Blackfriars Bridge. His huge collection had been sold off seven years earlier in an auction lasting 65 days.

On their eviction in 1827 from Johnson Street (p 113), the Dickens family took lodgings in The Polygon, at No.17 near its northwest corner. It was in the Polygon that Charles, in *Bleak House*, set the dilapidated 'down-town' residence of Harold Skimpole, commenting on 'the poor Spanish refugees walking about in cloaks, smoking little paper cigars'.

In 1823, Spaniards fleeing the oppressive regime of Ferdinand VII had found lodgings in Somers Town, reportedly over a thousand families. Despite finding the neighbourhood cold and inhospitable, Antonio Alcalá Galiano, a former member of the Spanish Cortes and founder in 1828 of the Department of Spanish at University College, London, wrote that Somers Town was known in his native land as 'a miniature constitutional Spain which made room for a great number of homeless Spaniards'. Like the earlier French émigrés they were given an allowance by the British Government, but whereas the French had generally been welcomed by the locals, the Spaniards were often treated with suspicion.

The engraver Samuel Mitan, who died in 1843 at No.8 The Polygon, was another founder member of the Artists' Annuity Fund (cf. Scriven, p 107). A later beneficiary was to be James Tibbitts Willmore (b.1800), considered by Turner to be one of six best engravers. Becoming paralysed in 1862, and so unable to work, he relied on a £40 income from the Fund to subsist until his death at No.23 the next year.

Lodging in The Polygon in 1848, with an allowance from his family and a landlady described as a 'dragoness', had been a young art student named James Collinson, 'an insignificant little man with a thick neck'. His proposal of marriage that year to the poet Christina Rossetti she reluctantly rejected because of his Roman Catholicism.

Affixed to the west side of Oakshott Court's north wing is a brown plaque to Mary Wollstonecraft **[33]**, author of *A Vindication of the Rights of Woman*. Erected by Camden Council in 1979 after pressure from Claire Tomalin, her biographer, the plaque was presumably placed where it would be most noticeable, as Mary actually lived at No.29 near the Polygon's north*east* corner. This was home for a decade to the novelist, atheist and proto-anarchist political philosopher William Godwin (also pp 78&98). In his *Political Justice* he condemned the institution of marriage as 'the worst of all laws', but that didn't stop him marrying twice. His first marriage – to Mary

33 Mary Wollstonecraft, and husband William Godwin

– was in 1797. She died of puerperal fever in the same year, shortly after giving birth to a daughter, Mary, the future wife of Shelley and creator of *Frankenstein*. Godwin remarried in 1801, to his neighbour at No.27, the enigmatic Mrs Mary Jane Clairmont, who moved in with her two existing offspring; 3-year-old Jane would later become, as 'Claire' Clairmont, the mother of Lord Byron's ill-fated natural daughter, Allegra. William Godwin Jr (b. 1803) and Fanny Imlay, Wollstonecraft's daughter from an earlier liaison, completed a most peculiar family in which none of the five children had the same two parents. All moved on in 1807, settling in Skinner Street, Holborn.

Next, return to **POLYGON ROAD** and walk east along the part that once formed the north side of Clarendon Square. On the left is the south end of the new building of St Mary & St Pancras C of E Primary School (p 116). The delightful fish mosaic, *A Drop in the Ocean* (2009), was inspired by pupils and realised by Amanda Parker and Sally Kendal. Beyond, the playground of the new school occupies the site of the old school it replaced. St Mary & St Pancras was formed by a merger in 1951 of the two local church schools. St Mary's had its origins in the Polygon Infant School, an early-Victorian offshoot of the Somers Chapel (p 115). To make way for its single-storey building a slice had been removed from the north side of The Polygon 'cake'. The later Victorian school across the road was designed by the church architect Sir Arthur Blomfield and opened in 1896.

Overlooking the present school playground is the visual highlight of this walk, the latest manifestation of the magnificent **Somers Town Mural**. Intended to be both decorative and educational, it was first conceived by the Somers Town Environment Association and then commissioned by the Greater London Council. Measuring 1,452 sq. ft, the mural is the work of Karen Gregory, who first painted it over three summers (1984-86) on the old school's east wall. It was threatened with destruction when the vacant plot it overlooked was needed for development. Claire Tomalin led a successful campaign to save the mural, which by 1995 had been repainted on the west wall by the original artist, with funding from the Gulbenkian Foundation. The later demolition of the old school building necessitated the mural's relocation for a second time. In 2007 Ms Gregory was back yet again to repaint it on the end wall of No.99 Chalton Street, whose construction had led to its first displacement.

The mural is an imaginative assemblage of images depicting three centuries of local history. A haymaking scene evokes the area's peaceful rural past; brick kilns, dust heaps, smoky factories and a railway viaduct intrude. All human life is here. The poet Shelley courts Mary Godwin on a little bridge across the River Fleet, spied on by Frankenstein's monster! Ragged children rub shoulders with (real) modern schoolchildren; a boy chimney sweep, a dustman and flower seller with local personalities from Godwin, Wollstonecraft and Dickens through Elizabeth Garrett Anderson to the 20th-century activists of SPH. Added to the latest version of the mural were images of Claire Tomalin, of the school's headmistress, and of a teaching assistant who had known all three of the artwork's incarnations.

Reaching **CHALTON STREET**, glance across to the right, where its east side is lined by the west face of Walker House (p 101). Initially known as Upper Evesham Buildings, this part of the street was soon renamed as the east side of Clarendon Square (p 102), whose houses were numbered anticlockwise from its southeast corner. At No.6, the Cornishman Henry Bone, a prolific miniature and enamel painter to Georges III and IV and William IV, died 'of paralysis' in 1834. The artist George Sidney Shepherd (p 112) moved into No.10 in 1822.

Turn left along the northern stretch of Chalton Street, here originally named Union Street, possibly celebrating the 1801 Act uniting Great Britain and Ireland. In 1813 a

French émigré, Général Darican, was killed when he and his horse fell headlong into a hole 20ft deep, which had appeared in Union Street during one of the River Fleet's regular inundations of the area. In 1823 the hydrographer Felipe Bauzá lodged at the then No.48 before settling round the corner in Johnson Street (p 113). The street was also home for many years to the bass singer George Smith (1777-c.1836), a regular at Drury Lane. Union Street was later renumbered as part of Stibbington Street (p 132), which was, in turn, absorbed into Chalton Street in 1938.

On your left at No.99 is **Mary Wollstonecraft House**, built in 1992 as nine flats for people recovering from mental illness, funded by the health authority and designed for SPH by Gordon Fleming. It is now a 'care home with nursing', run by the One Housing Group. The block covers the site of No.20 Clarendon Square, which from c.1852 was Lord Shaftesbury's London Female Dormitory, a refuge for 'unfortunate females from the streets or prisons'; and of No.19, later to become one of the several local bases of the Magdalen Mission (p 90).

At Nos.**103-117** are flats and houses of 1989-90, designed by Jim Monahan for the Covent Garden Housing Project. Beyond, on the corner of Aldenham Street (p 115), is **Phyllis Hodges House** (1993), named in honour of a tireless worker for SPH for some 40 years and its Estates Manager in 1973-75. The flats replaced the Lord Somers Arms at No.115, one of the first buildings to be erected in this northern part of Somers Town. Developers of middle-class estates often built a church to attract builders and house buyers; here a pub was a higher priority. To the north, at No.17 Stibbington Street, the engraver Richard Golding (p 37) died aged 80 in 1865. He was buried at Highgate Cemetery, from which his body was exhumed, amid suspicions he had been poisoned by his doctor, who inherited most of his property; but the inquest ruled that despite small traces of arsenic in his stomach he had died from natural causes.

Diagonally opposite at **No.130** is the former Anchor, one of two local establishments which functioned c.1930 as 'restaurant-pubs' (see also p 131). Most local watering-holes were then 'horrid little places' that encouraged insobriety. Both Father Basil Jellicoe and Miss Edith Neville were supporters of the Restaurant Public Houses Association (RPHA), whose aims were to open public houses with inexpensive wholesome food – places where even a clergyman would feel comfortable. Whitbread was persuaded to refurbish the Anchor as a restaurant-pub, and it opened as such in 1929. Jellicoe became the licensee and moved in. An oak-panelled bar, by Hamilton, served only beer (no spirits), and drunkenness was taboo. Above was a restaurant where lunch could be had for 1s 4d (7p). In its short life, the restaurant-pub was blessed by the Archbishop of Canterbury, and royally visited by Queen Mary and the Prince of Wales. It was handed back to Whitbread in 1933, when the RPHA gave up running pubs to concentrate on the training of aspiring licensees. The Anchor has now been converted as housing, but still sports its old sign.

At **No.134**, faced in yellow brick, is the hangar-like Somers Town Youth Community Sports Centre, built (1996-97) in the grounds of the then South Camden Community School (p 129), jointly funded by University College and Camden Council, and run by a charitable trust. The centre is used by the community, the local school and students from UCL. Adjoining it is a contemporary grey-and-white building designed by Theis & Kahn as the Council's Somers Town Youth Centre, with sports facilities, a cafe and an internet room. Ahead on the right, and fronted by twin Doric porticoes, are the privately-built, interwar flats of **Sussex House**. Born hereabouts at No.58 Stibbington Street, the son of a railway porter, was the Middlesex and England cricketer Fred Titmus (1932–2011) who in a first-class career spanning five decades took 2,500 wickets and made 20,000 runs.

Off the west side of Chalton Street are the flats of SPH's **Sidney Estate** (1931-38). It took its name from vanished Sidney Street, which previously ran east-west across the site, bisecting it. At first also referred to as the 'Garden Estate', it comprises six blocks in stock brick surrounding a generously large courtyard with trees and play areas. Designed by Ian Hamilton, the flats were the first to be all-electric, and although spartan by modern-day standards, were a far cry from the insanitary and overcrowded houses they replaced, where whole families had lived in a single room and children had slept five to a bug-infested bed.

The Sidney Estate was refurbished in 2017-18 and its central courtyard redesigned with seating. As you walk around the Estate, don't miss the colourful Doultonware lunettes above some of the 2nd-floor windows, designed by the sculptor Gilbert Bayes and mostly featuring scenes from the fairy tales of Hans Christian Andersen and the Brothers Grimm. Bayes also designed the charming finials of the washing-line supports in the drying-yards. Though all of these were lost in the later 20th century through vandalism or theft, some have since been replaced with reproductions.

Opposite the sports centre is a rather grand iron-gated forecourt, with St Anthony's Flats (p 116) to the left and **St Francis' House** (of 1938) on the right. Set in a niche above the central archway of the connecting block is a small statue of a saint with his donkey. Long assumed to be St Francis, he is actually St Anthony of Padua. Notice also the ring of concrete posts, still bereft of their Bayes finials, which here had a *Mother Goose* theme – 'four and twenty tailors went to kill a snail'.

Continuing north, turn left along **BRIDGEWAY STREET**, named Bridgewater Street until 1937, possibly after the canal-building 3rd Duke of Bridgewater (d.1803). An early resident was John Greig, a writer on arithmetic and astronomy, whose *Young Lady's Guide to Arithmetic* (1798) ran to sixteen editions, and who died in 1819 at No.12.

The north side of Bridgeway Street is now lined by routine St Pancras Council flats of 1960, numbered but not named, while opposite are further SPH blocks on the Sidney Estate.

On 23 January 1930, Lord Monk Bretton (Chairman of the LCC), detonated a small charge of dynamite in the chimney stack of No.23 Bridgewater Street to signal the start of the building work on the new estate. **St George's House**, the first block to be built, was opened later that year by Lady Cynthia Colville, lady-in-waiting to Queen Mary. **St Christopher's House**, beyond, was begun in January 1931, when General Sir Ian Hamilton (a namesake of the architect) lit a bonfire made of old wood from demolished houses, and giant effigies of a rat, flea, bug and cockroach were ceremonially burned **[34]**. The SPH nursery school (founded at the Charrington Hall, p 130) moved onto the roof of the newly completed block where, renamed St Christopher's Nursery School, it was opened by Princess Arthur of Connaught in January 1932.

Turn left again along **WERRINGTON STREET**, where **St Nicholas' Flats** were completed two

34 Sidney Estate, 1931: effigies of vermin ceremonially burnt

years later and blessed by the Archbishop of Canterbury. Note the imposing entrance and iron gates. Sidney Street had been closed and its houses pulled down to enable construction of the building. The nursery school spread onto the roof of St Nicholas', where a roof garden was installed, with 'Hans Andersen' reliefs by Lady Allen and a fountain by Gilbert Bayes. In its heyday the garden boasted a paddling-pool and sandpit, eventually abandoned for health and safety reasons. Decent clothing for the children was provided by a Guild of Needlework, which was founded in 1930 by Amy Gedge and flourished until 1957; hundreds of garments were made each year. A financial burden to SPH by 1970, the nursery school was handed over to the Inner London Education Authority (ILEA). Later, under Camden Council's control, budgetary cuts led to its closure in 1992. Rescued through a partnership of various local bodies, it was reopened on 12 May (St Pancras Day) in 1997, and now functions as a nursery at the Somers Town Community Centre in Ossulston Street (p 117). 2001 saw the reinstatement of the lost finials in the St Nicholas' drying-yard, recreated to Bayes' original design and in the form of painted sailing-ships.

Before 1938 this stretch of Werrington Street was called Clarendon Street, and the numbering on the east side ran northwards. Trading in the 1830s at the then No.24 was Hugh Powell, a notable maker of 'mathematical, optical and philosophical instruments; he supplied microscopes to his neighbour Cornelius Varley (p 105). Living at No.15 in 1816 was the sculptor William Scoular, who in 1821 was commissioned by the Duke of Clarence (later William IV) to take the death mask of his infant daughter, Princess Elizabeth, and whose carved figure of the child asleep on a couch is now at Windsor Castle. Sharing the house was fellow sculptor Edward Hodges Baily, best known for his statue of Nelson atop the column in Trafalgar Square. The draughtsman and watercolour painter George Sidney Shepherd (1784-1862) was living at No.9 Clarendon Street in 1817. Like his younger brother Thomas Hosmer Shepherd, he created numerous topographical views of London and elsewhere. In 1822 he moved to Clarendon Square (p 109).

The west side of Werrington Street is lined by Camden Council's **Somers Town Estate**, six stock-brick blocks with balcony access, built progressively in 1928-31 by St Pancras Borough Council. Demolished to make way for them was former Little Clarendon Street, a notoriously mean street which ran north-south through the middle of the site. Living there, three years before his death in 1838, was Sebastian Gahagan, a sculptor of Irish descent who created the statue in Park Crescent (Marylebone) of Queen Victoria's father, the Duke of Kent. The street's mid-19th-century inhabitants included a considerable colony of clay tobacco-pipe makers. At No.22 was a pub called the Bricklayers' Arms. On Booth's 1898 poverty map Little Clarendon Street is shaded 'dark blue barred black', just short of the worst colour-coding, a 'vicious, semi-criminal' black. In his notebook, Booth's informant Edward Aves describes it as 'a narrow thoroughfare of bad repute... the worst spot in the immediate neighbourhood, and a good many prostitutes and amateurish thieves are living here. ... The local name for the street is "Little Hell" and prisoners, on being discharged, often describe themselves as living in this byway of the nether regions'. Policemen were said to venture along it only in pairs.

Little Clarendon Street was later renamed Wolcot Street, after the satirist John Wolcot, alias Peter Pindar (p 88). Wolcot House, at right angles to Werrington Street and one of the first two estate blocks to be built, was opened in 1928 by Mary, the Princess Royal. Despite the regal ceremony, 'economy' was the watchword here: the utilitarianism of these council blocks contrasts starkly with Hamilton's more ambitious work on the Sidney Estate opposite.

Turn round and walk northwards, beside low hedges fronting **Clarendon House**. Out of sight behind it is **Morland House**, named after the artist George Morland (1763-1804), who lived and painted in Camden High Street. Beyond, and set back from the road, is **Gladwin House**, commemorating Grace Gladwin, who in her will of 1860 bequeathed 'the residue of certain stocks for the poor of Somers Town'. Finally, reach **Johnson House**, so named because when built it faced onto Johnson Street (now Cranleigh Street, ahead).

On the right-hand corner, at **No.51** Werrington Street, is the terracotta-faced former Neptune public house. This had been licensed since at least 1848, so that the inscription '1900' in its north-facing gable must refer to a rebuilding at that time. Quite recently closed, the pub has been converted into luxury apartments and renamed Doltan House.

Beyond Cranleigh Street lies the 1970s Mayford Estate (p 132). The original Werrington Street ran northeastward through its site to meet Goldington Crescent (p 123), across land owned by the Duke of Bedford (p 120). The manor of Werrington, on the Devon-Cornwall boundary, was another ducal property. Clarendon Street was renamed in 1938, assuming the name of its northerly continuation. When the two sections were later severed by the building of Mayford, the Werrington name was left stranded in Somers Town where it doesn't belong.

Turn right and walk along the eastern half of **CRANLEIGH STREET**, the former Johnson Street. Property developer John Johnson was official paviour to the Somers Town Paving Board in the early years of the 19th century. Jacob Leroux (p 102) had died in 1799, and his property was sold off in lots three years later. Johnson bought the leasehold of most of northern Somers Town. He sublet to various (often local) builders, who in turn erected the terraced houses eventually to be demolished in the various 20th-century slum clearance schemes.

Early Johnson Street residents included Sidney Richard Percy, a prolific and popular landscape painter of the Victorian era, living at No.11 in 1842, and two of the many Spanish refugees who fled to London in 1823 (see p 108). Antonio Puigblanch, philologist, Hebraist and author of *The Inquisition Unmasked*, lived at No.51, dying there in 1840. Felipe Bauzá, a naval officer, hydrographer and cartographer under sentence of death in his homeland, settled at No.58, where he died in 1834. The Bauzá Collection in the British Library contains hundreds of the maps of Latin America he had brought with him from Spain.

On the north side of Cranleigh Street today are the flats of 4-storey **Cranleigh House** (originally 'Houses'), eventually purchased by the Council but privately built. The potential monotony of its long brick façade is relieved by intermittent rendering and tiers of slightly protruding windows. The inscription 'GB 1934' on the small central gable relates to the death that year of George Burgoyne. A self-made man, he had worked successively as a farm hand, coachman and butler, before becoming an estate agent and successful property developer, with a local office at No.1 Stibbington Street (p 132) and a fine house on a residential estate he created in the Chilterns. Around 1930, he bought up and demolished all the houses on Johnson Street's north side, and replaced them with the present-day flats. The Cranleigh name is puzzling: Burgoyne hailed not from Cranleigh (Surrey) but from the Bedfordshire village of Cranfield. The flats' name was transferred to the whole of the street on its renaming in 1937.

The eastern part is still cobbled, as if in deference to Charles Dickens, who in 1825-27 lived as a boy with his parents at No.29 (later No.13) Johnson Street **[35]**. Having ceased work at the Charing Cross blacking factory, he was now a pupil at the Wellington House Academy in Hampstead Road. After Lady Day 1827 the family were evicted for non-payment of rent and rates, moving on to The Polygon (p 107). Their house was acquired in 1921 by Rev. J Brett Langstaff and the Children's Library Movement. Here they opened the

35 The house in Johnson Street where Charles Dickens lived as a boy

David Copperfield Library, for the use of poor local youngsters and as a memorial to the novelist. The house was given to St Pancras Borough Council which, however, declined to take on the library, and it closed after ten years for lack of support.

Near the entrance to flats 17-24 are two blue plaques, erected in 2013 by the Brook & Cranleigh House Residents Association. One of them, unsurprisingly, honours Charles Dickens. The other commemorates the Trinidadian George Padmore, journalist, author, Communist Party member and leading Pan-Africanist. He lived in Flat 22 from 1941-57 with his collaborator and common-law wife, Dorothy Pizer, a British Jewish anti-racist activist.

After noting small Stibbington House ('1930'), ahead on the corner of former Stibbington Street, backtrack to the western end of Cranleigh Street. For Booth, in 1897, Aves wrote: 'The W end is the worst. 3 and 2½ st[orey] houses; tousled haired women standing at open doors, bare-armed; dirty children; too many broken windows stuffed with temporary mendings; but nothing is charged against this street worse than roughness and drunkenness. ... Some of the houses are clearly occupied by well-to-do folk, including a showy undertaker's establishment.'

On the north side today is **Brook House**, another George Burgoyne development; the significance of its name is a total mystery. Here a third plaque recalls two former residents: the actress Alison Steadman, and Mike Leigh, film and theatre director (and local tenants' champion), who in the early 1970s lived together in a top-floor flat; they married in 1973.

Regain **EVERSHOLT STREET**, where **No.188**, on the right and now a bicycle shop, was the 1940s base of the George Burgoyne Estate Trust. Turn left, and walk south along what was known until 1865 as Upper Seymour Street (USS). Opposite, long-demolished No.61 USS was home in the late 1830s to the still-life painter George Lance. Surviving on the east side is a row of renovated 19th-century houses, of which **Nos.170-180** sport curly 'balconets'. The lexicographer James Knowles was living at No.44 USS (now **No.166**) when his renowned *Pronouncing Dictionary* was published in 1835. The **Pack & Carriage** (No.162), known in recent years first as Rowley's and then as the Elixir Bar, was for most of its long existence called the Seymour Arms, and as such was licensed as a theatre in 1855-57. Around 1851, the artist George Sidney Shepherd (p 112) was living at No.40 USS (now **No.158**). Nos.140-158 Eversholt Street were refurbished by SPH as the first phase of **Irene Barclay House**, which was opened in 1977 by Princess Margaret. Victorian shop-fronts were removed and stuccoed residential ground floors reinstated. Mrs Barclay (p 92) had retired in 1972, having served as SPH Estates Manager for half a century.

Now lining the west side of the street is a long range in stock-brick, entered through three imposing rusticated doorways labelled

Nos.203, 183 & 163. This was once part of the Railway Clearing House (RCH). Begun in 1842 in Drummond Street (p 72), with just two clerks, it was formally established by Act of Parliament eight years later. The RCH was to oversee all transactions between the then numerous private railway companies, dealing with through-ticketing for passengers and goods, harmonisation of safety practices and lost property found on trains. 2,500 clerks were eventually employed, enough to support a thriving dramatic society. The RCH finally ceased to exist in 1963.

The original building here was built in 1849 to designs by Philip Hardwick, but was demolished as Euston Station expanded. The present range dates in part from 1874-75 to designs by James B Stansby, architect to the LNWR; he also built the two lodges on Euston Road (p 157) but was stood down by the Company when his newly constructed roof at Huddersfield Station collapsed. The building was extended in similar style southwards in 1882 and northwards in 1896 and again in 1901-02. After the Railway Clearing House's demise the building was renamed Eversholt House. Its offices were refurbished in the 1980s, and in 1992, by then called Carriage Row, served also as a temporary home to Britain's first cartoon gallery, the Museum of Cartoons. Extensively renovated by Hale Brown architects, the three numbered blocks now contain a wide variety of offices and studios, and venues for corporate events.

Use the pedestrian crossing to cross over to the west side of the street and continue south. Despite their size, the surviving RCH buildings were only an annexe. The original premises of 1849, designed by Philip Hardwick in a similar neo-Georgian style, stood just to the south at No.101 USS (later No.123 Eversholt Street). On their site today, and rounding the corner into **BARNBY STREET** is Royal Mail's 1960s NW1 delivery office at No.1. Now largely a service road for the Ampthill Square Estate (p 133), Barnby Street was once a shorter, residential street providing access from the east into erstwhile Ampthill Square. With a Russell Arms pub on the north side, it was originally called Duke Street but soon rechristened Bedford Street. In 1896 it was renamed again, after Sir Joseph Barnby, an eminent organist and choral conductor and composer, best remembered for his part-song *Sweet and Low*; he had died that year.

Turn right, walk a few metres along Barnby Street, and turn round to view, across **EVERSHOLT STREET**, the façade of **St Mary's Church**. Built in rather grim, plain stock brick, with a square tower topped and flanked by pinnacles, this was designed, like the new St Pancras Church, by William and Henry Inwood, though in a very different style. It was mocked by Pugin, and criticised by Pevsner as 'thin and papery'. A parish church from 1868, it originally opened in 1826 as a chapel-of-ease, known as the Somers (Town) Chapel. Dickens worshipped there as a boy. The chapel was at first hugely popular, thanks partly to its controversial attempts at converting local Catholics; services at which they publicly renounced their faith filled the pews to overflowing. An early incumbent was the Rev. T J Judkin, whose hymnal of 1834 consisted wholly of hymns no longer than four verses of four lines, 'a number sufficient for any tune to be sustained without wearying the congregation'. Originally nicknamed Mr Judkin's Chapel, St Mary's was later dubbed 'the Cabbies' Church' because of the aid it offered to cabmen plying for hire at the old Euston Station. In 2003 it was merged into the newly enlarged Parish of Old St Pancras.

Use the central refuge to re-cross Eversholt Street and turn left. Past the church, turn east along **ALDENHAM STREET**, here initially known as Upper Grenville Street. On the north side are the council flats of **Aldenham House**, 1928 and part of the Somers Town Estate (p 112). Opposite is **St Aloysius Catholic Primary Upper School**, previously named St Aloysius Junior School, and much earlier the elementary school for boys. Note the three statues, of Christ, the Virgin Mary and St Aloysius, and a plaque recording the (far from evident) rebuilding of the premises in 1927-29. Iron railings still guard the school's former rooftop playground. Following the 2019 closure of the Lower School (p 104), the Upper School temporarily remained open while places were found for the remaining St Aloysius pupils.

Pause at the next crossroads. Here are four rare early bollards, inscribed 'Sommers Town 1817'. They were first erected by the Somers Town Paving Board, the body then responsible for paving and lighting the estate.

Look across to the right along the east side of **WERRINGTON STREET**. Once situated here was the main hall of the Magdalen College Mission. Founded at Oxford in 1883, the mission first came to Somers Town in 1908 to help in the outreach work of St Mary's Church. Father Jellicoe, its leader, opened the hall in 1924 at what was then No.5 Clarendon Street (and later No.83 Werrington Street). Here were run a nursery school, a soup kitchen, and various clubs, including one for boys which Jellicoe had founded earlier in Little Clarendon Street. Holidays were organised for the nursery school children, while older boys were helped to emigrate to Australia. Jellicoe headed the mission from 1921 until 1927, when he resigned to work full time for SPH, and was succeeded by the Rev. Percy Maryon-Wilson, later Vicar of St Mary's. The mission building was later lent to the Church for use as a community centre, and during WWII hosted various SPH activities displaced from the Basil Jellicoe Hall (p 93), which was in use at the time as an air raid shelter. Taken over in 1967 by the ILEA, the Magdalen clubhouse closed two years later.

Now covering its site is the new building of **St Mary & St Pancras C of E Primary School**, designed by Shepheard Epstein Hunter and built in 2005-06 to replace the old Victorian school in Polygon Road (p 109). Brightly coloured panels enliven the long, partly timber-clad façade. The school's signboard features a 'healthy school' mosaic designed and created by the children.

The school occupies two floors of an L-shaped block rounding the corner into **ALDENHAM STREET**, along which we continue. In the remainder is a Unite Students residence called **Somerset Court**, with an entrance along on the right. Lady Henry Somerset (1851-1921), philanthropist, temperance leader and campaigner for women's rights was also, as the co-heiress of the 3rd Earl Somers, the ground landlord of much of Somers Town.

Somerset Court covers the site of erstwhile Grenville Mews. Until 1867 this portion of Aldenham Street was called Grenville Street, possibly after Lord Grenville, prime minister in 1806-07. Living there in 1818 at No.2 were James Howe, the Scottish painter of horses and cattle (and of the Battle of Waterloo); the genre painter Alexander Carse, a fellow Scot; and his art student son, the future landscape painter William Carse (p 86).

On the left is SPH's Sidney Estate (p 111). In the drying-yard here is a full set of reproduction Gilbert Bayes finials, 13 more galleons encircling an elaborately embellished centre post. Beyond are **St Michael's Flats**, opened by the Duchess of Gloucester in 1938, where dolphins once adorned the washing-line posts; and **St Anthony's Flats** (the last block to be completed that year), where devils were the order of the day.

Aldenham Street is another local street name that is now out of place. The street once ran across the whole width of Somers Town, having originated on the Brewers' estate to the east (p 125), which endowed Aldenham School. Over time the eastern parts of the street have gradually vanished, leaving its name behind in alien, Somers territory. Ahead, across Chalton Street, the middle section of Aldenham Street, long downgraded to a footpath, was totally extinguished in 2018. Cross over to the right and enter **Polygon Road Open Space**. Dating from its relandscaping in 2001, the boundary railings, with their 'human hand' motifs, were designed with the help of local children. Follow the path running diagonally across the site. The children's play areas are successors to an adventure playground, begun in the 1970s by the Plot 10 Community Play Project, which in its early years was blest with a small city farm. The project is still active (in premises over on the left), providing after-school and breakfast clubs for local schoolchildren, and basic sports facilities. Completed in 2020, on the site to your left, were a 6-storey block of flats above a new 'community hub' and a new building for Plot 10, with a multi-use rooftop sports pitch and a very distinctive parapet resembling a stylised crown, designed by Adam Khan. This is all part of Camden's Community Investment Programme for 'Central Somers Town'.

Emerge into a section of **POLYGON ROAD** known until 1937 as Hampden Street. In the earliest days of Somers Town, before its rapid decline, there were actually detached villas here. In 1812, in London, the parliamentary reformer Major John Cartwright founded the first Hampden Club, named after John Hampden (1594-1643), the leading Parliamentarian mortally wounded in the Civil War. Cartwright's main aim was to unite middle-class moderates with radical members of the working class. This worried the authorities and led to his arrest the next year. Nevertheless, further Hampden Clubs sprang up, including, soon after the Napoleonic Wars, one of them here in Hampden Street.

Turn left and then pause where **OSSULSTON STREET** intersects. Its northernmost tip, on the left, has long been pedestrianised, surviving only as a footway through to Charrington Street (p 128).

Look southward along its east side. The former houses there were known until 1867 as Somers Town Terrace, where the singer and organist Frederick Charles Reinhold died in 1815, aged 74 and separated from his wife. In his will he asked that his memorial stone should read 'Professor of Music and principal vocal performer under the immortal Handel' (to whose music he had been devoted, since appearing as a teenager in the chorus at the Foundling Hospital's *Messiah* performance). Ann Woodbridge, who inherited Reinhold's Somers Town house, was seemingly his mistress.

The romantic fiction writer Henrietta Mosse, whose first novel, *Lussington Abbey*, was published anonymously in 1804, ended her 'harrowing career' as a novelist in 'a miserable attic' at No.6 Somers Town Terrace, dying there in 1834 'in a state of great destitution' (ODNB). When the doctor who attended her appealed to the Royal Literary Fund for money to enable a decent burial, his request was ruled 'inadmissible'.

Much later, the terrace gave way to six small blocks erected by the Hampden Residential Club (see below) to accommodate its young professional men. Agincourt, Baltimore, Cleveland, Doncaster, Edinburgh and Frankfort Houses (a motley assortment of names) were alphabetically arranged along the street from south to north. On their site today is the thriving Somers Town (formerly Hampden) Community Centre, along on the left at No.150, with a café and the nursery relocated from St Christopher's House (p 111).

On the near corner, at No.80 **POLYGON ROAD**, is the Council-run **Hampden Nursery** (previously the Hampden Children's Centre). Formerly on this site, and dominating the whole block southward to Phoenix Road, were the sprawling premises of the Hampden Residential Club. Founded in 1882 to meet what the Duke of Westminster described as 'a great want', and run by a company called Hampden House Ltd, it offered affordable accommodation for young trainee professionals, especially those 'up from the country'. The president was Viscount Hampden, whose portrait shared the Club's letterhead with that of the 17th-century John Hampden. Other patrons included Lord Derby,

Lord Shaftesbury, the newsagent W H Smith, and Samuel Morley MP. The attractions of Somers Town for such an institution were presumably the cheapness of land and its nearness to three mainline stations. Strangely, in an appeal for share capital in 1892, the Club saw fit to claim that 'the effect of the Midland [MR] clearances ... has been to make this neighbourhood one of the healthiest parts of London'. The Club included a Masonic Temple, and ran a dozen clubs and societies, athletic, social and professional, with such appropriate names as Circle of Science and Chapter of Literature. Pageboys with brightly buttoned uniforms were recruited from among local school leavers. Locals irreverently nicknamed the Club the Toffs' Doss House.

The international chess player George William Richmond (1877-1941) lived at the Hampden Residential Club for many years.

In 1906 a resident, Dr Charles Dumbleton, the first medical officer of Singapore, committed suicide. Two decades later another resident, Hans Herzl, the son of Theodore Herzl, the founder of political Zionism, was also to die by his own hands. In 1930 he attended his sister's funeral in Bordeaux, after which he shot himself there. Although he had converted to Christianity, his body and that of his sister were reburied in Israel in 2006.

By 1950 the Club had become a hostel for British Railways employees, most of the rooms occupied by permanent residents, many of them from Commonwealth counties or Poland, but some reserved for train crews from the North stopping overnight in London between shifts. In 1972 it was used to house Ugandan Asian refugees. Camden Council then acquired the site for a mixed development in red brick, including the aforementioned community centre and the sheltered housing of Monica Shaw Court (p 119).

Walk on along Polygon Road. The local Presbyterian congregation quickly outgrew their premises at Goldington Crescent (p 123), and a new Somers Town Presbyterian Church was erected, facing onto the north side of what was then Hampden Street. Designed by George Lethbridge and opened in 1882, with Rev. Woffendale as minister, it flourished here for over 70 years.

Soon reach the spot where, also on the north side, the Cooper's Arms once stood. Its landlord was fined 10 shillings (£0.50) in 1893 for selling diluted whisky. Opposite, having bisected the Hampden Club site, the north end of long-lost Middlesex Street (p 72) emerged. This had two tiny tributaries, Parker's Place off the west side, and Harris's Place off the east (labelled, probably wrongly, on an 1834 map as Paris Place).

Here today are the grounds of **Edith Neville Primary School**. Named after the ubiquitous local reformer **[36]** who died in 1951, this is a successor to a Victorian Board School that had faced onto the now vanished end of Aldenham Street (p 127). The present school's 'lightweight' one-storey buildings were erected in 1971 with a life expectancy of only 25 years. Under Camden's Central Somers Town proposals, a new school is to be built on the

36 Edith Neville addressing an open-air meeting in 1939

east side of the site, funded by the Council's proceeds from the Brill Place Tower scheme (p 101). Also planned is a green corridor to run along the site's south side, linking the Polygon Road and Purchese Street Open Spaces.

PURCHESE STREET, ahead, dates only from 1895, shortly before the building of the MR coal depot (p 126). Frederick Purchese, of Ossulston Street (and later of Platt Street), was a St Pancras Churchwarden at the time and in 1900 became the LCC member for St Pancras East. Although the roadway's original cobbles have been largely preserved, today's speed humps and asphalt cycle lane have diminished their nostalgic effect.

On the street's west side to your right is the 1970s sheltered housing of red-brick **Monica Shaw Court**. Dr Shaw was a much loved GP, who from her Eversholt Street surgery served local people for half a century, often waiving her fees in pre-NHS days.

Cross over and enter **Purchese Street Open Space**, sometimes known as 'Somers Green'. Follow the path running south-eastwards across it. Once traversing this site, from north to south, was Brill Path. This old footpath, a continuation of Brill Row (p 76), followed the eastern boundary of Lord Somers' estate. By 1834 it had been built up, with Brill Terrace on the west side and Dear's Place opposite, as a narrow, mostly residential street with a sprinkling of corner shops. John Revett and his family were living at No.13 Dear's Place in 1822 when a fire broke out. They gave evidence against a young servant, Eleanor Shrieves, who was convicted on flimsy and contradictory evidence of arson. She was sentenced to death but her father, an army veteran, petitioned the Home Secretary and got the sentence commuted to transportation to Van Diemen's Land. The artist and engraver Charles Hunt was living at 'No.11, Dear's Cottage', Brill Terrace in the 1840s. He was well known in the sporting print trade for the precision of his engravings, which were usually of racing scenes.

Somers Town housed not only refugees from the French Revolution but also some people who supported it, including members of the London Corresponding Society (LCS). Inspired by Thomas Paine, and with 10,000 adherents, this agitated for parliamentary reform and for the abolition of both the nobility and the clergy. Many of its members chose to live locally, close to town yet well away from the eagle eye of the authorities there. Living in 1810 at No.10 Brill Terrace was John Gale Jones, a radical orator and a leading LCS activist. That year he was summoned to the bar of the House of Commons to defend his authorship of a 'libellous pamphlet', and then twice imprisoned. Jones was also the proprietor of an apothecary's shop in Wilsted Street (p 70).

Brill Terrace was subsequently twice renamed, first as Brill Street and later as part of Goldington Street (p 127). At its south end, at its junction with Phoenix Street (now Brill Place), was an east-facing Brill Crescent, and a pub called the Duke of York. Both Crescent and Street were demolished to make way for the MR coal depot, and the substitute Purchese Street was constructed on a more westerly alignment. After the depot's closure in 1968, it in turn was pulled down.

A decade later the eastern side of its site eventually became the Coopers Lane Estate (p 126), and the remainder was transformed into the much cherished green oasis that is the present Open Space.

Just before you leave, note the small plaque on the boundary wall, close to a bench over to your right. It is to the murdered teenager Richard Everitt (p 129). Now turn left along Brill Place, a right turn at the end of which will bring you back to our starting-point at St Pancras International.

Route 7

Bedford New Town and the Brewers' estate

Circular walk from Mornington Crescent Underground Station

Here we explore two areas widely regarded as part of Somers Town, but historically quite distinct – one developed on fields owned by a peer of the realm, and the other on land vested in a City livery company for the endowment of a public school.

We begin at Mornington Crescent Station, in the northwest corner of the former Fig's Mead estate of the (Russell) Dukes of Bedford, a tract of farmland extending from the Hampstead Road east to Old St Pancras. Around 1826, with development of their better-known Bloomsbury estate largely complete, the Russells turned their attention to their more northerly property. They may have wished to create a second Bloomsbury here, but realising that 'first rate' houses would not sell in such an outlying area, settled for what was meant to be a model middle-class suburb. In 'Bedford New Town' there would also be housing for the better class of artisan or clerk.

Crescents or squares would ensure that the area's character was superior to that of the adjacent, and earlier developed, Somers and Camden Towns. Much thought was given to the names of the proposed streets, which it was decided would be borrowed from places on the Russells' estates in various parts of the country. The first plans for the new suburb, drawn up in 1826 by the Duke's surveyor Thomas Stead, were radically revised in 1834 by Christopher Haedy, his London steward. Haedy's plans, in turn, needed further alteration when the London & Birmingham Railway cut a gash through the west side of the estate. Delayed first by this intrusion, and then by a building slump in the later 1840s, the development of Fig's Mead was not fully complete until 1859.

Exiting from the Tube station, turn right and then quickly right again. Facing north up Camden High Street, past the well-known Richard Cobden statue, is the diminutive and now unlabelled **MILLBROOK PLACE,** named after a Bedfordshire village near Ampthill. Only one of the original three houses survives, as a coffee shop; the others were pulled down for the building of the station. Demolished Millbrook House at No.1 was the long-term home of the alliteratively named Dr Claude Clarke Claremont, the public vaccinator for St Pancras for thirty years, who died in 1900 soon after retiring to Bognor.

Approaching from the east, to the right of the Koko nightclub, is Crowndale Road, which we will visit shortly. Intersecting from the south is the north end of **EVERSHOLT STREET**, which takes its name from a village near Woburn Abbey, the Duke of Bedford's principal seat. The name at first applied only to this north end of the street; in 1937 it was extended southward along the road to Euston Square, absorbing former Seymour Street.

Cross over to the Crowndale Road corner, where a fearsome lion's head surmounts the door of the former Camden Town Post Office (relocated to the High Street in the 1990s). Turn south beside the massive building, in red brick and stone, of which it was part. As the **Crowndale Centre**, it now houses various Camden Council offices, and on the ground floor **Camden Town Library**, which moved here from the High Street in 1996. The building was converted in 1987-88, to the award-winning plans of Charles Thomson of Rock Townsend. First erected in 1912, it had previously served as the (second) North West District postal sorting office, whose predecessor had stood a few doors to the south. Once running beneath Eversholt Street, and linking the sorting office with Euston Station, was the first phase of the Pneumatic Dispatch Railway **[37]**. This operated from February 1863, using compressed air and carrying mailbags in trucks through horseshoe-shaped tunnels just 4½ft high.

It was extended to Holborn later that year and a further section from Holborn to the General Post Office in the City was added by 1869. Built as a speculative private venture, the railway was not a success: its tunnels leaked and trucks got stuck, and having failed to impress the Post Office, it was abandoned in 1874.

Pass a large metal gate marking the onetime entrance to Eversholt Mews, whose site is now occupied by the Ampthill Practice (formerly Ampthill Square Medical Centre), with pedestrian access from Crowndale Road. On the west side of Eversholt Street, at **Nos.235-277**, is a plain terrace of old 4-storey houses, with small shops and eateries on the ground floor and a continuous range of curly iron balconies above. Built as Bedford New Town's local shopping centre, the street was once lined here on both sides by all manner of 'useful' everyday shops.

37 The Pneumatic Dispatch Railway: dispatch of mailbags from the district office in Eversholt Street

At **Nos.210-214**, are the premises of funeral directors Leverton & Sons. Founded in 1789 in Henry Street (off the southwest end of Hampstead Road), the prestigious family firm moved to Eversholt Street in 1888, initially a few doors to the north. When in 1933 they acquired their first Rolls-Royce hearse, its earliest passengers included none other than Henry Royce, whose body was brought from Sussex to London for cremation. More recently the company has organised the funerals of Diana, Princess of Wales (1997), the Queen Mother (2002), and Baroness Thatcher (2013).

Turn left along the quiet northwest side of **OAKLEY SQUARE**. Glance to the right across the **Oakley Square Gardens**, pleasantly leafy and with many very tall trees. First laid out in 1845 for residents' use only, they were ceremonially reopened, after wartime damage, in 1953. Under Haedy's 1834 plan there would have been no open space here. Streets of terraced houses would have criss-crossed Fig's Mead in an 'X' formation; and the modern street map would have featured such unfamiliar names as 'Kingston Street' and 'Kingston Place'. From the later revision of Haedy's plans emerged Oakley Square, named after the Russells' Oakley House near Bedford, and developed gradually, in 1845-59. It takes the form of a slightly angular crescent. In its final form, the New Town consisted of three 'squares', none of which was even a rectangle.

At **Nos.53-69** is an apparently continuous range of partly stuccoed 'second-rate' houses with Doric-columned porticoes. Like virtually all of the surviving mid-19th-century buildings on this walk, they are Grade II Listed. Above the first-floor windows, triangular and segmental pediments alternate, all flanked by small scallops (a Russell family emblem). Indicative of the Square's piecemeal construction is **No.57**, a curious, narrow-built intruder of only 3 storeys and in a homelier style. George Rowney, the manufacturer of artists' materials, was living here in 1861. Note the series of coal-hole covers set in the pavement, bearing the names of the ironmongers who supplied them, several with local addresses.

At **No.52** is a neo-Gothic building, now a private house, with a squat pyramidal steeple inexplicably topped by a gilded sailing-ship and a tiny golden yacht. A lamb-and-flag insignia above the doorway suggests a former religious use and this was, indeed, the vicarage (1871) of St Matthew's Church. The modern 5-storey block of flats at No.50, named **St Matthew's Lodge**, stands on the site of the church, part of whose ragstone churchyard boundary wall may still be seen rounding the corner ahead. The architect of both vicarage and church was John Johnson of the Adelphi, who also designed St Luke's Church, Euston Road (p 19). The church, in a Decorated Gothic style, was erected in 1852-56 on a plot donated by the Duke of Bedford. He gave £1,000 to the building fund, a quarter of it conditional upon the erection of a steeple. The spire, which was duly built, lost its pointed tip during WWII, when the church was severely damaged. Although restored, it was later declared redundant, and in 1977 pulled down.

Cross over to the right to view **The Lodge** at No.40, a stuccoed one-storey building at the northeast end of the gardens. Here, until 1893, vehicular access to the two sides of Oakley Square was restricted by a pair of Bloomsbury-style bar gates **[38]**, overseen by a uniformed gatekeeper. No.40 was his lodge. Just visible through foliage above its Crowndale Road frontage is the Duke of Bedford's coat of arms. After serving for years as a glorified garden shed, the building now serves as a residential 'cottage'.

38 Oakley Square bar gates and lodge, with St Matthew's Church on the right (photo, 1893)

Next, turn west along the south side of **CROWNDALE ROAD**, which formed the northern boundary of the Fig's Mead estate. First made up in 17th century, this was long known as Fig Lane. Here was found the empty coffin of thief-taker Jonathan Wild, after its illicit exhumation from nearby St Pancras churchyard in 1725. For many years the lane was the only east-west route in St Pancras parish. In 1863, after tolls were removed, it was renamed Crowndale Road, after a Bedford property near Tavistock (Devon) that was reputedly the birthplace of Sir Francis Drake.

The north side of the road, built up at its west end by 1801 and there known as Gloucester Place, lay on the southern edge of Lord Camden's estate and so is, properly, part of Camden Town. We shall therefore focus on the south side, developed in the 1840s as part of Bedford New Town. The surviving terrace on your left at **Nos.31–53**, with recessed sashes and delicate cast-iron balconies, was at first named Kingston Russell Place after a Russell-family property in Dorset. The vicar of St Thomas', Agar Town, Rev. Robert Clemenger (p 65) lived at No.2 from the late 1850s. Edward Peron Hingston, who died in 1876 at **No.49**, had a remarkable CV: 'play writer and actor, traveller, spiritualist, Indian chief, Fiji courtier, agent and accountant, pedestrian, manufacturer of Dutch clocks, journalist, Cincinnati pig-raiser, notable "brave" amongst the Maoris and South Sea Islanders, sheep shearer in New Zealand, and store keeper in 'Frisco'. Thus was the globetrotting Hingston described in a report of his death in the *London West End News*. He had eventually settled down, spending his last 20 years as a theatre manager in London.

Beyond, on the same side of Crowndale Road, was a shorter terrace initially called Crowndale Place. March 1883 saw the death there, in comparative poverty at No.55, of William Desborough Cooley, FRGS, a geographer who in spite of his fellowship was ever at odds with his peers, who considered some of his notions absurd. He is best remembered for his founding in 1846 of what became the Hakluyt Society, still publishers today of primary accounts of historic voyages and exploration.

Retracing your steps, and crossing both Oakley Square carriageways, reach a stretch of Crowndale Road once lined by a terrace named Thorney Place, named after the Duke of Bedford's estate in the Fens. Born at No.1 Thorney Place in 1863 was Ernest Claremont, one of ten children of the surgeon, and later vaccinator, Claude Clarke Claremont (p 120). Ernest was to become the only true partner of a certain Henry Royce. In 1884 the pair together founded F H Royce & Co., a firm making electric lamps and bells. Only two decades later, having turned to making motorcars, did Royce meet Charles Rolls, and when Rolls-Royce Ltd was formed in 1906, the two men were not partners but co-directors in a limited company.

Looming on the right today is 6- to 8-storey **Godwin Court**, one of two tall red-brick blocks erected by St Pancras Council in the 1950s to replace bomb-damaged houses, and taking its name from William Godwin (p 98). Located here in the 1960s was Camden's local children's library. Beyond is the slightly less lofty **Crowndale Court**, covering the site of another old terrace, called Wansford Place after a Russell estate near Peterborough.

Reach **GOLDINGTON CRESCENT**. Built on the eastern edge of a field called Little Fig's Mead, it took its name from a village near Bedford. The nearby horse trough was erected by the Metropolitan Cattle Trough & Drinking Fountain Association, along with a drinking fountain for humans, now long gone; the water for horses has been replaced by flowers.

Enter, and walk to the middle of, **Goldington Crescent Gardens**. The amorphous sculptures ahead, cast in aluminium in 2010 and entitled *Silver Clouds*, are the work of Robert Worley. One 19th-century source asserts that this spot was traditionally known as Gooseberry Green, and had reputedly been 'one of the worst resorts of bad characters'. The reason for the name is unclear. Did it simply reflect the green space's elliptical shape? Did gooseberries once grow here? Or were stalls selling gooseberry fools set up to tempt patrons of the Adam & Eve pleasure gardens opposite (p 37), just as they were near the their namesake at Tottenham Court (p 136), where the fabled Gooseberry Fair was held. Although the Crescent's first houses appeared only in 1849–50, its enclosure may have been laid out earlier, appearing on an 1834 map as an elliptical patch of green. Four years before that, a builder called Soward had been seeking leave to develop 'The Oval', as he called it. In 1854 an address in the Crescent was a temporary home to the St Pancras National School for Girls while it awaited completion of its new building.

Turn right to emerge from the Gardens into the Crescent itself, opposite the north end of Chalton Street. To your right, at **No.17** Goldington Crescent, is a new 2-storey block of flats completed in 2018. It replaces the post-WWII version of the Prince Alfred pub, named after Queen Victoria's second son, located before the war at No.13 Crowndale Road and when first built at the end of Wansford Place. Turn left along the Crescent, past **Nos.5-16**, the one range of houses here to survive heavy wartime bombing. These have been knocked together as flats, so that between the 12 addresses there are only five doorways; the Camden Council project won a Civic Trust award in 1961. Norah Murray (d.1989), who lived at **No.11**, was nicknamed the 'Russian Queen of St Pancras': recruited as a Soviet spy, she had been the first Russian war-bride to come to England in 1942.

Just around the next corner, at the end of Goldington Street (p 127), a locked metal gate guards an old alleyway that once led to a place of worship. Tucked away behind the Crescent, it was built in 1852 by Rev. James Nunn as a replacement for the old Baptist meeting-place in Chapel Street (p 71). The new Zion Chapel was later taken over by the Presbyterians, after the demolition of their Middlesex Mission hall (p 72), and served as their Goldington Crescent Church until their new 'Somers Town' building (p 118) was ready. The minister, Rev. W Ewart, was noted for the mission services he held in the railway arches on Pancras Road. From 1884 the Zion Chapel was occupied by the Aldenham Institute, founded in Aldenham Street (p 115) two years earlier, by the Rev. Woffendale, for the 'social, mental and religious improvement' of young men. Besides Bible classes and prayer meetings, it offered a wide range of sporting activities, and an educational programme covering subjects both academic and practical, from the '3 Rs' to violin-playing and plumbing. The institute closed in 1900, and the building was later acquired by the Unity Theatre (p 130).

Now complete your rounding of the Crescent and turn south along the west side of **PANCRAS ROAD**. The underlying field here was a narrow one called 'The Slip': bordering the flooding-prone River Fleet, it was doubtless often waterlogged. The houses later built along Old St Pancras Road were called Chenies Terrace (after a Tudor manor house in Buckinghamshire once owned by the Dukes of Bedford).

In 1864, the landlord of the Crown, which stood here on the corner at No.179, applied unsuccessfully to the Vestry to install a horse trough outside his pub, to cater for the increase in traffic along Old St Pancras Road after the removal of the turnpike gates which had stood outside the churchyard opposite. Traffic certainly did increase: by the next decade there was a regular omnibus service between Kennington and Kentish Town which passed along the road. This was soon supplemented by horse-drawn trams from Holborn, which continued north up Great (now Royal) College Street. When the line was electrified in 1909, a new link was installed along Crowndale Road enabling the trams to serve Camden High Street.

Overlooking Pancras Road today are two cliff-like blocks of flats, **Cecil Rhodes House** and **The Chenies**. Dating from 1948-50, both were designed for St Pancras Council by Thomas Sibthorpe; in both, the glass-fronted stairwells and lift-shafts serve as a pleasing vertical architectural feature. Cecil Rhodes

39 St Pancras Ironworks' patent coal-hole cover

House was briefly known as Grangefield, but the Council changed its mind. The local field name was transferred to a different block in Marquis Road (Camden Town), while the Pancras Road building was renamed in honour of the founder of Rhodesia, who raised the memorial to his local family in St Pancras Gardens opposite (p 35). In 1983 Camden councillors took exception to the colonialist name, proposing to rename the block again, a move scotched by objections from residents. Suggested replacement names had been Zimbabwe Court and Robert Mugabe House. Still known as Cecil Rhodes House, the block was home in 1986 to the journalist John McCarthy, shortly before his fateful journey to Beirut and his 4-year incarceration there as a hostage.

Part of its site was once occupied by the foundry at No.171 of Messrs Cottam & Cottam's St Pancras Iron Work Co. Described as iron founders and engineers, they were based here for well over 40 years, making all manner of iron products, from stable fittings and agricultural equipment to street furniture **[39]** and fencing. As engineers, they made road vehicles, and in 1907 exhibited their medal-winning 5-ton 'St Pancras Steam Wagon'. They also had a foundry in Belle Isle (p 61).

A square-cut opening through Cecil Rhodes House is on the line of a short pre-WWII street of 12 terraced houses called Chenies Place. Continue past The Chenies to reach its post-war substitute. Dating only from 1949, present-day **CHENIES PLACE** cut through the site of bombed Metropolitan Buildings, London's first ever purpose-built flats, and the capital's first block of 'model dwellings' for the 'deserving poor'. Financed under the system known as '5% philanthropy' (whereby subscribers received a modest dividend), they were built in 1847 by the Metropolitan Association for the Improvement of the Dwellings of the Industrious Classes, of which Dr Southwood Smith was a leading light. The architect was William Bonython Moffatt, once a partner of Sir George Gilbert Scott. The Buildings **[40]** comprised 110 two- or three-roomed flats, built as a range of eight distinct double houses, facing north onto Platt Street, with two projecting wings. The flats were built to a high standard: accessed from an internal staircase, each had running water, a scullery and WC. The rents were too high to attract the poorest people for whom the dwellings had originally been intended. Most early residents were respectable, better-off working people, and some were even middle-class. Robert Ablett, a porter's son, and the founder of the Royal Drawing Society, lived at No.108 Metropolitan Buildings in 1848-50. A mid-19th-century visitors' book includes the names of Prince Albert, Lord

40 Metropolitan Buildings, Pancras Square (drawing from *The Builder*, 1847)

Shaftesbury and the King of the Hawaiian Islands.

The Buildings' forecourt subsequently became known as Pancras Square – not to be confused with its present-day King's Cross Central namesake. In April 1941, a parachute mine landed in Pancras Square, causing 200 casualties and 77 deaths. The devastated Buildings were demolished, and the new Chenies Place was opened up across the site.

Crossing Chenies Place and continuing south along **PANCRAS ROAD**, we reach a stretch that formed the eastern boundary of the Brewers' (or Aldenham School) estate. In 1575, a benevolent London brewer called Richard Platt gave land he owned locally to endow a public school to be founded at Aldenham (Herts.), his birthplace. Described as 'all those 3 pastures of ground lying nighe the Churche of St. Pancrasse... containing an estimacion of 20 acres, more or less', the property was vested in the Brewers' Company as trustees. Its southeast corner, on the site of St Pancras Station (p 21), was the earliest to be developed for housing, from 1811. The later-built houses here, fronting onto Pancras Road, were known as Aldenham Terrace. At No.26 (later No.151) a Brewers' Arms public house stood on the corner of the now long extinct eastern extremity of Aldenham Street (p 115).

Here today, and now containing workshops, are the Gothic-style former offices of the Midland Railway's Purchese Street Coal Depot. The word 'Hope' is painted in large white letters on the parapet. Opened in 1898 and extending west to Purchese Street, the two-level depot covered seven acres. A bridge carried coal trains across Pancras Road to a fan of 11 elevated sidings, from which wagons were hauled by capstans to their final resting-place in one of the sidings ranged crosswise across the upper level. Pancras Road, hereabouts, was once spanned by no fewer than five railway bridges. Immediately after the coal depot bridge it passed under part of a viaduct leading to the Somers Town Goods Depot. A little to the south – before the remodelling of St Pancras Station and still following its traditional course – the road snaked through a gloomy chasm beneath three further bridges, two of them carrying trains in and out of the passenger terminus, and the third crossed by trains using the tunnel link to the Metropolitan Line (p 21).

Turn right into **BRILL PLACE** (p 101), near the corner of which yet another bridge delivered goods trains to their final destination in the Goods Depot then lining the street's south side. This eastern extremity of Brill Place began as Elstree Street, a cul-de-sac off Old St Pancras Road; the Brewers' Company was at first reluctant to join it to Phoenix Street (p 102), on the troubled Somers Town development to the west, although the link was eventually made. On the Brewers' Field to the north was an L-shaped street, whose two arms were called Stanmore Street and Watford Street, where building leases were let in 1824. Like Elstree Street, both took their names from places within a few miles of Aldenham. Watford Street was pulled down when the bridge into the Goods Depot went up, while Stanmore Street gave way a few years later to Purchese Street Coal Depot. This closed in 1968 and was, in turn, sometime later pulled down.

It was from Coal Depot's abandoned upper level that in May 1969 – and watched by an excited crowd on the roof of The Chenies – Tom Lecky-Thomson in his RAF Harrier jet took off, to land in Manhattan barely six hours later, and so win first prize in the *Daily Mail* Trans-Atlantic Air Race (see also p 74). By the following year, air travel from Somers Town was less frenetic. Installed on the coal depot's Phoenix Road (now Brill Place) frontage for much of the 1970s was the rather basic Euston Air Terminal of Britannia Airways; many a foreign package holiday began with a coach ride from here to Luton Airport.

Between 1978 and 1981 this east side of the depot site was redeveloped as Camden Council's **Coopers Lane Estate**. High-rise housing was by then out of favour, and the intention here was to create a more traditional street environment. **NEVILLE CLOSE**, the unlabelled service road immediately on the right, is named after the oft-mentioned reformer, Edith. Just beyond, turn north along a footway leading to **COOPERS LANE** itself. Lined by houses and blocks of maisonettes in brown brick, this is the estate's mostly pedestrian spinal route. The Lane has a tranquil, 'suburban' feel: much of the coal depot's Pancras Road frontage (out of sight to your right) was retained partly as a buffer against noise from the main road and railway. The Lane's name might commemorate the erstwhile Coopers Arms pub in nearby Polygon Road; or could equally honour the makers of wooden casks, once so essential to the brewing industry.

At a crossing of paths by a 'No Ball Games' notice, turn left through (here unlabelled) **HAMPDEN CLOSE**, whose name derives from that of former Hampden Street (p 117). At **No.2**, on the south side, as you emerge from the Estate, up a ramp, is the Estate's tenants' hall. Camden Council's proposals for Central Somers Town include the erection here of a new 3- and 4-storey block of flats around a community garden. On the north side is Clyde Court, 46 units of sheltered housing for the elderly. The block's name recalls the Lord Clyde pub, which once stood nearby at No.29 Phoenix Street, and whose sign honoured a veteran of the Crimean War.

Reach **PURCHESE STREET** (p 119), opposite the grounds of Edith Neville Primary School. The promised new school and children's centre (p 118) are to occupy this frontage. Turning right, we soon re-cross the line of the extinct eastern end of Aldenham Street (p 115). Its easternmost part was sacrificed to the coal depot, and the next section westward gave way to the present school. On the south side were its predecessors, the Aldenham Street Board Schools, opened in 1874. The architect was E R Robson, who designed several hundred buildings for the London School Board. George Girling, the headmaster in 1883, was the author of a textbook entitled *Outlines of the History of England.* Near the school, at No.49, was the 19th-century Aldenham Hall, used in the interwar years as a gospel hall of Christian Men's Union based in Chalton Street (p 96). The original No.16 had been the meeting-place in 1848 of the 'Camden Town' branch of the Mormon Church.

Continue north. The modern council flats on your left, Nos.9-15 Purchese Street, in stock brick and classically proportioned, harmonise nicely with the 19th-century houses in **GOLDINGTON STREET** ahead. Here, on the northwest corner of Chenies Place, is the modern **Doreen Bazell Hall**, its entrance topped by a miniature glass rotunda serving as a skylight. This is the tenants' hall for The Chenies and Cecil Rhodes House (p 124), of whose tenants' association the commemorated lady, who died in 1994, was a Secretary.

The east side of Goldington Street is dominated by the rear elevations of those two blocks of flats, with frontages on Pancras Road. Once standing almost opposite Platt Street was the Star public house at No.10, which functioned in 1866 as a music hall. The original houses here were built on Bedford land, but seem to have soon been sold to the Brewers' Company, the owners of the land on the opposite side. Surviving on the west side, beyond Medburn Street at **Nos.26-39**, is a pleasing terrace of renovated early-Victorian 3-storey houses, built in a style typical of the Brewers' estate. All have stuccoed rusticated ground-floor walls, round-arched doorways and ornamented cast-iron balconies, as specified by the Brewers' Company in its building leases.

Turn left into intersecting **MEDBURN STREET**, lined with similar houses on both sides and deriving its name from a farm at Aldenham. This part of the Brewers' estate was developed in 1849-54. Local 19th-century residents were typically upper-working or lower-middle class. On Charles Booth's 1898 poverty map, the locality was coloured pink, meaning 'fairly comfortable, good ordinary earnings'. Born at No.23 (on the left) was the songwriter and record producer Wally Ridley (1913-2007). Over the years he wrote a song for the 1937 film *Jericho*, starring Paul Robeson, coached a young Vera Lynn and found her the song *We'll Meet Again*, and was almost sacked by EMI for releasing Elvis Presley's 1956 hit *Heartbreak Hotel.* Very run-down after wartime bomb damage, the houses passed into the ownership of the Greater London Council (GLC). For a while in the early 1970s, some were colonised by squatters. At the time the Squatters Movement was very strong on the Brewers' estate. The Medburn Street houses were converted into flats and maisonettes as part of the GLC's 'rehabilitation' of the neighbourhood in 1972-73.

Halfway along, turn left into **PENRYN STREET**. Originally called Percy Street (for reasons unknown), it was renamed by the Metropolitan Board of Works in 1865 as part of a major exercise to reduce London's numerous street-name duplications. Many of the renamings were quite arbitrary: here, the new name was at least a partial anagram of the old. Penryn Street is delightfully intact, with two complete terraces of partly stuccoed houses, all retaining their decorative balconies. The four corner houses in the symmetrically designed street have porticoes. Stuccoed archways lead into secluded communal gardens, carved out of the houses' original private back gardens.

PLATT STREET, ahead, owes its name to the philanthropic brewer Richard Platt (p 125). Along on the left the street once continued east to meet Pancras Road, fronting Metropolitan Buildings but after WWII surrendered its eastern end to the grounds of The Chenies (p 124). On the north side are two further ranges of 3-storey houses in the, by now familiar, local style. In a squat here the former academic Robin Farquharson, author of the 1968 autobiographical book *Drop Out!* and a leading figure in the contemporary counter-culture, was badly burned in a fire in 1973; he was taken to the nearby Hospital for Tropical Diseases but died of his injuries. Two fellow squatters were convicted of his unlawful killing.

The houses on the opposite side have given way to the low-rise 1970s council flats of **Somers Close**. They cover the site of the former Somers Town Police Station, closed after nearly a century in 1946, and (on the southeast corner) the British Transport Commission's post-WWII St Pancras School for Apprentices.

Turn right to reach **CHARRINGTON STREET**, which took its name from the well-known brewing company (eventually merged with Bass). The east side of the street is lined by three pleasingly complete terraces dating from 1842-50, although here the original iron balconies have been lost and have plain modern replacements.

Firstly turn left, passing **Nos.1-17**. In the GLC's 1970s rehabilitation, each of the street's houses was divided into two maisonettes, and

41 Aldenham Street (1970), looking east towards the coal depot and railway lands gasholders, with Aldenham Hall on the right; on the corner at No.2 Charrington Street, funeral director H J Belch. Photo by Richard Lansdown

the street was renumbered, assigning a separate number to each. So, every door now bears two numbers. As part of Camden's strategy for Central Somers Town, this terrace is to be extended southward with three new-built houses, a belated replacement for the former Nos.2-6, demolished half a century ago. Ahead is the northern tip of Ossulston Street, as a continuation of which Charrington Street was built, and long since pedestrianised at much the same time as part of a traffic-calming measure.

Intersecting here until the 1960s was the former eastern part of Aldenham Street (p 115). On the southwest corner of the crossroads **[41]**, with an incongruously pastoral name, stood the Shepherd & Shepherdess pub at No.53. The next section of Aldenham Street westward survived as a footpath until 2018, when it was officially extinguished and absorbed into the Plot 10 redevelopment site (p 117). Housed alongside the path until autumn 2017, in temporary one-storey premises, was the now defunct St Aloysius Nursery; a 6- to 9-storey block of flats is to be erected in its place.

Turn round and walk back northwards beside the extensive campus of **Regent High School**. On the far side of its outdoor games area the community sports and youth centres (p 131) in Chalton Street which, like the nursery, were built in the grounds of the school, although not part of it. Around 1960 this large site was cleared, and in the process the entire west side of Charrington Street was demolished. Wholly expunged from the map were the 67 terraced houses of Barclay Street which, largely unscathed by the Luftwaffe, then still ran north-south across the site. Its name had derived from the brewing firm Barclay Perkins (later amalgamated with Courage). New school buildings were erected for the Sir William Collins Secondary School, until then housed in a Victorian building in Chalton Street (p 131). Its pupils would include Nasim Ali (OBE), who in 2003 became the first Bangladeshi Mayor of Camden and, at the age of 34, Britain's youngest ever mayor.

In 1991 it became South Camden Community School, where children and parents, from a multicultural and substantially Bangladeshi background, were to learn alongside each other. Tragically, in August 1994, Richard Everitt, a white 15-year-old pupil, on his way home was set upon by a gang of Bangladeshi youths, and stabbed to death. There was much racial tension in Somers Town at the time. The racially-motivated murder of a wholly innocent teenager shocked both white and Asian communities and prompted local groups to launch a Festival of Cultures aimed at bringing them together, and still flourishing today as START (p 98).

To counter 'negative perceptions', the school was again rebranded in 2012, as Regent High School, and then redeveloped at a cost of £25 million, with Walters & Cohen as architects. The cheerful multicoloured fins adorning the façade of the new main block (2014) are based on a music-to-colour synaesthesia of the song *Für Elise* by Beethoven. The new build included a theatre (p 131), drama workshops and studios, a large library and new science facilities. The school has 800 pupils, and partnerships with UCL, Rothschilds, and The Francis Crick Institute.

Pause opposite Medburn Street. Here before WWII, on the west side of Charrington Street, a 'Camden Gym' at the then No.57A offered courses in physical education. Earlier, in July 1881, the Brewers' Hall pub at No.59 played host to the Social Revolutionary & Anarchist Conference. Among those attending was the Russian scientist, philosopher and anarchist, Pyotr Kropotkin. The surviving terraces opposite appear somewhat grander than those in adjacent streets, each with a continuous stuccoed parapet and comprising 3½-storey houses (with semi-basements), designed for the slightly better-off with at least one servant. The two or three houses at the end of each symmetrical range have pedimented first-floor windows.

On the corner of **MEDBURN STREET**

(p 127), spot an antique blue metal street sign: marked 'Medburn Street NW', it must pre-date 1917, when postal districts were first numbered to speed the wartime mail. The street once continued part way across the Regent High School site to a right-angled junction with Barclay Street. Situated there was the entrance to the school's earliest predecessor, the Medburn Street Board Schools (p 131).

Northward along **CHARRINGTON STREET**, the novelist Doris Lessing lived in the 1960s at No.60 (now **Nos.47&48**), immensely proud of the central heating she had had installed. Other post-WWII Charrington Street residents included Charlie Charles (1945-90), drummer for The Blockheads, and the Australian actress and singer Laura ('Little Nell') Campbell while appearing in *The Rocky Horror Show* in 1973. Among the earliest inhabitants at No.74 (now **Nos.57&58**) was (Sir) George Samuel Measom, a wood engraver and compiler-publisher of railway guides and later treasurer of the RSPCA. The northernmost house, porticoed No.80 (now **Nos.63&65**) once housed the St Pancras Committee of the Charity Organisation Society (now Family Action), and in 1924 hosted the inaugural meeting of the St Pancras House Improvement Society (later SPH).

Today's *Camden City Learning Centre* opposite, another recent intruder onto the Regent High School site, offers computing curriculum support to all schools in the borough.

The T-junction ahead was once a crossroads. Charrington Street continued north across the site of towering Crowndale Court (p 123) to meet Crowndale Road. Once standing on the crossroads' northwest corner was Bedford New Town Chapel, erected by the Congregational Building Society and opened in 1851. The poet Robert Browning was a regular worshipper there for several years. Though restored in 1885, it was closed in 1908 and rebuilt as the Charrington Hall, successively home to a Conservative Club and, in 1930, to SPH's newly founded nursery school. From that same year it was licensed as a 'little' theatre. The St Pancras People's Theatre had been founded four years earlier at the Mary Ward Settlement in Tavistock Place by the energetic Edith Neville, who served as its director. Removed to the Charrington Hall, its repertory company staged three performances each week, with a change of programme weekly. Compared to that of the nearby, and unrelated, Unity Theatre (p 131), its repertoire was quite mainstream, including both light comedy and serious drama, from Shakespeare to Chekhov. The building was destroyed in an air raid in 1940.

Just short of Crowndale Road, behind No.93, was a small factory, which became the Crowndale Works of the Splinterless Anti-Mist Glass Syndicate and Life Saving Devices Syndicate; their 'Home Front' female workforce made gas masks there during WWI.

Having re-crossed the Brewers'-Bedford estate boundary, deviate eastward along a stretch of street that began in the mid-1840s as the *original* Werrington Street (cf. p 113), but is now a semi-detached part of **CHALTON STREET**. Along on the right is **Unity Mews**, a modern development of 15 houses and flats, built by SPH on the site of the old Zion Chapel (p 124). The Unity Theatre moved here in 1937, a year after its formation in Britannia Street, King's Cross. 400 volunteers collaborated in converting the old chapel for theatrical use. For some 40 years, the Unity **[42]** was renowned for its quality amateur productions of left-wing drama. It served as a training-ground for numerous well-known theatrical figures, including Lionel Bart, Alfie Bass, Michael Gambon, Bob Hoskins, David Kossoff, Warren Mitchell and Ted Willis. The black American singer Paul Robeson, then an international superstar, appeared at the Unity in 1938, unpaid and as an ordinary member of the cast. Renovated in 1966-68, the theatre was gutted by fire in 1975. By 1983 most of the company had dispersed, but productions continued at other venues, including the Lord Palmerston in Hampstead Road (p 137).
A circular plaque, recalling this 'theatre run for the people by the people' is mounted by the

42 Unity Theatre poster

entrance to Unity Mews, declared open in 1992 by Bill Owen, another of the theatre's 'alumni'.

Now turn and walk west, passing the site of the British Society's schools connected with the old Congregational chapel. Chalton Street soon becomes a footpath, following the southern pavement of old Werrington Street, whose roadway lies buried beneath a small football pitch in the grounds of Godwin Court (p 123). Until the 1960s the road continued straight ahead across the site of Mayford (p 132), but it now turns south as part of the more familiar section of Chalton Street.

On the near corner is the site of the Tavistock Arms, one of the two 'restaurant pubs' inspired by Basil Jellicoe (see also p 110). It was opened in that guise in April 1930 by Prince George (later Duke of Kent), who then walked up the street to the Anchor, accompanied by an enthusiastic crowd of locals. Less successful than its sister establishment, the Tavistock was soon forced to close when its manager Mr Sharpington fell ill and no replacement could be found.

Its site is now occupied by the 200-seat, state-of-the-art **Regent Theatre**, with a windowless, partly timber-clad façade, and belonging to **Regent High School** (p 129). Along on the left are the surviving Victorian buildings of its forerunner, the Medburn Street Board Schools. They first opened around the corner in Werrington Street in 1873, apparently taking over the British School there. Their next building, opened four years later, was approached from the east by Medburn Street (p 127), hence the schools' historically best-known name. The schools' frontage here in Chalton Street dates from 1880. A stone plaque, high up on the wall at the far end, records another of their several successive names. In 1904 they were renamed the Stanley Schools, after Lyulph Stanley (Lord Stanley of Alderley), the last vice-chairman of the London School Board. With 2,000 pupils and an annexe in Camden Street, they became the largest school in the borough, and before WWI also housed the St Pancras School of Art. The 'Stanley' name was subsequently dropped and transferred to the new Central Schools in Camden Street. A later 'Medburn Street' pupil was the singer Chris Farlowe (born John Deighton in 1940), whose hit single *Out of Time* topped the charts in 1966.

In 1958 the school became Sir William Collins Secondary School, named after the first chairman (in 1904) of the LCC's Education Committee, and soon expanded into its new premises off Charrington Street (p 129). The old Chalton Street building later became Camden Council's Medburn Centre, housing both education authority offices and the Somers Town Youth Club. Today it is once again part of the school behind, cleverly integrated by Walters & Cohen into the new Regent High School and lining one side of a top-lit, triple-storey internal 'arcade'.

On reaching the school's new entrance, 'flipped' here from Charrington Street, cross over and turn back north. Now converted into flats is the former Eastnor Castle pub (see roofline inscription), which closed in 2013.

Although its sign had depicted a medieval ruin on a coastal cliff-top, its name referred to Lord Somers' landlocked seat in Herefordshire, whose extravagant rebuild from 1812 was part funded by his Somers Town ground rents.

Before 1840, the original Union Street (p 109) terminated here. A turnstile at its dead end gave access to two official footpaths running diagonally across Fig's Mead to either end of what is now Crowndale Road; and to an unofficial path to Camden Street which locals used 'by sufferance' of the Duke of Bedford. Only people beating carpets were allowed to trespass on the ducal grass. Union Street was subsequently extended northward as Stibbington Street (named after a Russell property near Peterborough), which in turn became part of Chalton Street in 1937.

Next to the old pub, a closed gate protects the service road for Mayford (see later). Set in the brick wall along on the left is a now inaccessible stone plaque proclaiming that 'This fourteen-inch wall is the property of the Duke of Bedford, 1861'. The purposefully erected barrier was a potent symbol of the great social divide between the middle-class New Town and the Somers Town slums to the south. The gate also marks the site of vanished No.67 Stibbington Street, an early marital home of the Pearly King, Henry Croft (p 105) and his wife Lily.

Continuing north, bear left along a footpath, with one wing of lofty Godwin Court to your right. A ramp, beyond, leads up to the south side of **OAKLEY SQUARE** (also p 121). Turn left, and walk beside **Mayford**, entry to which is restricted by fob access gates. The labyrinthine complex of maisonettes, arranged in blocks lettered A to O, was completed by Camden Council in 1972. Despite a vigorous public campaign to save them, the houses it supplanted had been demolished c.1965. The roadway was adjusted to align with Lidlington Place (ahead), and now carries fast-moving southbound traffic emerging from the Camden Town one-way system.

Former residents (from northeast to southwest) included the printmaker and watercolourist John Wykenham Archer, who died in 1864 at No.31. The philosopher Herbert Spencer was living at No.24 in 1859 and Sidney Percival Bunting, who became a communist activist in South Africa, was born in 1873 at No.14. James Calkin, an organist and music teacher, whose organ transcriptions from the works of Mendelssohn were much admired, died in 1862 at No.12; his four musical sons included John Baptiste Calkin, a future organist at St Thomas' Church, Agar Town (p 65). Lenin occupied a flat at No.6 while on a visit to London in November 1911. No.1 was, from 1908, the headquarters of Magdalen College Mission (p 90), and served later as the first registered office of the St Pancras House Improvement Society. In 1912 the St Pancras (and Northern) Dispensary (p 81) moved to No.39 from Euston Road. Here it provided a specialist tuberculosis dispensary among other services; in the interwar period St Pancras Borough paid its staff.

On regaining Eversholt Street, notice that the stretch of road across on the right is actually labelled 'Oakley Square', and that porticoed **Nos.71-76** are numbered as the Square's west side. In the 1960s, **No.72** was the headquarters of International Voluntary Service.

To your left is a part of **EVERSHOLT STREET** originally named Crawley Street, after Husborne Crawley, a village 2 miles from Woburn Abbey. Mayford covers the sites of onetime Crawley Mews, and of the Duke of Bedford (aka Bedford Arms) which stood at No.204 Eversholt Street. Whereas pubs were a rarity on the Russells' Bloomsbury estate, in the New Town there were three, each with a family-related name.

Opposite, above shops, are **Holmrook flats**, of 1973. On the site of the convenience store at Nos.207-211, No.13 Crawley Street was the final home of Joseph Timothy Haydn. From Ireland and no relation to the composer, he is chiefly remembered as the compiler of the hugely popular *Haydn's Dictionary of Dates* (1841). Having fallen on hard times and after suffering a stroke, he was granted a Civil List pension of £25 a year (a 'paltry reward for merit' of 1s 4½d *per diem*, as a friend put it in a letter to *The Times*). Moving to No.13, ironically from Carey Street, he died here in poverty in January 1856. A personal gift of £100 from the Prime Minister, Lord Palmerston, had enabled Haydn's wife Mary to acquire the shop at No.13, where she scraped a living as a stationer and newsagent; one of her two boys did the paper round.

At the former No.219 Eversholt Street was a baker's shop long run by the Stanley family. With ovens extending beneath the pavement; this was reputedly, at the time of its closure in 1966, the last surviving underground bakery in the old borough of St Pancras.

Cross over to the north side of **LIDLINGTON PLACE**. The boxy Escape Sports Bar at No.2 opposite was built as an unworthy 1960s replacement for the Russell Arms in Barnby Street (p 115). Among the nine houses once standing on the south side, No.8 was home in 1859 to the marine painter Oswald Brierley. The portrait and subject painter Charles Baxter, whose work is represented in the V&A, lived at No.6 until a few months before his death in 1879.

Arriving at Harrington Square (see later), stop at its near (southeast) corner, where until 1893 stood another Bloomsbury-style bar-gate. From here, look across to the **Ampthill Square Estate**, a Camden Council development of the late 1960s designed by Eric Lyons & Partners. Security gates now limit public access. Although the eponymous Square has not existed for half a century, some flats on the Estate still have '**AMPTHILL SQUARE**' as their postal address. In the foreground are three 20-storey tower blocks, distinguishable only by their late-1980s trimmings in different primary colours, and immortalised in paint of a different kind by local (Mornington Crescent) artist Frank Auerbach – red-capped **Oxenholme**, yellow-trimmed **Dalehead**, and tucked behind them blue-topped **Gilfoot**. Dalehead overlooks a stretch of Hampstead Road (round the corner) once known as Bedford Place, with 12 terraced houses erected in 1838 by James Sim, the builder responsible for Bloomsbury's Woburn Square. A fire in Gilfoot in May 2011 destroyed two flats and caused the evacuation of 50 people. Tests on the blocks' external cladding in the wake of the Grenfell tragedy in North Kensington in June 2017 found it to be of 'solid aluminium' and so not a fire hazard. All three towers have Lake District names, Camden having continued the St Pancras Council policy of naming blocks in this part of the borough after Lakeland locations.

Also with Cumbrian names are the several low-rise, brick-built flats in the Estate's interior: **Mickledore**, **Glenridding**, **Calgarth**, **Stockbeck**, **Beckfoot** and **Brathay**. Swept away in their construction, despite fierce objection, was erstwhile Ampthill Square. Dating from 1844-53, this had been built on a part of the Duke of Bedford's Fig's Mead estate called Pond Field, lately farmed by the Rhodes family (pp 50 & 141). Thomas Stead's plan of 1826 (p 120) would have placed here an elongated square with rounded ends, on an axis linking Euston Grove (p 157) with Camden High Street. Haedy's 1834 revision proposed a 'Russell Crescent', aligned contrariwise SW-NE and flanking a through route from Hampstead Road to Camden Street. Linking the crescent to Eversholt Street would have been a short Cople Place (named after a Bedfordshire village where the Duke of Bedford owned land). With the advent of the London & Birmingham Railway, plans were changed once again. When the crescent finally materialised, it was as the slightly angular, inaccurately named Ampthill Square, after Ampthill Park, another ducal property in Bedfordshire. At their south end the Square's two carriageways crossed the railway cutting over brick arches, replaced in 1896 by girders. Much of the Square's east side was lined by carriage sheds of what had become the LNWR. Blighted by smoke from the railway, the central communal garden was perennially grimy.

The Square was once inhabited by a number of minor authors and artists, and several notable thespians. Among the latter was Frederick Robson, a master of burlesque at the Olympic Theatre, and resident at No.19 in 1859-64. Living at No.20 from 1904-13 was Rev. Silvester Horne, minister of the Whitefield Chapel in Tottenham Court Road, St Pancras councillor and later Liberal MP. The youngest of his seven children was the BBC radio comedian, and businessman, Kenneth Horne (1907-69).

At No.30, on Ampthill Square's east side **[43]**, lived the fraudster William George Pullinger. Employed as chief cashier by the Union Bank of London, he used a bogus pass-book to embezzle from them over £¼ million. After his conviction in 1860, he was lambasted by Charles Dickens in his periodical *All the Year Round.* Nine years earlier, Elizabeth Dickens, the novelist's newly widowed mother, had moved into nearby No.33 to lodge with a nephew. Another neighbour was the engraver William Holl the Younger installed at No.36. Next door at No.37, from 1857 until his death in 1874, was the actor (and child prodigy) William Henry West Betty, nicknamed the 'Young Roscius' after a sensational stage debut in 1802 at the age of 11. The actor and theatre producer Charles Farley, who had once mentored the pantomime clown Grimaldi, died in 1859 at No.42.

Running from the north end of the Square to meet Harrington Square (just south of where you stand), was the short street named Houghton Place, taking its name from Houghton House, a now ruined Russell property near Ampthill. Living at No.2 in 1861-65, with her thespian mother, was Ellen (Nellie) Ternan, the young actress with whom Charles Dickens had fallen passionately in love as his marriage failed and to whom he left £1,000 in his will. The house purchase had almost certainly been paid for by him. The same house was occupied in 1911-13 by the painter Spencer Gore. From a window or balcony there he painted several of his well-known works, including *Down the Garden* and *A London Sunset.*

HARRINGTON SQUARE took its name from

43 East side of Ampthill Square viewed from Houghton Place, 1900s (photo by E J Lambert)

Anna Maria Stanhope, daughter of the 3rd Earl of Harrington, who in 1818 married the 7th Duke of Bedford. Under the plans of both Stead and Haedy (p 120), the Square would have been a crescent, balancing Mornington Crescent (over to the left), across whose garden enclosure Carreras' Black Cat cigarette factory, now Greater London House, was controversially built in the 1920s. The Russells' new crescent was to be named Ridgmount Place, after Ridgmont *(sic)*, a village adjoining Woburn Park, their Bedfordshire seat. By the time it materialised, the crescent had changed both its name and its shape. The triangular gardens were laid out in 1843.

In spite of public protests, the Square's south side was pulled down by Camden Council in 1967-68. As in Oakley Square the roadway here was nudged southwards. Among the houses demolished was No.2, where Edward Doubleday, a renowned lepidopterist, died young in 1849. The author and journalist William Mudford had expired the previous year at No.5, having latterly edited the *John Bull* magazine. No.9 was home in the 1860s to the coal merchant and future MP, Samuel Plimsoll (p 48). The painter Walter Sickert lived at No.14 Harrington Square with his second wife Christine after their marriage in 1911. He and Gore were thus near neighbours when that year, with others, they established the Camden Town Group of artists. In 1877 another pair of newlyweds had turned up in Harrington Square in an overloaded cab. (Sir) Oliver Lodge, the physicist and pioneer of wireless telegraphy, stayed here with his artist bride Mary for only one night. The landlady took umbrage at the amount of luggage they'd brought and obliged them to move on.

Continue along Harrington Square's northeast side, where a terrace of original houses remains, part stuccoed and with Doric-columned porticoes, not all in good condition. **No.15** was home in 1855 to Dr John Saunders Muir, vice-principal of the North London Collegiate School for Boys. **Nos.17-18** have been knocked into one. No.18 was once the residence of Alexander Melville Bell (1819–1905), a Scottish-American elocutionist and phonetician who devised *Visible Speech*, a graphical representation of speech sounds based on the position of the vocal chords, used to teach the deaf to speak; Alexander Graham Bell, the telephony pioneer, was his son. E V Lucas, the journalist, essayist and *Punch* contributor, later lodged in the Square in 1892.

Hurdwick House flats were built by St Pancras Council on a site ravaged on one of the earliest nights of the Blitz. On 9 September 1940 a German bomb landed here, opening a crater in the road and famously up-ending a double-decker bus against the façade of the houses, three of which were destroyed. If you cross over into **Harrington Square Gardens**, the public gardens of the square, the first bench is dedicated to the memory of Pinkus Nierenstein and ten other people who died when the bomb struck. At No.35 most of his family perished but his daughter, Phyllis Hillel, had been evacuated. She was to win an Exceptional People in Camden award shortly before her death in 2006 for her tireless and selfless work with young schoolchildren.

North of the gardens is **HURDWICK PLACE**, a short surviving terrace of 4-storey houses facing onto the end of Hampstead Road, and named after a farm near Tavistock on the Bedfords' Devonshire estate. It leads us back to our starting-point at **Mornington Crescent Station**, which first opened on the 'Hampstead Tube' (now the Northern Line) in 1907. After a lengthy closure for refurbishment, it reopened in 1998, its oxblood-red tiles restored, and its interior tiling reproduced from Leslie Green's original designs. The reopening ceremony was performed by cast members of BBC Radio 4's *I'm Sorry, I Haven't a Clue*. They returned on 17 March 2002, unveiling a Comic Heritage plaque to the satirist Willie Rushton (1937-96), a past master of the programme's spoof parlour game, 'Mornington Crescent', which has brought national fame to this otherwise unsung part of north London.

All change at Euston

Serpentine circular walk from Warren Street Underground Station. Much of the area is affected by preparatory works for the High Speed 2 railway (HS2). The whole of our itinerary was open to pedestrians in early 2020, but if access arrangements change, the walker should heed the latest signage.

Emerging from Warren Street Underground Station, turn left. Cross straight ahead at the pedestrian lights and pause on the bridge above the Euston Road Underpass. Quite recently dubbed **EUSTON CIRCUS**, the wide intersection here dates only from the 1960s, when the underpass was created and this part of Euston Road was trebled in width. The two-lane westbound carriageway we just crossed reflects the previous width of the highway, which opened as the New Road in 1756. Here, where it crossed the ancient route north to Hampstead, were two pre-existing public houses. Respectively on the northwest and northeast corners at the crossroads were the Adam and Eve and the King's Head **[44]**. Both hostelries feature in Hogarth's 1750 painting of *The March to Finchley*, showing Grenadier Guards, in some disarray, setting off northward in 1745 to deal with Bonnie Prince Charlie. A rebuilt Adam & Eve survived, at No.284&286 Euston Road, until about 1961.

By that time this spot had become an important tramway terminus. Horse-bus services had run up Hampstead Road to Camden Town as early as the 1840s. Horse-drawn tramcars of the London Street Tramway Co. had arrived in 1871-72, when the single fare was 1d outside and 2d inside. Electric trams were introduced in 1909. Euston Road was as far towards the West End as 'working-class' trams were allowed to penetrate, and those running south from Camden Town and beyond came to an abrupt halt here at the south end of Hampstead Road, their so-called 'Tottenham Court Road' terminus.

Continuing across the second slip road, head towards a new local landmark: Gary Hume's vibrantly coloured, 20-panel *Pecking Bird* (2017), installed 14m above the pavement on the corner of Brock Street. Stop short of it, however, and pause again in the wide space on the present-day southwest corner of **HAMPSTEAD ROAD**.

The huge mirror-glass building on the opposite corner (see p 152) marks the probable site of the manor house of Tottenhall, also known as Tottenham Court. Excavation here in 1979 yielded evidence of early Saxon and 13th- and 14th-century activity. Also found were remains of medieval and Tudor walls and a garderobe pit, part either of the manor house or of the adjoining Tudor farmhouse. The former has been depicted as a very slender building of timber and brick, standing in 1½ acres of ground with an orchard, and surrounded by a moat. A plan by William Necton dated 1591 shows the house as belonging to the Crown. Occupants included Daniel Clarke, Master Cook to Queen Elizabeth. The manor later passed into the hands of Charles FitzRoy, Lord Southampton, in one corner of whose 'Southampton estate' the streets we are about to explore were first developed, mostly in the early 19th century. The manor house – which was demolished in 1808 – was popularly known as 'King John's Palace', though there is no evidence that the Plantagenet king ever lived here.

For 18th-century Londoners Tottenham Court was a favourite rural retreat, surrounded by pleasant meadows and country lanes. At Easter and Whitsuntide the rural calm was shattered by the Tottenham Court Fair, which spread itself southward along Tottenham Court Road, then a lane lined by hawthorns. Notorious for its 'vice and immorality', the fair featured bear-baiting, bull-fighting, penny theatres and boxing-booths (with female boxers); while 'stalls of gooseberry-fool vied with 3d [threepenny] tea-booths'. Suppressed by Parliament in 1808, the event was later revived as a slightly less rowdy Gooseberry Fair.

It is time to strike north along Hampstead Road. Although in this book we focus on the even-numbered east side, we will walk up the west side, observing the buildings opposite.

Swept away during and after the Euston Road widening were Nos.2-38. Photographed by Ernest Milner in 1903 was the shop of Grafton Dairies at No.26. Adjacent was the covered entrance to Grafton Yard, occupied by a succession of cowkeepers in Victorian times and by a cream dealer in 1898. Originally built beside the eponymous public house in Palace Row (p 152), the yard was at first known as Grafton Head Yard.

44 No.2 Hampstead Road and the Old King's Head, and on the right the junction with a narrow and barely visible Euston Road (photo Ernest Milner, 1903)

The present-day east-side numbering in Hampstead Road begins at No.40. At Nos.50&52, beneath 1980s social housing, is the Hopscotch Asian Women's Centre. The name comes from a club founded by the Save the Children Fund in 1943 to offer activities for orphaned and homeless children. In 1982 the club's Hopscotch name and its premises, a derelict butcher's shop in Eversholt Street, were taken over by the present charity, which having moved to Hampstead Road by way of Phoenix Road (p 102), continues to offer help and support to mostly Bangladeshi women and their families.

With Tolmers Square (p 150) to the rear, the original terrace here was briefly known as Tolmer(s) Place. In 1863 all the named terraces that lined the main road were numbered as part of Hampstead Road, with even numbers on the east side. At No.42B in the 1890s was the factory of harmonium manufacturer Richard Franklin Stevens. By 1920 the Western Skin Hospital was at Nos.44&46; founded as a dispensary in 1851, and moved here from Great Portland Street, it closed in 1948. Among the great variety of useful shops that once lined both sides of Hampstead Road was that of linendraper Tom Boocock at Nos.52-58.

Reach the junction with Drummond Street (p 147). On the southeast corner at **No.60** Hampstead Road, dating from at least 1869 but closed by 1984, is the very run-down former Lord Palmerston pub. The high-level fascia lettering 'Truman, Hanbury, Buxton & Co.', and the pub name below, were re-exposed in 2015, after the departure of a Chinese medicine centre that had substituted its own signage. On the ground floor is the Camden People's Theatre, founded here in 1994 by a splinter group from the Unity Theatre (p 130), with the aim of working with 'traditionally disenfranchised groups' and being affordable for local people. It had help from the West Euston Partnership, and attracted funds from Sir John Gielgud, Bob Hoskins and large corporate organisations.

Opened in 2010 on the opposite corner at **Nos.62&64** was the Green Light Pharmacy, previously three doors away in Drummond Street. The modern fascia bears the legend 'Laurence Corner', in memory of the Army Surplus store of that name which had traded here for 54 years until its closure in 2007. It also had a fancy dress department, from which were sourced the outfits that inspired the uniforms worn by the Beatles on the cover of their *Sergeant Pepper* album. The shop was a haunt of various other well-known pop stars, and fashion designers such as Vivienne Westwood, and provided some of the props for *Star Wars*.

Crossing Drummond Street, walk on along

the west side of Hampstead Road. The dental practice opposite at **No.66** fronts a gem of a 4-storey house, a remarkable survival of the late Georgian terraces that once line the road. In the 1990s it housed the Ethiopian Community in Britain, an organisation now relocated to West Hampstead.

Beyond is 1980s social housing accessed from George Mews (p 150). The original terrace here was known until 1863 as St James' Place. Living there at No.4 in 1851 was the copper-and steel-plate printer Thomas Ross, whose firm, founded in 1833, became famous for its fine art reproductions. Its co-founder had been Thomas Dixon, who lived next door at No.3 (which became No.70 Hampstead Road). Apprenticed to the firm was his nephew, the photographer Henry Dixon, best known for his work for the Society for Photographing Relics of Old London.

Sharing No.4 in 1851 were the fruit and flower painter Anne Gaugain, and probably her husband, the portrait painter Philip Augustus Gaugain (though he was recorded elsewhere on census night). The same house had earlier been home to the funerary sculptor Charles Regnart (no relation to Sir Horace, p 146), whose work can be found in churches and cathedrals nationwide, and in Jamaica. On the death of his first wife he had married Jane, the family cook, and around 1817 set up home with her at No.4.

45 Celebrity pugilist Bill Richmond

Living at No.6 in the mid-1840s was the artist Edward Henry Corbould; the son-in-law of the engraver Charles Heath (p 83), he was later to serve for 21 years as historical painting instructor to the Royal Family.

Having crossed William Road and then Netley Street, pause on reaching Prince of Wales Passage. Opposite is a red-brick building at No.108, a former orphanage to which we will return (p 142). Until recently, a path to the left of it led into the lamented St James' Gardens, originally the overspill burial ground of St James', Piccadilly. The first burial on the 4-acre site took place in 1790.

Notables buried here included the local landlords, Charles and George FitzRoy, 1st and 2nd Barons Southampton; Lord George Gordon, who had infamously incited the anti-Catholic Gordon Riots in 1780; the explorer Matthew Flinders (p 159); the dissolute artist George Morland and his wife; and John Hoppner, the portrait painter. A local worthy also buried here was John Leverton, founder of the funeral directors (p 121), who died in 1843 aged 80.

The bare-knuckle fighter Bill Richmond **[45]** was born a slave in New York in 1763. He came to England in 1777, where his education was paid for and he eventually married an Englishwoman, living first in Yorkshire and later in London. Nicknamed 'the Black Terror', he won all but two of the 19 bouts in his boxing career. Becoming the world's first black sporting celebrity, he mixed with the nobility, and was one of the pugilists chosen to act as ushers at the coronation of King George IV. Dying in 1829, Richmond was buried at St James', Hampstead Road.

Closed in 1853, the burial ground lost a quarter of its area when in 1883 the London & North Western Railway was empowered to acquire an acre on the eastern side, for a westward expansion of Euston Station. The St Pancras Vestry then obtained powers to acquire the remaining ground and lay it out as a public garden. St James' Gardens were formally opened in 1887 by Olive, wife of Harry Lawson, then the Liberal MP for St Pancras West (and later, as Viscount Burnham, involved in formulating the

Burnham Scales for teachers' pay). Most of the gravestones were moved to the perimeter, where a few survived, along with a handful of more substantial monuments. One of these was an obelisk topped with a Celtic cross **[46]**, commemorating members of the Christie family, including James Christie (d.1803), the founder of the world-famous auction house.

The announcement that St James' Gardens were to be destroyed, to make way for new HS2 platforms at Euston, sparked vociferous local protest. Objectors decried the threatened loss of a valued green space and the proposed felling of numerous mature trees in an area with a high level of air pollution. Their campaign ended in 'yarn-bombing' – wrapping long hand-knitted scarves around the trunks of trees to signal their impending fate.

46 The Christie family monument in the now destroyed St James' Gardens (photo Stephen McKay)

Nevertheless, the site was flattened in 2018 and archaeologists, within a huge white marquee, began work on exhuming up to 60,000 bodies for reburial in consecrated ground elsewhere.

We will venture no further north along Hampstead Road, the eastern side of which has become one vast HS2 demolition site. To read about the complex history of the cleared area, you may wish to rest on one the benches conveniently sited beyond Robert Street beneath a prominent willow tree.

Just north of here stood the Hampstead Road turnpike (or tollgate), as depicted in a cartoon by Thomas Rowlandson **[47]**. Also shown is St James' Chapel. Set back from the main road, designed by Thomas Hardwick and consecrated in 1791, this was the chapel of the adjacent burial ground. Notable organists here included (Sir) George Smart from 1796, later personally acquainted with Beethoven, and the conductor of the first English performance of the latter's 9th symphony. Another was Samuel Sebastian Wesley (1810-76), thought to have been born at the southwest end of Hampstead Road, at No.11 Adam's Row, a natural son of the composer Samuel Wesley (1766-1837) and his housemaid. Trained as a child chorister, Samuel Sebastian was appointed organist at St James' when aged just 15. In 1864 the chapel was relinquished by its mother church in Piccadilly, becoming the parish church of a new local ecclesiastical district. In 1879 the novelist George Gissing was married to Nellie Harrison at St James' Church. Declared redundant, it was closed in 1954 and demolished ten years later.

47 The Hampstead Road Turnpike, looking south; St James' Church with its cupola, centre left (Thomas Rowlandson, 1798)

Initially built north of the church, and eventually wrapping round it, was the National Temperance Hospital. In the face of antagonism from many in the medical profession, apothecary Dr C H Yewen had suggested founding a temperance hospital in which the use of alcohol would be discouraged. In 1873, the London Temperance Hospital admitted its first patients to premises at No.112 Gower Street, with 12 beds. Funds subsequently raised enabled purchase of the Hampstead Road site. The east wing, designed by F R Barker of Manchester as a 2-storey pavilion-style building with 100 beds in wards arranged north-south (for sunlight), was opened by the Lord Mayor of London in 1881. The west wing was opened in 1885 by the Bishop of London, Frederick Temple. Patients were accepted from all parts of the UK; and as the first hospital ever of its kind, it attracted international interest. One of the fundraisers for the hospital in its early days was the first Pearly King, Henry Croft (p 105). Wards were named after major donors, as in 1892 when the Duchess of Westminster opened the Grosvenor children's ward.

In 1928 a new nurses' home was built as a memorial to a former Lord Mayor of London and Privy Councillor, Sir Thomas Vezey Strong. In 1932 the hospital was renamed, as the National Temperance Hospital (NTH). Opened that year was the Insull Memorial Wing at No.110 Hampstead Road, designed by William Binnie, later the architect of the east stand of Arsenal's former Highbury Stadium. $160,000 had been donated to the hospital by the Chicago businessman Samuel Insull, the London-born son of a Congregational minister and temperance advocate. His American business empire, founded on electrical utilities and rail transport, was soon to collapse, and he died penniless on a Paris Métro station in 1938. A glazed corridor was installed to link the Insull Wing with the hospital's older buildings, bridging the entrance to its courtyard, which was also used by churchgoers until St James' was finally pulled down. During WWII, the NTH served as a casualty station. After bomb damage – sustained in October 1940 and three times in 1941 – patients always returned within a few days; sadly, in January 1941, a cleaner nicknamed 'Tom Thumb' was killed.

The coming of the NHS in July 1948 saw the transfer of the NTH to the North West Metropolitan Regional Hospital Board, under the care of the Paddington Group Hospital Management Committee. Although Ministers of Health were sympathetic to retaining the hospital's name and identity, subsequent health policies and reorganisations led to a dwindling in patient numbers. In 1968, the hospital came under University College Hospital (UCH) management and its casualty department was closed. Closure as an acute hospital came in 1990. The buildings were used thereafter as offices by UCH and for local health service clinics, and latterly as a local base for the developers of HS2.

Housed in a box-like temporary building on the site is the **HS2 in Camden** Information Centre. A small pop-up skip garden alongside, with historical display boards and two memorial stones from the NTH, closed in February 2019 but another site was found for it further north on the west side of Hampstead Road.

The next traffic lights northward mark the junction with former **Cardington Street**, now reduced to an access road for HS2 lorries. The street was begun on the southern edge of the Duke of Bedford's estate (p 120), hence its name, derived from a ducal property near Bedford. When the London & Birmingham Railway out of Euston was constructed, landowners insisted that bridges be built to carry as yet undeveloped streets across the line. One such was Wriothesley Street, intended to run diagonally from the junction of Hampstead Road and Cardington Street, meeting today's Eversholt Street opposite what is now Polygon Road. (Wriothesley was the family name of the 17th-century Earls of Southampton, whose Bloomsbury estate the Russells acquired by marriage.) According to a map of 1843 the street had by then become a more pronounceable Willington Street, renamed after a village near to Cardington where the Duke of Bedford was Lord of the Manor. When in 1845-46, extra tracks were added to the railway out of Euston, the 'Wriothesley Street Bridge' was pulled down and the eponymous street was closed, apparently with no houses built, not having appeared in any contemporary parish rate-book.

Subsequently built along part of its course, off the north side of Cardington Street, was a short, and short-lived, terrace of houses named Birchmore Place (or Terrace), after another of the Duke's fiefdoms, the manor of Birchmore (or Birchmoor) adjoining Woburn village.

The southern (Southampton estate) side of Cardington Street was once a hive of industry. The directory listing in 1846 included a coachmaker (James Wright), a coach painter (James Lemmon) at No.6 and the coach factory of David Ivall at No.18½. The wood engravers John Jackson and Mason Jackson were at No.12 from 1846-63: John had learned his craft from Thomas Bewick in his native Northumberland, later trained his brother, and both were prolific in work for books and periodicals. Daniel Fryer and Henry Jacobs, pianoforte makers, had workshops at No.24½. Several prominent makers of stained-glass windows were at No.24A: Abate & Clerville and Clayton & Bell being joined there (c.1858) by Heaton & Butler, and in 1862 by Robert Bayne. At the same address were Rand & Co., makers of metallic collapsible tubes for artists' colours; having patented his invention in London, the American artist John Goffe Rand (1801-73) moved his firm from Fitzrovia to Cardington Street in 1848, staying here for 20 years. A Fitzroy Arms pub at No.19 became No.42 when the street was renumbered in 1874. On the corner beyond, where L-shaped Cardington Street turned south to meet Melton Street (p 148), was the large works of McCorquodale & Co., once well known as printers to the rail industry, producing tickets, timetables and posters. They sold up in 1966. Later occupying the war-damaged site was the Thistle Euston (formerly Kennedy) Hotel, in a forbidding grey 1970s building.

On Hampstead Road, north of erstwhile Cardington Street, the whole east-side frontage has vanished. No great loss to the streetscape was the monotonous range of post-WWII buildings at Nos.132-142, which served as a warehouse and offices of British Home Stores. In 2010 Derwent London, the buildings' new owners, were granted planning permission for redevelopment of the site with a mixed-use development of offices, described as a 'White Collar Factory' and a tall wedge-shaped apartment block at the north end. This scheme had to be abandoned when the site was required by HS2. The block was subsequently let to UCL as a temporary home for The Bartlett, its faculty of the built environment. In early 2017 the freehold of the site, and of the petrol station just beyond, was sold to the Department for Transport for around £130 million. In the 'Euston Stations Masterplan' published in late 2017 by the Greater London Authority (GLA), land thereabouts is earmarked for a new 'North City Park'.

Historically, this frontage lay on the western edge of Pond Field (or Close) on the Duke of Bedford's local estate (p 120). The meadow (see inside front cover) had long been farmed, along with nearly 300 acres elsewhere in the parish, by the influential Rhodes family. William Rhodes, who came to London from Staffordshire in 1720, became an Overseer of the Poor. His grandson Thomas, a notorious St Pancras vestryman, was the great-uncle of the colonialist Cecil Rhodes (p 35). Dairy cows still grazed in Pond Field when the young Charles Dickens was a pupil at the Wellington House Academy across the road. By the mid-19th century the remaining local farmland had given way to house-building.

Built north of Cardington Street was a short terrace named Maulden Row, after a village near Ampthill (Beds.). James Francis Danby, an artist noted for his paintings of sunrise and sunset, was at No.9 in 1848. Surviving beyond was the farmhouse of 'Rhodes' Farm', actually more like a gentleman's villa. This became No.138 Hampstead Road, and by 1860 was one of several local premises of Henry Brooks & Co, makers of piano actions. A decade later, pianoforte makers George Challenger & Co. were listed at Nos.136&138. The little industrial enclave to the rear was officially named Wembley Yard in 1909, for reasons unknown. Meanwhile, No.138 Hampstead Road had become the West St Pancras Conservative Club. During WWII the former farmhouse was bomb-damaged 'beyond repair', to be marked as a 'ruin' on a post-war map. Left intact, at nearby No.130, was the Sultan, a longstanding beershop turned pub.

Beyond was the exceptionally wide entrance to Ampthill Square (p 133), on the north corner of which was a substantial detached house (No.1). Based here from 1912 was the School for Mothers (p 100), later to evolve into the St Pancras Maternity & Child Welfare Centre.

Northward was a short terrace named Ridgmount Place, after Ridgmont *(sic)*, a village on the Duke of Bedford's Woburn estate. 'Ridgmount House' at No.1 was the final home of Lt-Col Robert Batty FRS, an army officer wounded at Waterloo; also an amateur artist noted for his paintings of continental scenes, he died here, paralysed, in 1848. Renumbered as No.140 Hampstead Road, the house was acquired in 1910 by the artist Walter Sickert, who moved his etching school here from No.209 (just opposite). In homage to the Georgian caricaturist Thomas Rowlandson (p 139), he renamed the building Rowlandson House. He entrusted management of the school to one of his pupils, Madeleine Knox, who put her own money into the enterprise but, aged only 20, was unable to cope with Sickert and soon gave up. The baton passed to her fellow pupil, the older and more resilient Sylvia Gosse (1881-1968), later well-known as printmaker and painter. Miss Gosse became Sickert's business partner and managed the etching school until its demise in 1914.

Four doors away, No.148 had been home to the line engraver Edward Goodall; the father of the better-known painter Frederick Goodall RA, he died there 1870.

We will now resume our walk, returning south to the pedestrian lights by Prince of Wales Passage. Cross over to reach the red-brick Edwardian Baroque building at **No.108 Hampstead Road**, also known as St James' House. As a (damaged) inscription still declares, this once housed the St Pancras Female Orphanage & Charity School, founded in 1776 'to maintain, clothe, educate and train for domestic service' female orphans belonging to the parish. Its original building on the site was erected in 1790 on land donated by the ground landlord, Lord Southampton. The 1881 Census records 42 'inmates' in residence, with their Matron, 29-year-old Fanny Turner. The foundation stone of the replacement building was laid in 1904 by the 4th Baron Southampton and the vicar of St Pancras, the Rev. Henry Luke Paget. The architects were E W Hudson and S G Goss. In 1930 there were still 46 girls in the orphanage, which was sold to the NTH in 1945 and subsequently passed to the NHS. A Drug Dependence Clinic was started in 1971, also working with problem drinkers. The building now houses local health service administration offices, and the Margarete Centre which runs several health clinics.

The neighbouring Euston Saree Centre at **No.100** occupies the only shop unit provided in the 1980s redevelopment of the southward stretch of Hampstead Road, once lined by small shops of many kinds. Notice the adjacent old St Pancras lamp-post, a rare survival.

Once running east from this point was Little George Street, a long cul-de-sac of terrace houses, passing the north end of Cobourg Street (p 147), as a continuation of which it was renamed in 1911. The street was shaded black on the Booth's poverty map, as being of the very poorest class. His researcher described it as 'dirty and squalid', with 'sodden looking women talking at the doors, a pitch and toss lot', and 'plenty of beer and fried fish'. There was a beerhouse at No.52. The street was destroyed in a pre-WWII northward extension to Starcross School (see below).

Take the left fork into a pedestrianised section of **NORTH GOWER STREET**. The road was originally called George Street, probably after George FitzRoy, 2nd Baron Southampton. During the 1820s it was known as Great

48 Sir Edward Pellew, later 1st Viscount Exmouth, by Thomas Lawrence c.1797

George Street. Listed in the 1851 Census at long-vanished No.52 on the left was Henry Haynes, a gilder aged 53, employing six men; the artist John Powell Frith used Haynes as a frame-maker. Opposite, the then No.33 George Street was home in the mid-1850s to the geographer and cartographer Ernst Ravenstein, who founded the German Gymnasium (p 23). Where the pedestrian section ends, to our right, is an entrance to George Mews (p 150).

Pause here to look east along the turning to our left, **STARCROSS STREET**. Originally named Exmouth Street after Admiral Lord Exmouth **[48]**, a hero of the Napoleonic Wars, it was renamed Starcross Street in 1937, after a Devon village facing the *town* of Exmouth across the Exe estuary. Police Inspector Wait told Booth's researcher that the street 'really wants three men to look after it – not so much criminal as rowdy and drunken, with boys gambling at the corner'.

For a century the north side of Starcross Street was occupied by a collection of school buildings. Pulled down to make way for the earliest of them had been Little Exmouth Street, a north-south link between Little George and Exmouth Streets that Booth had described as likewise extremely poor. The first school building was opened by the LCC in 1916, as its Exmouth Street Myopia School (for myopic boys). In 1937, it was recommended that the name be changed to Starcross LCC School for Boys, only for the senior boys to be moved to Medburn Street (p 131) the following Easter, and senior girls to move in from nearby Stanhope Street School. On the outbreak of WWII, the girls were evacuated to schools in Bedford and Ickleford (near Hitchin), but Starcross reopened in January 1940 as an emergency school for children remaining in London. After the war it became Starcross (Senior Girls) School with 289 pupils. A post-war increase in pupil numbers led to the older girls moving in 1959, a mile southeast to a new building in Sidmouth Street, taking the 'Starcross' name with them at the teachers' insistence. In the early 1990s, Camden Council granted a 30-year lease of the North Gower/ Starcross Street site to Maria Fidelis Catholic School as an annexe housing its Lower School. This relocated in 2019, joining the Upper School in its new premises in Drummond Crescent (p 92). Though the site was intended to become an open space, replacing some of that bulldozed locally by HS2, a planning application reported in September 2019 was for its redevelopment as a training centre for HS2 construction workers, with a community hall and only a small amount of green space.

At the far end of Starcross Street and preserving the street's original name, the **Exmouth Arms** pub was rebuilt following WWII bomb damage, and has miraculously escaped erasure by HS2. Opposite the pub at a former No.23 was the warehouse of cable manufacturers Connolly's (Blackley) Ltd, who despite their important export role were refused permission to redevelop. Although the local Initial Development Plan of the 1950s had zoned the area for commerce and permitted the development of warehouses, repositories and wholesale trade, the Plan was amended in the 1960s, re-zoning the neighbourhood as 'West End'. At the time, No.23 was the only property in the street not to have been bought up by Joe Levy (p 151). The south side of Starcross Street comprises two ranges of 4-storey terraces in different-coloured brick, one of Renton Howard Wood Levin Architects (RHWL)'s several attractive developments for Camden Council. Here too is one entrance to the three addresses in **EXMOUTH MEWS**. The small modern brick building at the western end of Starcross Street is the entrance to the **Shahjalal Jame Masjid E-Noor (Euston Mosque)**. It is numbered 204A North Gower Street, but also occupies Nos.202&204. Continue south along **NORTH GOWER STREET**, most of whose early-19th-century buildings are Listed, being noteworthy for the variety of their balcony and railing designs. As a London Borough of Camden green plaque testifies, **No.200** (on the even-numbered east side) was the workplace of the West Indian physician and civil rights campaigner Lord Pitt of Hampstead (1913-94); his surgery occupied the ground floor from 1950 for 34 years. The basement served, in 1959-60, as the HQ of the fledgling Anti-Apartheid Movement. The North Gower Hotel at **Nos.190-198** occupies what were once five houses. **Nos.231&233**, opposite, is a post-WWII block replacing demolished houses and seeming to blend in well with both its Georgian and newer neighbours.

George Street was renamed in 1937 as a northern continuation of Bloomsbury's Gower Street. The 'North' prefix was added to the name in 1966, after the Euston Road underpass severed the two parts of the street, but the 3-digit Gower Street numbering was retained. **Nos.203-209**, on the southwest corner at the crossroads, has in recent years been turned into flats. In the 1990s and early 2000s, it was Al-Ahram House, the London office of the Cairo-based Arab newspaper, and before that, as Drummond House, housed offices of the Transport & General Workers' Union (TGWU, now Unite).

On the other side of North Gower Street, **Nos.184-188** in yellow stock brick are notable for their cast-iron balconies and railings with flame finials, and form an attractive group with the Crown & Anchor pub (p 149). At the end of the 1970s, No.188 housed the offices of SWAPO: the South West Africa People's Organisation of Namibia. Behind its narrow plate-glass front **No.180** is home to the law practice Hodge, Jones & Allen LLP, founded in 1977 by Henry Hodge, Peter Jones and Patrick Allen; its first offices were in Camden High Street. The firm has represented victims of the King's Cross fire (1987) and the *Marchioness* disaster (1989). Previous occupants included the advertising firm Mediacom. To the rear in mid-Victorian times was a large sawmill belonging to Henry Hopton, 'timber bender'.

Stand at the corner with Euston Street to look at **No.195**, which might easily be dismissed as routine 1960s, but in fact dates from 1938-39. A building ahead of its time, it was designed by Maxwell Fry (a specialist in social housing), its blue panels a then innovative use of colour. The block was built as one of several houses for homeless young women run by Cecil Houses, a charity founded (in Boswell Street, Holborn) in 1926-27 by Mrs Cecil Chesterton, journalist, drama critic and author of *Darkest London.* The building has for some time been a UCL hall of residence, Prankerd House, presumably named after Professor Thomas Prankerd, clinical haematologist, author of *The Red Cell*, and a former Dean of the college's Medical School.

Past the first of two approaches to Tolmers Square (p 150), original early-19th-century houses survive at Nos.185-191, with particularly fine continuous cast-iron balconies. From 2010, the doorway adjoining Speedy's Café at **No.187** posed as that of No.221B Baker Street in the filming of the cult TV series *Sherlock*. The Café has become something of a tourist destination, with the owners reporting a huge increase in sales and also in post addressed to Mr Holmes. **No.185** bears a blue LCC plaque to the exiled Italian patriot Giuseppe Mazzini, who lodged here when he first arrived in London in 1837 and was working as a journalist; at that time, this house was No.9 George Street. Living here with him until 1840 were three compatriots: the poet Giovanni Ruffini, who drafted the libretto of Donizetti's opera *Don Pasquale*, his brother Agostino and the writer Angelo Usiglio. In 1835 the Glaswegian portrait and figurative sculptor Patric Park had established a studio next door at No.8 George Street (now **No.183**); his bust of Napoleon III is in the V&A.

Continue past Euston Street and Stephenson Way, just beyond which on the corner of Euston Road, is the Euston Square Hotel at Nos.152-156 North Gower Street, whose iron railings have been preserved. Known as the Gower Hotel before WWII, the building later became the Gower Hostel of University College Hospital.

Demolished houses opposite included No.171, which as No.4 George Street was the hospital's birthplace. Founded in 1828 as the North London Dispensary, to provide clinical experience for UCL medical students, it remained here for six years while funds were raised for a purpose-built hospital to be erected to the south in Gower Street, opposite the parent college. At No.2 George Street, around 1824, was the engraver John Henry Robinson, one of nine engravers who petitioned the House of Commons in 1836 to investigate the state of engraving in Britain; he eventually became a Royal Academician in 1867.

Retrace your steps and turn right into L-shaped, still partly cobbled **STEPHENSON WAY**, named after Robert Stephenson, the celebrated civil and railway engineer. The street's east-west section was originally called Southampton Mews. Off its north side until at least 1835 was an early National School, associated with St Pancras New Church and reported in 1819 to have been 'lately established ... for the education of 1,400 children'. Nearby was the livery yard of Aldridge's, the once famous horse mart based in Upper St Martin's Lane, near Seven Dials; its premises here were auctioned off in 1869.

The street was renamed Euston Buildings in 1882. Seven blocks of working-class housing were erected on the south side, named after royal dukes and owned by the Castle Martin Trust. On their site today is the back of the former Cambridge University Press block in Euston Road (p 154), which retains the publisher's coat of arms. The north side of the street was once synonymous with furniture making: **Nos.24-32** was Maple's bedding factory until its closure in 1972, after which it became well-known as the Charity Centre, housing the Institute of Family Therapy, various mediating bodies and the National Training Organisation, and the Directory for Social Change (which began in Hampstead in 1977). A planning application was lodged in mid-2018 for a 7-storey block if student accommodation on the vacant plot opposite Nos.24-32 (which is behind Nos. 210 and 222 Euston Road).

No.22 is the national office of the GMB union; it has recently been named Mary Turner House, in memory of the Union's President who died in 2017. Now based at **No.18** is the Royal College of Ophthalmologists, the professional body for medically qualified ophthalmologists; founded in 1988, it was previously in Cornwall Terrace, Regent's Park. No.18 had been home to Arthritis Care, which has since moved to Saffron Hill. A fairly recent newcomer at **No.14** is the Royal Asiatic Society, a forum for those 'interested in the languages, cultures and history to meet and exchange ideas' at lectures and symposia. Founded by Sanskrit scholar Henry Thomas Colebrook in 1823, it received its Royal Charter from King George IV in 1824. Members have included explorer Sir Richard Burton, and writer and poet Rabindranath Tagore. The present building at No.14 (incorporating a modern version of a taking-in door) was designed by Jestico & Whiles and served as their offices from 1986 until 1998. **No.12**, another contemporary building, has been home to the Magic Circle since 1998; the wall plate bears the signs of the zodiac. Once standing opposite, at Nos.31-39 Euston Buildings, was the London factory of Besson and Co., an Anglo-French firm making brass musical instruments of all kinds, advertising as suppliers 'to the Armies and Navies of the World'. In 1894 they employed 131 workers, producing 100 instruments a week and supplying some 10,000 musical ensembles. The firm had been founded by Gustave Auguste Besson at No.198 Euston Road in 1858. His redoubtable daughter Marthe Josephine Fontaine-Besson managed the business until 1895, when she became embroiled in a very acrimonious court case with her husband who claimed she had stolen thousands of pounds from him. Dying in 1907, she was buried in Highgate East Cemetery, where her elaborate tomb is now Grade-II Listed.

Ahead of the left turn in the L-shaped street was UCL's Wolfson House, a 1970s office building of brick and concrete which housed various College departments. In August 2019, HS2 was granted planning permission to erect here a monolithic white-tiled block, 5 storeys high and likened to a giant sugar cube, to house a ventilation shaft and a huge fan to blow air into the Tube tunnels below. Critics have claimed that the countless holes in its fretwork tiled façade will attract nesting pigeons and litter, and that the white tiling will soon be stained.

The left turn in the street has been closed, so retrace your steps back to North Gower Street. Turn right, and then right again, along **EUSTON STREET**, here known as Crescent Street until 1867, leading, as it did, to erstwhile Euston Crescent (p 159). On the north side, **No.100** was home to the Agency for Legal Deposit Libraries (formerly the Copyright Libraries Agency), to which copies of all UK publications (including this one!) are sent for legal deposit in the five designated copyright libraries other than the British Library (which operates its own scheme). Insufficient capacity led to the Agency relocating to Edinburgh in 2009. Beyond are more RHWL-designed houses.

On the opposite side of the street, the red brick building at **Nos.105-111** was, from 1952, the Castle Works of Cooke, Troughton & Simms, York-based makers of optical instruments, especially famed for their theodolites. Born on the site in 1845, at the then No.24 Crescent Street, was Marie Bethell Beauclerc, probably the country's first female reporter. Having worked on the *Birmingham Morning News* when it started in 1871, she went on to pioneer the teaching of Pitman's shorthand in the Midlands, instructing some 4,000 people. In 1888 she was appointed to teach shorthand at Rugby School, making her 'possibly the first lady teacher at a boys' public school'.

At Nos.81-103 is **The Wesley**; its railings incorporate pretty foliage designs. Previously known as the Methodist International Centre, the hotel has won awards for green tourism. Originally completed in 1939 to the designs of architects Munby & Smith, it housed the laboratories and office of the British Non-Ferrous Metals Association until 1974, when the latter moved to Bayswater.

Ahead, at the now extinct eastern end of Euston Street, all the old properties were compulsorily purchased by HS2 for demolition in 2019. Brought up on the right at No.75 was the sculptor Andrea Carlo Lucchesi (1860-1925), a son of an immigrant Italian plaster figure moulder. Though his statue of a (fully clad) Queen Victoria adorns the Art Gallery in Bath, he specialised in the female nude. The early-19th-century house became part of the Cottage Hotel at Nos.67-75, an 80-year-old family-run concern which came to an end on the proprietor's eviction in late 2017. Emerging from the right **was** the north-south part of Stephenson Way (p 145), originally called Little Crescent Street. There, at No.3 from 1850-55, were piano makers Ennever & Steedman (predecessors of Sandon & Steedman, p 99).

Where Euston Street now ends, turn right into **REGNART BUILDINGS**, an L-shaped cul-de-sac originally Southampton Buildings and renamed after either Sir Horace Grece Regnart or Clare Henry Regnart: both were presidents of Maple's the furniture-makers whose factory we encountered in Stephenson

Way. Continue a few paces to view 4- and 5-storey converted brick warehouses with a mix of offices and apartments.

Returning to Euston Street, continue ahead up **COBOURG STREET**. Known until 1911 as Coburg Street (without the middle 'o'), it dates from 1816, the year in which Princess Charlotte married Prince Leopold of Saxe-Coburg-Saalfeld. On its demolished east side, at Nos.59-67, was an attractive terrace of early-19th-century houses. At No.69, a public house stood on the Euston Street corner from the time when the area was first developed, originally called the Jolly Gardeners; the name may have recalled the several nursery gardens which previously adjoined the New Road (p 155). In more recent years, it was greatly transformed as the Bree Louise **[49]** (renamed after the publican's daughter who had died shortly after birth). In 2016 it was CAMRA North London Pub of the Year, but this accolade did not prevent the closure forced on it by the HS2 scheme in February 2018.

Pause at the junction with Drummond Street. Ahead, at the top end of the north part of Cobourg Street, facing the Exmouth Arms (p 143), demolished red-brick No.1 started life as railway company stables, and so was one of the few buildings to survive from the earlier years of Euston Station. For many years, it was home to Collectors' Corner, which sold railway memorabilia and had its entrance in Cardington Street; it has since moved to the National Railway Museum in York. The architectural practice of Jestico & Whiles sympathetically renovated the building as its base in 1998, but had to relocate in early 2018, this time to Clerkenwell. Remaining intact on the west side of this part of Cobourg Street are more examples of RHWL housing. Under plans for HS2, Cobourg Street will be transformed from a quiet backwater into a busy city centre street, with a taxi rank fronting the western edge of the new station, whose proposed western portal will be located where you stand. Now turn your attention to **DRUMMOND STREET**, which took its name from Lady Caroline Drummond, a great-granddaughter of 2nd Duke of Grafton. The part of the street east of Cobourg Street has recently been reduced to a footway between hoardings. Walk through this corridor to where it meets Melton Street, and then pause for a while.

Before the 1960s, when it was buried beneath the redeveloped Euston Station,

49 The Bree Louise pub, compulsorily purchased and demolished in 2019

Drummond Street continued east to Eversholt Street, and beyond it along what is now Doric Way (p 90). En route it passed the sites of the Drummond Arms pub/hotel at No.54, the ill-fated 'Euston Arch' (p 161), the original location of the Royal George (p 86), and an early short-lived Drummond Mews. The young Charles Dickens once walked this way to school at Wellington House Academy in Hampstead Road. In Drummond Street, he and his school chums would amuse themselves by pretending to be beggars, asking old ladies for charity, then running away laughing at their victims' surprise. In *Sketches by Boz,* Miss Amelia Martin, 'The Mistaken Milliner', lives at No.47. Ahead of you, and offering step-free access to Euston Station is the last vestige of the street's extinguished eastern end.

To your left is the now sealed-off south end of **former Cardington Street**. To the left is the site of the Hotel Ibis; originally to be called the Euston Hotel, the 4-storey 1987 building, in an attractive peach shade of brick, was the first newly-built hotel in central London for ten years. Out of sight beyond the barrier is the east side of the lamented St James' Gardens (p 138), while on the right is Euston Station. In its 1880s westward expansion, when the former burial ground was reduced in size, Cardington Street gained a new arm, running south to join Melton Street along the western edge of a newly expanded Euston Station. Railway Mews, which had begun life as Alfred Mews, was swept away in the process.

So too was the whole of Whittlebury Street, which had thitherto run southeast between the original Cardington Street and the now extinct part of Drummond Street. Whittlebury Lodge, on the Fitzroy family's Northamptonshire estate was the sometime home of the fox-hunting third Lord Southampton, and 'Ranger of Whittlebury Forest' was among the hereditary titles of the Dukes of Grafton. The writer and journalist Peter George Patmore (c.1786-1855) was father of the poet Coventry Patmore, a friend of William Hazlitt and Charles Lamb, and later a close acquaintance of Leigh Hunt. He edited the *New Month Magazine* from 1841 to 1853, and died two years later on 25 December at his home, No.49 Whittlebury Street. All the houses on the east side had by then been pulled down for the first enlargement of Euston Station. Railway employees and others continued to live in the street until the 1870s; it was also home to several firms of coachbuilders. A Southampton Arms pub at No.41 subsequently became No.20 in the new section of Cardington Street.

Turn round to look south along **MELTON STREET**. Charles FitzRoy, the third Baron Southampton, was a keen huntsman and from 1827-31 was Master of the Quorn Hunt, based around Melton Mowbray, Leicestershire. The eponymous street now faces near-extinction, almost all of its buildings having been pulled down.

Still standing in early 2020, on what was the corner of Drummond Street, with its distinctive arched windows and oxblood-red tiles, was the original Euston station of the Charing Cross, Euston & Hampstead Railway ('the Hampstead Tube'), now the Charing Cross branch of the Northern line. Designed by Leslie Green and opened in 1907, the surface building here was closed in 1914 together with that of the Bank branch station (p 85). The Melton Street building latterly housed a giant fan in its lift shaft, ventilating the tunnels below.

Until renamed in 1836, Melton Street was called Euston Street. Long-gone No.16, on the old Tube station site, was the 1820s home of Samuel Wesley (1766-1837). Separated from his wife, the bipolar organist and composer lived here in genteel poverty with Sarah Suter, now his lifelong-partner, and his second family of natural children. He was briefly imprisoned for debt, pursued by his legal wife's creditors.

Two adjacent terrace houses, Grade-II-Listed Nos.14&15, survived until 2019. Now vanished Walkden House, a 1960s building southward at No.10, was once the HQ of the Transport Salaried Staffs' Association (TSSA), the white-collar rail union, and also a conference centre for Age Concern.

Across the road, the demolished 10-storey Grant Thornton House at No.22 was the London office of the eponymous accountancy firm, now moved to Finsbury Square. On its site, from at least 1825 to 1961, the Euston Arms pub stood at No.33, on the corner of Melton Mews, originally known as Euston Mews. In 1884, the cabmaster Henry Neate of No.6 was gaoled for a week with hard labour for cruelty to his horses. A few years later Booth's researcher said the Mews was full of costermongers, who were 'rowdy and troublesome'.

Now turn back west along the walkway to Cobourg Street, with smart panels provided by HS2, and identified as part of the 'Euston Green Link', a newly designated 'healthier' walking route between the mainline station and Regent's Park. Other panels draw attention to the independent businesses still trading in the now cut-off westerly part of **DRUMMOND STREET**. Continue west along the latter's south side.

In 1898 Charles Booth's researcher wrote of the street's hotels and coffee houses being a haunt of prostitutes. Since the 1970s, the draw to Drummond Street for many people has been its profusion of food from the Indian sub-continent. The shop at **No.115** has on display examples of the range of food and spices sold in the street. The Diwana Bel Poori at **No.121**, opened in 1972 and renowned for its Indian vegetarian cuisine, is just one of the several Indian restaurants still in business in Drummond Street today, although fearful for their future.

Look across at the other side of the street, where there are two shops selling Indian confectionery: at **No.100** Gupta Sweet Centre, and Ambala Sweet Centre at **Nos.112-114**. Indicative of the increasingly cosmopolitan nature of the street is 'African Arts and African Kitchen' at **No.102**. Between No.108 and No.110 is a second entrance to Exmouth Mews (p 144), while next to No.114 is the square-cut opening to **CHARLES PLACE**, called Charles Mews in its earliest days. The adjacent part of Drummond Street was named Charles Street East when first developed in the 1820s, probably in honour of Charles FitzRoy, 1st Baron Southampton. The whole street was renamed in 1857 after Lady Caroline Drummond, one of his great-nieces. Among the businesses that once thrived in Charles Place were timber storage, cabinet-making, engineering and stained-glass painting.

The north side of **DRUMMOND STREET** has been fortunate to retain its 19th-century domestic architecture. The street did not escape bomb damage in WWII and, in common with much of the locality, was later threatened by wholesale redevelopment, many of the properties having been bought up from the 1950s by Levy's Stock Conversion Company (p 151).

Continuing along the south side, we come to **No.129**, now a fried chicken outlet. Founded here in 1975, in a squat previously occupied by a radical bookshop, was a women's centre that began as the Wages for Housework Campaign. Among other women's organisations formed at this address were the English Collective of Prostitutes and Women Against Rape (WAR). Evicted in 1977, they moved along to No.138 (p 150) – from where WAR organised its first public rape 'trial', in Trafalgar Square – only to be evicted again the next year. The women's centre moved on, first to Tonbridge Street, King's Cross, and then to Kentish Town where it still thrives today, offering support to women of all ages and backgrounds, and renamed 'Crossroads Women' in honour of the female squatters at Crossroads township in Cape Town, who had famously refused to be moved.

On the southwest corner with North Gower Street, at No.137, is the Crown & Anchor pub, in a Listed building dating from the 1820s. Beyond the junction, on the south side of Drummond Street, the flats and shops at **Nos.141-153** (named The Proximity Building) are on the site of former No.57, which housed the Railway Benevolent Institution. It was rebuilt in 1877 as the Tolmers Square Institute and School (also known as Tolmers Hall). Its foundation stone was laid by Samuel Morley MP, a wealthy hosiery manufacturer, who devoted £14,000 of his fortune to erecting chapels and who gave his name to Morley College in Lambeth. The Institute opened in 1879, and among its early occupants was the Euston Middle Class School for Girls, founded in 1880. From 1925, the building became known as Fred Tallant Hall (*alias* 'The Meeting Place'): it served both as the base of the London Esperanto Club, and as the regional office of the London CHA Club Ltd. Until his death in 1934, Fred Tallant was the Secretary of the latter, which had been formed in Red Lion Square in 1901 as the Co-operative Holidays Association. The Club was one of seven organisations which founded the Federation of Rambling Clubs in 1905. With rooms for hire at reasonable rates, the Hall was much favoured as a meetings venue for more than 20 other organisations. A dwindling, ageing membership led to the CHA's decision to close the Hall in 2004.

In 1958, opposite at **No.134**, Laxmishanker G Pathak opened a shop selling Indian goods and groceries. He and his wife Santagaury had started making authentic Indian foods in the kitchen at their home in Queen's Crescent (Kentish Town), to sell to the local immigrant population. To use up surplus vegetables from the shop, a factory was opened in Northamptonshire and the firm Patak Foods established, selling pickles, curry pastes and spices. Moving production to Wigan, the business gained an eventually international clientele. The Euston shop had closed in 1982, but the Patak's brand continues today as part of Associated British Foods.

Adjoining No.134 is an entrance to **GEORGE MEWS**: its delicate wrought-iron gateway is surmounted by a spearhead design, incorporating the name of the mews, now occupied by 1980s social housing. Here, in the late 19th century and until at least WWII, there was a timber yard which served upholstery, furniture- and cabinet-making factories in Hampstead Road. Later, disinfectant and battery factories occupied the yard until 1960. To the left of George Mews, **No.138** is surmounted by a parapet, bearing the inscription (obscured by white paint) 'Duke of Edinburgh': the building was a former late-Victorian beershop, named as if it was a pub, a common practice at the time. Now a dry cleaner's, the address was the second squat of the aforementioned women's centre (p 149).

Off the south side of Drummond Street, an arch takes you into **FOUNDRY MEWS**, its modern name recalling Wailes' nearby iron foundry off Euston Road (p 152). Through a further arch, we come to **TOLMERS SQUARE**. In 1797, long before the square was ever developed, the New River Company leased land on its site and built a circular reservoir there, within 'a grassy mound', to serve the West End; later, an artesian well was sunk. In 1845-46 a large range of baths and wash-houses was erected around the three sides of the reservoir at its east end, with entrances in adjacent streets. Funded by voluntary contributions (with Prince Albert as patron and Lord Southampton as president), the baths catered for all classes. As well as first- and second-class cubicles for men and for women, there were 'vapour' and plunge baths. The charity also embarked on a programme of disinfecting the houses of the local poor.

The baths were demolished when, in 1863, the Square was laid out for housing. It took its name from a mansion at Tolmers Park, near Cuffley (Herts.) owned at the time by Thomas Mills MP, a Deputy Governor of the New River Company. The present footway into Tolmers Square from Hampstead Road lies approximately on the line of the original road entrance. Stuccoed terraced houses built by William Sawyer on the north and south sides of the new square were intended to be more 'genteel' than those on streets to the east. The 1871 Census, however, reveals 364 people in the 28 houses, almost all of which were in multiple occupation; Booth's map of 1890 indicates 'poverty and comfort mixed' and his researcher comments on the prostitutes living there.

A Congregational Church was built in the centre of Tolmers Square at the same time as the houses. A successor to an earlier 'Albany Chapel' in nearby Frederick (now Longford) Street, it was designed by John Tarring (known as the 'Gilbert Scott of the Non-Conformists') and boasted a 120ft spire **[50]**. The church was believed to be haunted after a minister had hanged himself, and strange lights were seen. When it eventually closed, in a remarkable change of use, it became the Tolmer Cinema, opened in 1924 by George Smart; the spire survived for 4 more years. The building suffered bomb damage in 1944, and was bought by the Ponson family who, trading as New Tolmer Ltd, continued to run the cinema as a traditional, 'popular and lively but not at all elegant' fleapit. In 1968, an application to rebuild the cinema was refused, as it would 'prejudice an overall development scheme'. It closed in 1972.

During the 20th century, half of the Square's south side was taken over by Sanger's, the pharmaceutical company (p 153), and converted to factory and warehouse use. The Square became a cause célèbre in the 1970s, when the Tolmers Village Action Group and squatters led community opposition to Joe Levy and his Stock Conversion Company, who were intent on further Euston Tower-style developments. Since the late 1950s, Levy had been buying up properties very cheaply, not just in Tolmers Square, but also in Hampstead Road, North Gower Street, Starcross Street, Cobourg Street, Drummond Street and Euston Street. In September 1973, Camden decided to embark on a joint scheme with Stock Conversion, but a ratepayer immediately threatened the Council with a writ. The following month, many prominent Labour and trades union figures supported Tolmers Square residents against the scheme. The situation was resolved only with the passing of the Community Land Act 1975, which enabled Camden to purchase properties from Stock Conversion for £4 million. The controversy ended in a compromise: social housing would be built in the Square itself, while adjacent land alongside the widened Euston Road was designated for commercial development.

The Square as redeveloped for the Council in 1975-82 by RHWL is of a shape quite different to its predecessor: 4-storey houses and flats on the north and east sides, and the back of Hampstead Road housing on the west side, have as their focal point two octagonal shapes, one a grassy knoll (possibly recalling the old raised reservoir), the other a brick-paved sunken area. The Square's traffic-free environment is enhanced by plane trees, rowans and shrubs. **The Square Tavern** was built as part of the development. Leave the Square by the footpath next to it, to emerge onto a wide pavement on the east side of Hampstead Road and, turning left, regain Euston Circus. Cross the slip road and the bridge above the underpass. Then either turn immediately left along the footway beside the latter, where Route 9 begins; or veer right to return to our starting-point at Warren Street Station.

50 Tolmers Square Chapel

Euston Circus to Euston Station

Short linear walk between Warren Street Underground Station and Euston Station

On exiting from Warren Street Station, cross at the lights straight ahead of you by the road junction now known as Euston Circus (p 136) to the corner of University College London Hospital (UCLH, see *Streets of Fitzrovia*). Turn to the left and cross the roadway fronting the hospital at the pedestrian lights. Turn right along a curved footway, with a bike park and seating, that runs east beside and above the **EUSTON ROAD** underpass.

Over to your left is the vast building at **No.250** Euston Road, described by Pevsner as 'a disturbing faceted cliff of glossy mirror glazing'. Designed by RHWL and erected in 1975-82, this was the commercial part of the Tolmers Square compromise (p 151). The first occupants were Prudential Assurance ('the Pru'), relocated here from their better-known headquarters at Holborn Bars. No.250 now houses various departments of UCLH, including its Education Centre, Institute of Nuclear Medicine and Centre for Medical Imaging. Extending east as far as North Gower Street, the building lines the post-1960s northern frontage of Euston Road.

Walking on the south side of the underpass, we follow roughly the line of the road's pre-widening north side. This stretch of the original New Road was called Palace Row – from 'King John's Palace', the spurious *alias* of the adjacent Tottenhall manor house (p 136). The Row was renumbered in 1857 as part of Euston Road.

At No.1 Palace Row, the Old King's Head (p 136) protruded into the New Road, causing a narrowing of the carriageway, and so did its Victorian rebuild. This much disliked obstacle to traffic was finally removed only in Edwardian times when, as No.282 Euston Road, the pub was demolished and replaced by a bank. At No.3 was the Duke of Grafton pub, mentioned in 1787 and at first called the Grafton Head; as No.278 Euston Road, it survived until the 1960s road-widening.

Palace Row was already part-commercialised by the early 19th century. There was a 'Swan' brewhouse there until 1809, when its owners went bankrupt. Cowkeeping was a major local occupation, and a cow-yard was noted in 1820, with space for 120 cows. By the 1830s there were several statuary and masons' yards off Palace Row, including at No.5 that of John Mullane (d.1837).

At No.6 was the works of William Croggan, who had taken over the running of the business of his partner Eleanor Coade upon her death in 1821. Croggan supplied Coade stone decorations for the new Buckingham Palace but went bankrupt in 1833.

Only a few of the Palace Row properties were conventional New Road houses with front gardens. They included No.7, home in the early 1850s to William Francis Burdett, an exhibitor of panoramas who was a partner in the Diorama in Blackfriars Road.

Cowkeeping persisted, and by the 1860s dairyman William Mundy was at No.270 Euston Road, at the entrance to a presumably eponymous Mundy's Yard. Adjoining No.262 was Palace Yard, home in the mid-19th century to a Wesleyan Chapel.

In 1825, at No.10 Palace Row (the future No.258), Charles Rich began his business as an engineer, millwright and iron founder. Adjacent was a court of ten houses, owned by Rich and known as Selby (or Silby) Place. After 1855, the enterprise was carried on by George Wailes, whose foundry was built on a site to the rear. Rex Wailes (a well-known writer on the history of engineering) was the last managing director of the business, which closed in 1960 when Euston Road was widened.

The 1870 directory lists a mixed bag of small tradesmen along the main road here, among them two bootmakers, a milliner and staymaker, a zinc worker, a coachsmith and maker of ladders, and a photographic artist, John Ward. There were also several timber yards, including that of mahogany merchant Charles Snewin. By the end of the century, Maple's were trading as timber merchants at No.248 and No.254. The same company later had furniture repositories at Nos.262-270 (and Nos.8-12 Hampstead Road), vacated by their Tottenham Court Road neighbours and rivals, James Shoolbred & Co., on that firm's liquidation in 1931. Another major local employer, Sanger's the wholesale 'druggists', had premises at Nos.252-258.

On the North Gower Street corner at No.234 stood the Victorian rebuild of the Orange Tree pub **[51]**, dating from at least 1791 and originally close by at No.16 Palace Row. When it was demolished in 1963 for road widening, the Beatles visited the site and a photo of the group jumping over rubble was chosen for the cover of their *Twist and Shout* EP.

At the end the curved footway, cross at the pedestrian lights. Here we encounter the south entrance to **Euston Square Station**, set in the corner of the Wellcome Trust's Gibbs Building. Opened in 1863 on the Metropolitan Railway, the station was more appropriately called Gower Street Station until 1909. Its surface buildings have been rebuilt several times.

51 The Orange Tree public house

From beside the Gibbs Building, look across to the opposite side. None of the original buildings on the next stretch of the road survive, although some still stood in 1945. Built by local developer James Haygarth, who died here in 1794, the houses with garden plots in front formed Southampton Place, until renumbered as part of Euston Road in 1857, and were first advertised as having fine views across open countryside to Hampstead. An early resident at No.3 was the surveyor and architect William Inwood, who co-designed nearby St Pancras New Church with his son Henry, the ratepayer at No.5 in 1832. Nos.18-19 served as studios of the early-19th-century engravers Edward and William Finden. For his engraved portrait of King George IV, after Sir Thomas Lawrence, William received 2,000 guineas, the highest sum ever paid for such a work. No.19 had initially been home to Lt Gen. Andrew Gammell (d.1815), who was buried at Westminster Abbey.

From No.212 Euston Road in 1888 the young magician David Devant was advertising magical séances, 'delightful delusions suitable for the drawing room'. He went on to become 'the prime minister of magic' giving performances to royalty; he was also an early pioneer of cinema in London, showing the first films in the UK in 1896.

No.208 was home from the late 1850s for three decades to the sculptor brothers David and William ('Mynorydd') Davies, who worked at both St James' and Kew Palaces. In 1890 Dr L S Forbes Winslow opened a clinic in 'a modest building in Euston Square', one of the first to provide outpatient psychiatric care to the poor. It soon moved to No.208, becoming the British Hospital for Mental Disorders & Brain Diseases. By 1913 it had relocated to Camden Road, where it later became known as the Camden Clinic.

No.206 was the home in the early 1880s to Horace Wigan, an actor known for his detective roles.

Moving into No.200 in 1858, from Grafton Place (p 87), was the London Female Preventive & Reformatory Institution, which had its headquarters here until the 1920s when it transferred to Birkenhead Street, just south of King's Cross Station. Its dozen reformatory homes across London, aimed to 'afford temporary protection to friendless young women whose circumstances expose them to danger, [and] to rescue fallen females, especially those decoyed from the country'. After WWII the organisation was renamed the London Haven for Women and Girls; it was wound up in 1976.

At Nos.194-198 before WWI were the offices of brass instrument makers Besson & Co. (p 146), next door to the Accordion Pleating Co. at No.192, which exhibited its Permanent Pleating Machine at the 1887 Jubilee Exhibition. In the 1850s, as No.21 Southampton Place, the building had housed Thomas Spencer, an analytical chemist then credited with inventing electroplating.

Walk on along the south side of Euston Road (see *Streets of Bloomsbury*), with a good view of the architectural features of the present-day buildings opposite, which we will describe from west to east. **No.222** was built by Moiret & Wood in 1954-58 as the headquarters of the National Union of Mineworkers; in 1983 they decamped to Arthur Scargill's home territory of Sheffield, taking with them the sculptures and mirrors that had adorned the façade. Following refurbishment, the building housed the Medical Research Council (MRC)'s Clinical Trials Unit. Here from March 2014 was the Farr Institute of Health Informatics Research, an MRC-funded collaboration of 21 academic institutes and health-related organisations (including UCL and Wellcome), to analyse data 'to better understand the health of patients and populations'. When Farr's funding ceased in October 2018, the Institute's functions transferred to the newly formed body Health Data Research UK, with accommodation at the same address.

No.210 originated as Gestetner House, for many years the offices of Gestetner Ltd; their stencil duplicating machines were once so ubiquitous that 'to gestetner' was used as a verb. It was erected in 1953 as a Modernist building designed by Verity & Beverley but was later given its present post-modern marble cladding. In 2002 the building contained the Two Ten Gallery, where the Wellcome Trust mounted temporary science and art exhibitions. The block's latest occupants, the Institute of Ismaili Studies, moved to the Aga Khan Centre (p 58) in 2018, and the block was undergoing full refurbishment at time of writing.

At **No.200** is the Portland-stone façade of former Bentley House, built in the late 1930s as the London base of Cambridge University Press (CUP); the architects were Messrs W Curtis Green, RA, Son and Lloyd. Note the obelisks surmounting the tower-like sides. Although CUP moved out at the end of the 1970s and the building was renovated in 1990, the name Bentley House was retained: Cambridge University gave one Richard Bentley a free hand in setting up the Press at the end of the 17th century. The National Union of Railwaymen (NUR, now RMT and based in Chalton Street, p 99) used No.200 during the rebuilding of its short-lived Unity House headquarters, completed in 1983 on the site of the Gibbs Building (beside us). During the latter's later construction, No.200 was temporarily occupied by Wellcome Trust staff. Erected since 2013, behind the preserved façade of the building and backing onto Stephenson Way, has been a 7-storey block of student accommodation. The design of No.200 was influenced by its neighbour at No.194, long a local office of the former War Pensions Agency and its predecessors. With its giant Ionic columns and pilastered ground-floor windows, this was built in 1932 by W H Gunton as an extension to the building round the corner at **No.30** on the west side of **EUSTON SQUARE**.

This was built in 1906-08 for the London, Edinburgh & Glasgow Assurance Company (LE&GAC), to the designs of Arthur Beresford Pite. The building, of load-bearing Portland stone and brick masonry, with steel and concrete floors, has a Grade-II* Listing, unlike its abovementioned non-Listed annexe, for which Pite's services were not retained. In 1912, the LE&GAC became part of the National Amalgamated Approved Society, a joint venture of a dozen major insurers, set up to administer statutory benefits; No.30 became its headquarters. After 1948, the building was taken over by the Ministry of National Insurance, later subsumed into the Department of Health and Social Security, under which it became 'Nos. 1-9 Melton Street'; it then passed into private hands and lay empty for some time. In 2010, the Royal College of General Practitioners acquired the building, which was refurbished by Tilney in 2012, carrying out conservation work on interior features such as the green and cream Doulton Parian Ware tiles, and also the original board room. Cross to the far corner of Gordon Street, from where you can see the building's east-facing façade, ideas for which derived from the Temple of Apollo Epicurius at Bassae.

Continue along the south side of Euston Road, walking alongside the Friends' House, the Quakers' HQ. On reaching its garden, stop to admire how the two lodges in Euston Grove opposite so beautifully frame the War Memorial beyond (p 158). Take advantage of the seating in the Friends' House garden to consider the history of Euston Square.

Created in 1811, it was designed as a centrepiece of Lord Southampton's local development, and as a northward extension of Bloomsbury. Previously occupying its site had been a large nursery garden, latterly known as Montgomery's Nursery and owned by Robert Montgomery, also the landlord of the satirist 'Peter Pindar' (p 88). The Square extended on both sides of the main road until 1879, when the southern half was renamed Endsleigh Gardens. Later, in the 1920s, its garden enclosure was controversially built over.

The mid-19th-century cast-iron railings around present-day Euston Square and fronting Euston Road are original (and Listed), although some are damaged. Other than Nos.70&71 on the east side (p 84), none of the Square's original real estate has survived: most of it was demolished in 1937, probably to make way for a proposed rebuilding of Euston Station which did not materialise.

Once lining the north side of Euston Square were distinguished Regency stuccoed and pilastered terraces of c.1811, designed either by C A Busby or James Burton. These two blocks of 15 and 13 houses (separated by Euston Grove) were built by Thomas Jennings of Upper Marchmont Street and John Knight of Kenton Street. At first-floor level, the French windows with roofed balconies were 'of exceptionally beautiful design'. The house numbering ran anticlockwise from the northeast corner.

No.4 was the scene of the notorious unsolved 'Euston Square Murder'. Living there in 1878, with his wife and children, was Severin Bastendorff, a bushy-bearded bamboo chair maker born in Luxembourg. Miss Matilda Hacker was one of their lodgers. The next year, when the cellar was cleared out, her decomposing body was discovered under a heap of coal, and investigations began. Hannah Dobbs, a former housemaid at No.4, found to have pawned some of Miss Hacker's property at a local pawnshop, was tried for murder at the Old Bailey, but acquitted for lack of evidence. Some say that Bastendorff knew more about Miss Hacker's death than he made out in court, and that he had used his maid (and mistress) Hannah to get rid of her belongings.

By the end of the 19th century most Euston Square properties had been converted into apartments, boarding houses or private hotels, but in its heyday the Square had many distinguished residents. The prolific furniture and interior designer Bruce Talbert lived at

52 Frederic Harrison ('Ape' caricature, *Vanity Fair*, 1886)

No.5 Euston Square from 1875 until his death. Thomas Leigh Hunt, a journalist writing for *The Spectator, Morning Chronicle* and *Daily Telegraph* and eldest son of the essayist-poet Leigh Hunt (p 95), lived at No.6 (1863-65) and at No.26 (1866-72). The many clergymen attracted to Euston Square included Rev. Henry Stebbing, the incumbent of St James', Hampstead Road (p 139) and chaplain of UCH, who lived at No.16 (1836-56); he wrote extensively on church history and in periodical literature, being instrumental in founding *The Athenaeum* in 1828 and editing its earliest issues. His fourth son, Thomas, born in the Square in 1835, also became a clergyman, but his religious views were considered 'unorthodox': he was eminent as a zoologist, specialising in crustacea and an early convert to Darwinism.

Born at No.17 in 1831 was the Positivist Frederic Harrison **[52]**, who co-founded the bizarre Church of Humanity in Holborn, and served as an alderman in the LCC's early years (from 1889), contributing to initial plans for Kingsway.

Montague David Eder, born in 1865 at No.19, was the first doctor in England to practise psychoanalysis, and a founder-member of the London Psycho-Analytical Society in 1913, which was soon disbanded and later re-formed by a rival (Ernest Jones). During WWI, Eder served as a temporary captain in the Royal Army Medical Corps: his book, *War-Shock* (1917), called for a psychotherapeutic approach to what was then known as shell-shock. He corresponded with George Bernard Shaw, and was friends with Dorothy Richardson, Rebecca West and D H Lawrence.

Sir Claudius Stephen Hunter, a relative of Sir Hans Sloane, lived at No.23 (1838-51). He was a solicitor and City alderman who served as Sheriff (1808) and Lord Mayor (1811). Thomas Hancock Nunn, a pioneer of social work, was born at the same address in 1859. He combined public and voluntary sector interests, first at Toynbee Hall and in Stepney; he went on to found the Hampstead Health Institute in Kilburn (in 1913), to bring social services and public health interests together as a means of disease prevention.

John Payne Collier was a Shakespearean critic who also rescued many famous authors from oblivion: he was responsible for an outstanding edition of the works of Edmund Spenser. However, this resident of No.25 (1834-39) was at other times something of a rogue, forging works by Shakespeare, *inter alia*. His work led to his appointment as secretary to a royal commission on the British Museum in 1847.

On the west side of Euston Square, former No.30 was home to the scientific writer Charles Tomlinson, a lecturer at UCL, who in 1838 published *The Student's Manual of Natural Philosophy*. Next door at No.31 lived George Bullen, Keeper of Printed Books at the British Museum; his house would later become the Griffins Hotel.

Now cross at the pedestrian lights to the north side of Euston Road, to arrive at the eastern lodge of a pair of two, flanking the entrance to **EUSTON GROVE [53]**. The LNWR needed an Act of Parliament in 1869 to acquire the land here from Lord Southampton, and to build this 80ft-wide drive. Designed by the LNWR architect, J B Stansby, the **lodges** are the only buildings that remain from the old Euston Station as finally conceived. Each lodge is of 2 storeys, square in plan, faced with Portland stone, and with a low-pitched lead-covered roof. The quoin stones bear the names of stations served by the railway at the time. In the north and south pediments are sculptures by Joseph Pitts, representing England, Scotland, Wales and Ireland. In recent years the two lodges have been used as twin beer houses called the **Euston Tap**. The nearby lamp-posts resemble jousting lances and each is surmounted by a laurel wreath and helmet at lamp level.

Euston Grove bisects (or bisected) **Euston Square Gardens**, the two halves of which were once linked by a pedestrian tunnel under Euston Grove. The western half disappeared entirely in early spring 2018. Local conservationists had yarn-bombed the site (cf. p 139) and a group from Camden Civic Society

53 Euston Grove with Marochetti's statue of Robert Stephenson, 1939

(including Rev. Anne Stevens, vicar of St Pancras Church) had chained themselves to the plane trees that were about to be felled. Opened here at the end of 2018 was a new 'interim' taxi rank, with access for cabs from Melton Street.

The gardens on the east side had so far remained untouched, its trees still standing. Close to the southeast entrance, opposite the fire station, was an oak sapling (rather shaded by a large plane tree). An accompanying plaque read: 'In memory of the travelling public and Railway Workers who lost their lives or were injured travelling on the railway or working for the railway industry. This tree was planted by the rail unions ASLEF, RMT and TSSA on 29 March 2001, International Rail Safety Day.' During the 1920s, the railway company lent the Square to the St Pancras House of Fellowship (affiliated to the Shaftesbury Society), which ran an open air school for delicate children drawn from neighbouring schools. During WWII, the Open Air Centre continued to provide educational classes, activities such as Girl Guides and Junior Women's Air Corps, and health services (e.g. immunisation). The Fellowship's Chair of Council was St Pancras Housing stalwart Edith Neville (p 91).

At the time of writing, the eventual fate of the Gardens is unclear. The (much redacted) GLA Masterplan envisages a new approach to Euston Station along a pedestrianised Euston Grove, with the lodges and 'cenotaph' still in situ, and much reduced green space on either side; tall commercial blocks would be erected over the Gardens' east and west sides.

Since the 1970s, the north side of Euston Square has served as Euston's increasingly busy bus station. In the middle of a small roundabout stands the **war memorial**; cross to it if you can. The memorial was designed by Reginald Wynn Owen, architect to the LNWR, unveiled in October 1921 by Lord Haig and dedicated by the Archbishop of Canterbury; and it commemorates the 3,719 men of the LNWR who fell in WWI, including 3 VCs and 950 who gained other honours. With a granite base, the 13m-high obelisk of Portland stone has four relief carved crosses at the top with bronze wreaths on each side, beneath which are four bronze figures representing the Navy, Infantry, Artillery and Air Force; the latter is unusual, there being few WWI memorials that depict an airman. The bronze figures were modelled by Ambrose Neale, chief artist of R L Boulton & Sons of Cheltenham, contractors for the memorial, a noted firm of architectural masons and sculptors. The monument is Listed Grade-II*.

Overhanging the adjacent **bus station** is the 'bridge' building of 1974-78, designed by R Seifert & Partners and faced, like the rest of this 'estate', with a seemingly shiny black stone, actually some form of reconstituted rubble from South Africa.

Through a doorway in the hoardings to your left, you may catch a glimpse of ***Piscator*** (also known as the 'Euston Head'), a 16-ton sculpture in galvanised cast iron, intended to represent a man's head and shoulders, which until recently overlooked the western Euston Square Gardens. Commissioned by British Rail, it was completed in 1981 by Eduardo Paolozzi, who dedicated it to his friend, the German theatre director Erwin Piscator. The GLA plan suggests a possible future site for the sculpture beside Eversholt Street.

Euston Grove, as originally conceived, was a residential street continuing northwards to meet Drummond Street. No.2 was home to two eminent people of the 19th century: John Cooper, an actor very much in vogue for his Shakespearean roles at Drury Lane, lived there from 1845-53; while the comparative anatomist Robert Edmond Grant, a friend of Charles Darwin, Professor of Zoology at UCL and founder of the eponymous museum, was a resident from 1858-74. At that time No.7 was home to Francis Healey, a former Irish butcher who had made a fortune and retired to become chairman of the St Pancras Magistrates Board. Seven of the eight other properties in the street became private hotels – including Giffards at No.1 and the West Riding Hotel at No.4 – which also survived until the 1960s.

Now walk on through a covered way to Euston Station **Piazza**, where to your left Seifert's tower block variously known as No.40 Melton Street or 'oneustonsq', and at one time as Railtrack House, was undergoing demolition in 2019. Facing east is Marochetti's statue of Robert Stephenson, the engineer and main player in the building of the railway into Euston. In bronze and on a plinth of Aberdeen granite, it had been presented by the Institute of Civil Engineers. Baron Carlo Marochetti is noted for the realism with which he sculpted his subjects' clothing, and you may even glimpse daylight below the insteps of Stephenson's shoes. The statue originally stood between the two Euston Road lodges, and the GLA Masterplan suggests it may eventually return there.

When first installed in the piazza, the statue was at its eastern end. There, on the site of Café Rouge, was an 'ornamental pool', never very savoury and constantly strewn with cans. One spring in the 1980s, a family of mallard ducklings took up residence with their parents, but failed to survive in that inhospitable habitat. Nearby, two tall, dark concrete structures conceal ventilation shafts for the Underground station.

In the centre of the piazza, on a low stainless steel plinth, is the heart-warming bronze **statue of Matthew Flinders** and his faithful pet cat, Trim. Captain Flinders is half kneeling, dividers in hand, over a chart of the coastline of Australia that he circumnavigated and charted in 1800, also giving the continent its European name. The sculptor Mark Richards, FRBS, was commissioned by the Government of South Australia to create this memorial statue, which was cast by Castle Fine Arts at its Tanat Foundry at Llanrhaeadr-ym-Mochnant in North Wales. On 18 July 2014 the statue was unveiled by Prince William, Duke of Cambridge, at Australia House. Its subsequent move to Euston, first to the station concourse, and then outside, has brought it close to Flinders' final resting-place in St James' Burial Ground, unexpectedly unearthed by HS2 archaeologists in January 2019.

The picnic tables which had cluttered the piazza, hemming in Flinders' statue, were removed at Easter 2019. Less welcome has been the removal of the four low 'Time Benches' that stood in front of the station. Each was in a different type of stone, from a different part of England, with an inscription beneath, indicating its geological period. The benches' creator was Paul De Monchaux. Originally commissioned by British Rail's Public Art Development Trust, they were installed here in 1993. The HS2 developers have pledged that should the benches be removed during the station's reconstruction, they will be re-installed somewhere else on site. Find an alternative place to sit and consider the history of the Euston Station site.

The **Colonnade** fronting the station follows the line of an extinct eastern section of Euston Street, which once continued east to meet Eversholt Street. The first stretch was known as Melton Place, where the architectural draughtsman Michael Angelo Nicholson (1794–1841) set up a drawing school. The singer Janet Patey, considered in her day the leading British contralto, was born at No.13 in 1841.

Off Melton Place's north side, until demolished in 1937, was the attractive Euston Crescent. Horwood's map of 1813 shows it when newly built, an arc of 17 stuccoed houses with handsome railings, facing south across a semicircular garden enclosure. At first called Euston Crescent, it later became Melton Crescent before once again reverting to its original name. The literary scholar Sidney Walker had lodgings in Melton Crescent in 1836. East of Euston Grove (p 157) was a similar Seymour Crescent, pulled down by 1834 to make way for a hotel. There was originally yet a third crescent, Southampton

Crescent, to the east, off the north side of what is now Lancing Street (p 85). Euston Street's approach to the series of three crescents explains its original Crescent Street name.

North of Euston Street, and thus on the site of the present station concourse, Euston Grove opened out into Euston Place. This was lined on either side by the first two railway hotels ever built, in 1839, to the designs of Philip Hardwick. The Victoria Hotel opened at first as a dormitory, serving breakfast only, under the management of a former steward of the Athenaeum; bedrooms cost from 3s 6d to 5s (17p to 25p) per night. The Adelaide, later called the Euston, was a more conventional hotel. Charles Dickens and his much-travelled amateur thespian friends were no strangers to the Euston Hotel. In 1881, the two establishments merged and were connected 'in the modern French style' by a screen across Euston Grove, designed by Stansby with details by J McClaren. The hotel was closed in 1962 and pulled down to make way for the rebuilding of **Euston Station**.

The proposal for the original station and the London & Birmingham Railway – the first trunk line into London – passed as an Act in May 1833, after initial objections from the House of Lords. At first known as 'Euston Square', the station opened in 1837. Based around the present Platform 6, it was planned by Robert Stephenson. The platform shed **[54]** was designed by Sir Charles Fox, and featured a colonnade of Doric columns in cast iron, with iron roofs, a first in railway architecture. For the first 8 years, cables powered by a condensing engine hauled carriages up the incline to Chalk Farm, where a locomotive was attached. Queen Victoria and Prince Albert made their first journey from Euston in 1844.

Two years later, the London & Birmingham Railway merged with two other lines to form the LNWR. A large group of new buildings was proposed, designed on a Roman Baths model, and comprising a great hall, a grand staircase, meeting room, board room, general offices and new booking offices. The board room was graced by busts of both George and Robert Stephenson and of fellow engineer Joseph Locke, Robert's collaborator in the building of the railway. Philip Hardwick was the architect, but the work was carried out in 1846-49 by his son, Philip Charles Hardwick. The glorious Great Hall was inspired by the principal apartment in Peruzzi's Palazzo Massimo alle Colonne in Rome. Relief panels depicting the railway's various destinations and a representation of Britannia, accompanied by a lion, a ship, the Arts and Sciences and Mercury, were designed by John Thomas (1813-63). The Hall's walls were finished in grey Martin's cement, painted to imitate granite. Columns were finished in red granite, with white marble caps and bases. Around the sides of the Hall later stood coin-activated models of locomotives enclosed in glass cases. Surveying the scene was a second Stephenson statue, of 1852, this one depicting George, the engineer father of Robert, and sculpted in Carrara marble by E H Baily; it is now in the National Railway Museum (NRM), York. In 1912, the booking hall incorporated refreshment and dining rooms. In 1916, Edwin Lutyens advised on the redecorating of the Hall's walls, which were painted in white and gold. A previous offer by G F Watts to paint frescoes for nothing had been turned down.

54 Euston Station (lithograph, 1837)

At the same time as the acquisition of land to the south, the station was extended east in

1869-70. Some properties in former Seymour Street (p 92) and the 1836-37 carriage sheds were demolished, to make way for the construction of Arrival Platforms 1-3. The company's then engineer, William Baker, raised the roofline by introducing cast-iron pillars.

The expansion of the station continued in the 1880s, first with new offices in Drummond Street, finished in grey cement and stone, by architects Joseph & Smithern. At the same time, the Parliamentary powers to extend the station west to the newly extended Cardington Street (p 148) enabled Platforms 12-15 to be built, opening in 1892. Signal Box Euston No.2, brought into use the previous year, was the largest of its kind in existence.

Fronting the station was the famous 'Euston Arch' [55], which stood beyond Euston Place on the north side of the now vanished part of Drummond Street (p 147). More correctly a Propylaeum of the Doric order, its design by Philip Hardwick was inspired by that on the Acropolis in Athens. Arthur Mee called it one of the grandest English specimens of the Greek style. Built in 1836 of Bramley Fall stone (from a quarry near Leeds), it was immense – 72½ft high; its four columns were, at 44ft 2in, London's tallest, and hollow. There was a chamber in the roof, with very cramped office space, reached by spiral staircases. Marking the entry into the station were elaborate cast-iron gates, now on display at the NRM in York. On either side were four pavilions or lodges, not as attractive as those facing Euston Road. The Arch was restored and the station's name carved on the architrave in 1870. Eleven years later, the construction of railway offices destroyed the western lodge. The Arch gradually became surrounded by buildings, so that its grandeur could no longer be fully appreciated.

The original plans for the 1960s rebuilding of Euston Station included retention of the Arch. The LCC, however, had no objection to its demolition, provided it was erected elsewhere 'in an appropriate, dignified and open setting'. The British Transport Commission considered the £190,000 cost of relocating it to be excessive, and the fate of the Arch assumed a kind of inevitability. A vigorous campaign to save it, supported by the likes of Betjeman and Pevsner, culminated in a fruitless appeal to Harold Macmillan, the prime minister. Britain's 'worst act of corporate vandalism' began on 6 November 1961, and three months later nothing remained. Frank Valon (of the demolition contractors) so hated the job that he offered to number the stones and store them for re-erection on British Rail land elsewhere, but to no avail. Most of the stones were dumped in the River Lea in east London – bought as rubble to plug a hole in the river bed – from which some were dredged up in 2008 during the construction of the Olympic Park. Proposals to rebuild the 'Arch', perhaps between the Euston Grove lodges, remain only an aspiration at the time of writing.

Now enter the present Euston Station. For at least 50 years, there were plans to redevelop or rebuild Euston Station. An obscure Edwardian scheme came to nothing. Few details are known of a later plan in 1935, under which the station would have resembled a 1930s cinema! The Euston Arch would have disappeared with that scheme, too, but on that occasion it was saved. The project may have been shelved because of the railway company's poor financial results in 1938, after which WWII intervened.

The impetus for its construction was the electrification of the West Coast Main Line out of Euston, and building work began in 1962. Hardwick's architecture 'on the grandest scale' was swept away 'in the interests of modernity' (Pevsner). British Rail's London Midland Regional Architect, R L Moorcroft, produced a stark, utilitarian building, using the black polished granite and white mosaic finishes so beloved of 1960s architects.

The new station was built by Taylor Woodrow and opened by the Queen in October 1968. After rail privatisation, Railtrack cluttered the spacious 'Passenger Hall' with small shops, obliterating the daylight and leaving the station with a dearth of seating. A welcome recent innovation has been the mezzanine 'Food Terrace', offering not only a further choice of eateries but also welcome seats for waiting passengers, away from the bustle on the concourse. A new Fuller's pub, the Signal Box, opened in late 2018.

If all goes to plan, much greater change is in prospect over the coming years. Redevelopment plans current in 2019 included six additional platforms for HS2 to be built by 2026, and five more for completion in 2033. Catering for users of both high-speed and 'conventional' rail services would be a vast new single concourse, with a glass façade and set beneath a dramatic hemispherical dome. The major new transport hub would also eventually accommodate the planned subterranean Crossrail 2. In February 2020, the Government confirmed the HS2 project would continue; HS2 Ltd was to focus on its timely delivery with separate arrangements to be made for the redevelopment of Euston Station.

Easter 2019 saw the relocation of **Euston Underground Station** entrance from the mainline concourse to the Colonnade outside, enabling the Night Tube to be accessed externally. If you travel home by Tube, you may encounter final reminders in Euston's Underground, of the area's past. On the Northern line Charing Cross branch (Platforms 1 & 2), the platform walls, re-clad in 1987 (to designs of David Hamilton and Robert Cooper), incorporate the colours of the FitzRoy family's coat-of-arms, together with images of the same and an eloquent explanation of their local significance. On the Victoria line platforms, each seat recess sports a tiled motif. Tom Eckersley's design offers us a reminder of the Euston Arch, whose senseless destruction came to symbolise a turning point in town planning and conservation, and changes in attitudes to our historic buildings.

55 The Euston Arch or propylaeum (c.1900) with horse cabs

Sources

Books and pamphlets

Aston, Mark. *The cinemas of Camden*. L B Camden, 1997

Aston, Mark & Marshall, Lesley. *King's Cross: a Tour in Time*. Camden Local Studies, 2006

Barnes, Eric George. *The rise of the Midland Railway 1844-1874*. Allen & Unwin, 1966

Barty-King, Hugh. *Maples: fine furnishers*. Quiller P, 1992

Bebbington, Gillian. *London street names*. Batsford, 1972

Besant, Sir Walter. *London north of the Thames*. A & C Black, 1911

Blackwood, John. *London's immortals: ... outdoor commemorative statues*. Savoy Press, 1989

Booth, Charles. *Life and labour of the people of London*. Macmillan, 1892-97

Bradley, Simon. *St Pancras Station*. Profile Books, 2007

Brown, Stella. *A history of the London CHA Club*. The Club, 1965

Brown, W E. *Open spaces and disused burial grounds of St Pancras*. 1902

Cambridge University Press. *Bentley House and the evolution of Cambridge Publishing*. CUP, 1938

Camden History Society. *From Primrose Hill to Euston Road*. 1995

Carpenter, Kirsty. *Refugees of the French Revolution: émigrés in London...* Macmillan, 1999

Chambers, Colin. *The story of the Unity Theatre*. Lawrence & Wishart, 1989

Cherry, Bridget & Pevsner, Nikolaus. *London 4: North*. Penguin, 1999 (The buildings of England)

Christopher, John. *King's Cross Station through time*. Amberley, 2009

Christopher, John. *St Pancras Station through time*. Amberley, 2009

Clarke, Linda. *Building capitalism*. Routledge, 1992

Clinch, George. *Marylebone and St Pancras*. Truslove & Shirley, 1890

Clunn, Chris. *Eels, pie and mash*. Museum of London, 1995

Clunn, Harold. *The face of London*, new ed. rev. by E R Wethersett. Spring Books, 1962

Colvin, H M. *A biographical dictionary of British architects, 1660-1840*, 4th ed. Yale UP, 2008

Cooper, C S. *The outdoor monuments of London: statues, war memorials, tablets and memorial buildings*. Homeland Association, 1928

Darley, Peter. *The King's Cross story: 200 years of history in the railway lands*. History Press, 2018

Denford, Steven L J. *Agar Town: the life and death of a Victorian 'slum'*. Camden History Society, 1995

Denyer, C H (ed.) *St Pancras through the centuries*. Le Play House Press, 1935

Duncan, Andrew. *Favourite London Walks*. New Holland, 2007

Emery, Philip A & Wooldridge, Kevin. *St Pancras Burial Ground: Excavations for St Pancras International, the London terminus of High Speed 1, 2002-3*. Gifford Monograph, 2011

Essex Lopresti, M. *Exploring The Regent's Canal*. Brewin, 1987

Evinson, Denis. *Catholic churches of London*. Sheffield Academic Press, 1998

Fairfield, S. *The streets of London: a dictionary ....* Macmillan, 1983

Fletcher, Geoffrey. *London's Pavement Pounders*. Hutchinson, 1967

Fletcher, Geoffrey. *London at my feet*. Daily Telegraph, 1980

Frame, Joan E. *Alive and lively 100 years later: a centennial report on the National Temperance Hospital 1873-1973*. NTH, *1973*

Forster, John. *Life of Charles Dickens*. New ed.,1966

Foster, D. *Alehouses [etc]* (at Westminster Archives)

Gilbert, Bob. *The King's Cross Cut*... King's Cross Canal Project, 1985

Gough, Janine. *20 years of 'planning' the Tolmers Square development*. Middlesex Polytechnic, 1981

Greenwood, James. *In Strange Company, being the experiences of a Roving Correspondent*. Henry S King, 1874

Highmore, Anthony. *Pietas Londinensis:...public charities in or near London*. 1810

Hobhouse, Hermione. *Lost London: a century of demolition and decay*. Macmillan, 1971

Holmes, Malcolm J (comp.). *Somers Town: a record of change*. L B Camden, 1985

Holmes, Malcolm J. *Housing is not enough*. St Pancras Housing Assoc., 1999

HS2. *London-West Midlands environmental statement*, vol.5: *Technical appendices CFA1: Euston - Station and approach: Baseline report (CH-001-001): Cultural heritage (ES 3.5.2.1.3)*. Department for Transport, 2013

Hunter, M & Thorne, R. *Change at King's Cross*. Historical Publications, 1990
Inglis, Angela. *King's Cross: a sense of place*. Troubador, 2012
John McAslan & Partners (Jay Merrick, ed.). *Transforming King's Cross*. Merrell, 2012
Jones, Gareth S. *Outcast London*. Clarendon P, 1971
Joseph, Adam. *King of the Pearly Kings: the story of Henry Croft*. Cockney Museum, 1975
King, James Frederick. *Kentish Town panorama* [c.1848-55]. Facsimile ed., London Topographical Society, 1986.
Lansley, Alastair. *The transformation of St Pancras Station*. Laurence King, 2008
Le Faye, Deirdre. *Medieval Camden*. Camden History Society, 1975
Lee, Charles E. *St Pancras Church and Parish*. The Church, 1955
London County Council. *Survey of London*, vol. 19 (1938), vol. 21 (1949), vol.24 (1952)
Low, Crail. *Rock and pop London*. Handbook Publishing, 1997
Maple & Co. *The House of Maple*. [The Company], 1964
Mee, Arthur. *London*. Hodder & S, 1927 (The King's England)
Merrington, W R. *University College Hospital and its Medical School: a history*. Heinemann, 1976
Miller, Frederick. *St Pancras past and present*. Abel Heywood, 1874
Morrell, Conyers. *The story of Agar Town: the ecclesiastical parish of St Thomas*. Premo Press, 1935
Newton, Douglas. *Catholic London*. Hale, 1950
Norwich, John Julius. *The Architecture of Southern England*. Macmillan, 1985
Oakley, E R. *The London County Council Tramways*, vol. 2: *North London*. London Tramways History Group, 1991
Palmer, Samuel. *St Pancras: Being Antiquarian, Topographical, and Biographical Memoranda...* The author, 1870
Pevsner, Nikolaus. *London, except the Cities of London and Westminster*. 3rd ed., Penguin, 1973 (The Buildings of England)
Renton Howard Wood Partnership. *Tolmers Square development report ...* 1973-74
Richardson, John. *A history of Camden*. Historical Publications, 1999
Richardson, John. *Kentish Town Past*. Historical Publications, 1997
Robertson, Brian. *Roman Camden*. Camden History Society, 1977
Saint, Andrew (ed.). *Politics and the people of London: the LCC 1889-1965*. Hambledon Press, 1989
St Clair, William. *The Godwins and the Shelleys*. Faber, 1989
St Pancras Chamber of Commerce. *Introducing industrial St Pancras and its many industries*. [1938?]
St Pancras (Met. Borough). *The end of one story: a souvenir of the borough ...* 1965
Scholey, K A. *The railways of Camden*. Camden History Society, 2002
Simmons, Jack & Thorne, Robert. *St Pancras Station*. Historical Publications, 2003
Sinclair, Frederick (comp.). *St Pancras through the ages*. MB of St Pancras, 1938
Smithson, Alison & Peter. *The Euston Arch and the growth of the [LMS] Railway*. Thames & Hudson, 1968
Stewart, C J. *The housing question in London*. LCC, 1900
Tindall, Gillian. *The fields beneath*. Temple Smith, 1977
Tolmers Village Action Group. *The Tolmers people plan*. [1977?]
Townend, P N. *Top Shed: a pictorial history of Kings Cross Locomotive depot*. Ian Allan, 1989
Uwins, Sarah. *A memoir of Thomas Uwins RA*. 1859; EP Publishing, 1978
Wainwright, David. *The piano makers*. Hutchinson, 1975
Walford, Edward. *Old and new London*, vol. 5. Cassell, 1878
Wates, Nick. *The battle for Tolmers Square*. Routledge, 1976
Weinreb, B & Hibbert, C (eds). *The London encyclopaedia*, 3rd ed. Macmillan, 2008
Whitehead, Andrew. *Curious King's Cross*. Five Leaves, 2018
Whitehouse, Patrick. *LMS 150*. Ramboro Books, 1997
Wilson, Colin St John. *The design & construction of the British Library*. BL, 1998
Yalom, Marilyn. *Blood sisters: the French Revolution in women's memory*. Pandora, 1995

Also many individual biographies and institutional histories, in printed form or digitised

Maps

Rocque 1746; Horwood 1799; Thompson 1801/1804 (& terrier book); Davies 1834; Greenwood 1834; Britton 1834; parish 1849 & 1861; Stanford 1862; Cassell 1862; Ordnance Survey 1871 & later; Bacon 1888; Booth's poverty maps 1889/98; LCC bomb damage maps

Periodicals & Newspapers

Camden History Review (CHR)
Camden History Society. Newsletters
Camden Journal
Camden New Journal
GLIAS Newsletter
St Pancras Journal, 1947-1965

Articles

Denford, Steven. 'Luxury living for the lower classes', CHR 20 (1996), 9-13
Gobbi, Claire. 'The Spanish quarter of Somers Town', CHR 6 (1978), 6-9
Hayes, David A. 'Lyne's academy, Somers Town', CHR 42 (2018), 32-35
Howkins, C D. 'Somers Town between the wars', *Camden Journal*, Dec 1971
Symons, John, 'A Most Hideous Object: John Davies (1796-1872) and Plastic Surgery', *Medical History* 45 (2001), 395-402
Waterhouse, Paul. 'The Euston Road', *Architectural Review*, Town Planning & Housing Suppl. (Dec 1910), 303-307
Whytehead, R & Blackmore, L. 'Excavations at Tottenham Court, 250 Euston Road', *LAMAS Transactions*, vol.34 (1983)

Other records

Census returns, 1841–1911
Conservation Area Statements (L B Camden)
Crossrail and Transport for London publicity
Goad insurance plans, 1880s & later
Licensed Victuallers Recognizances, 1723 & 1760
London County Council/GLC street lists
London County Council: Education Committee & Housing Committee reports
Post Office London Directories (Kelly & Co.)
Registers of Electors, St Pancras and Camden
St Pancras Met. Borough: rate books
St Pancras Vestry: minutes; Poor Rate
School Board for London: annual reports
Theatre programmes

Websites

Numerous online resources, including websites of extant local institutions, and also:
Ancestry (ancestry.com)
The Bartlett (bartlett.ucl.ac.uk)
British History Online (british-history.ac.uk)
L B of Camden: Planning (camden.gov.uk/planning)
Charles Booth Online Archive (booth.lse.ac.uk)
Discovery: The National Archives (discovery.nationalarchives.gov.uk/)
Eustontowner (eustontowner.london)
Grove Music Online (oxfordmusiconline.com)
Historic England: Listed Buildings (historicengland.org.uk/listing/the-list/)
London Pubology (https://www.pubology.co.uk/)
London Transport Museum (ltmcollection.org)
Lost Hospitals of London (ezitis.myzen.co.uk)
Mapping Sculpture (sculpture.gla.ac.uk)
Music Hall & Theatre History (arthurlloyd.co.uk)
Old Bailey Online (oldbaileyonline.org)
Oxford Dictionary of National Biography (oxforddnb.com)
Times Digital Archive 1785-1985 (gale.cengage.co.uk/times.aspx)
UCL: Bloomsbury Project (ucl.ac.uk/bloomsbury-project)
UCL: Legacies of British Slave-Ownership (ucl.ac.uk/lbs)
Wellcome Library (archives.wellcome.ac.uk)

Archive centres

British Library
Camden Local Studies & Archives Centre, including Heal Collection
Guildhall Library
London Metropolitan Archives
Westminster Archives

Index

Streets included in the survey are indicated in boldface, as are the main entries for these and other selected subjects.
* = illustration
IFC = inside front cover
PH = public house